LIFE IN AN ENGLISH VILLAGE

The only identified photograph of Maud Davies (courtesy of William Seabrook and Cindy Hughes)

Life in an English Village

AN ECONOMIC AND HISTORICAL SURVEY OF THE
PARISH OF CORSLEY IN WILTSHIRE

MAUD F DAVIES

edited with an introductory essay by

JANE HOWELLS

First published in 1909 by T. Fisher Unwin of London and Leipzig
This reset edition, with new introduction and additional matter, first published in
the United Kingdom in 2013 by
The Hobnob Press, PO Box 1838, East Knoyle, Salisbury, SP3 6FA
www.hobnobpress.co.uk

British Library Cataloguing in Publication Data
A catalogue record for this book is available from the British Library

ISBN 978-1-906978-05-1

Typeset in Minion Pro 12/16 pt. Typesetting and origination by John Chandler
Printed by Lightning Source

Front cover illustration:
Photograph of Fiona Stansbury as Maud Davies, for the Available
Light Production television documentary, 'Death of a Sociologist' in
2001 outside Corsley Church (*photograph by John Chandler*)

Contents

Acknowledgements   *vii*

Original Preface, 1909, by Maud Davies   *ix*

Introductory Essay by Jane Howells   1

Family   6

London School of Economics   10

Victoria County History   13

Life in an English Village   18

Publication and reception   21

Fabian Society   25

School Care Committees   30

The white slave trade   34

The Writers' Club, Whitehall Hotel, and

    Wellesley Buildings   36

Final weeks   38

Life in an English Village, part 1, Corsley in the Past   47

1 The Parish under Cley Hill   49

2 Seignorial Unification   59

3 Cloth-making and its Effects in Corsley, 1660-1727   67

4 Industry and Agriculture, 1760-1837   81

5 The Religious Revival, 1760-1837   95

6   The House Famine and its Results, 1760-1837   101

7   Corsley under the Old Poor Law, 1760-1837   111

8   Corsley in the Nineteenth Century, 1837-1905   120

Life in an English Village, part 2, Corsley in the Present   **133**

9   Introduction: Method of Inquiry   135

10   Who the Corsley People are, and How they get a Living   140

11   Houses and Gardens in Corsley   165

12   Poverty   171

13   Character and its Relation to Poverty   182

14   Corsley Family Budgets   209

15   Ancestry and Children of Corsley   246

16   Social Life in Corsley   263

17   Conclusion   271

Appendices

1   Medieval and Stuart Records   276

2   Extracts from Overseers' Accounts   287

3   Extracts from Census Reports   290

4   Extracts from farming accounts of Mr John Barton   291

    List of References   292

Corsley: A Hamlet Parish in Wiltshire by Brian Short   **295**

Bibliography   306

Index   310

Ordnance Survey Mapof the Corsley Area, 1898   317

Acknowledgements

JOHN CHANDLER HAS been intending that his Hobnob Press should publish a reprint of *Life in an English Village* for many years. The original plan had been to mark the centenary of its first appearance in 1909, but circumstances conspired against us so here it is 100 years after the death of its author. More than a decade ago John researched and contributed to a television programme about Maud Davies which was very well received, and his enquiries revealed a continuing interest in Corsley and district. Not only did he offer me the enticing opportunity of investigating Maud's life and death, he put the results of his research at my disposal, and has offered further help throughout. In addition, John has been entirely responsible for the technical production of this new volume. Without him you would not have it in your hands to read.

When I succeeded in making contact with members of Maud's family they welcomed my approach enthusiastically. A particular moment of excitement was seeing her photograph for the first time. My thanks go to David Slatter, William Seabrook, Lucy Nisbet and Cindy Hughes. A family friend, Mark Walford, also generously shared his memories.

Any undertaking such as this is dependent on the assistance of many people. Alan Crosby visited Liverpool archives on my behalf, and I sent queries to maritime researcher Hannah Cunliffe. Anna Towlson at LSE archives, Steve Hobbs and Helen Taylor at Wiltshire & Swindon History Centre, Alwyn Hardy and Eric Peddle at Warminster Dewey Museum, all accepted enquiries and provided so many answers (and further questions). David Parker of Available Light Productions supported the original programme that started the project. John Beckett allowed me to read an unpublished paper on women workers at the early Victoria County History, and Matthew Bristow helped me around the VCH archive collection. Mark Freeman kindly encouraged the plan to reprint, and allowed us an early view of his comments on Maud's work. Brian Short willingly gave permission for us to include his case study of Corsley using the 1910 Valuation Office survey which provides an extra dimension to this analysis of Edwardian rural society.

Family and friends have supplied encouragement throughout. I extend grateful thanks to all. The errors, and of course the unanswered questions, are my own.

JEH
January 2013

Original Preface, 1909

IN 1905, WHEN a student at the London School of Economics, it was suggested to me by Mr. and Mrs. Sidney Webb that I should pursue my studies of economic history and social science by making an investigation into the history and present conditions of the parish in which I was living, and it is upon the research and investigations begun at that time that this monograph is based.

Everything that may be of value in the book is due to some suggestion of Mr. or Mrs. Sidney Webb, while to my own mistakes and failures in filling in outlines sketched by them must be ascribed all its shortcomings.

To Mr. and Mrs. Webb, moreover, I owe the most valuable advice on how to investigate and where to look for possible sources of information, historical or otherwise.

My thanks are due to many of the lecturers and staff of the London School of Economics for advice and criticism, especially to Mr. Hubert Hall, Dr. Lilian Knowles, and Mr. J. McKillop.

I am indebted to the Marquis of Bath for allowing me to examine various documents at the Longleat Estate Office, relating to the history of Corsley.

To the Rev. J.T. Kershaw I owe thanks for various references to manorial and ecclesiastical records.

I have to thank Canon Christopher Wordsworth, Mr. C.N. Phipps, Miss M. Calthrop, and many others for valuable information, advice, or the loan of documents or books, and Miss Winifred Mitchell for reading the proofs.

Last, but not least, my most hearty thanks are due to many friends and neighbours in Corsley, who do not wish to be mentioned by name, but without whose extremely valuable co-operation no attempt could have been made to describe village life in the nineteenth century and at the present day.

Maud F. Davies

Introductory Essay

MAUD DAVIES WAS born in London in 1876, the eldest child of Byam and Frances Davies. She died at the age of 37 on the railway line in a tunnel near High Street Kensington station. The book for which she is remembered today was produced as the result of research undertaken on the advice of Sidney and Beatrice Webb, who inspired many pioneering students at the London School of Economics of the time, including Maud Davies who was said to have 'entered heart and soul into Economics and Social subjects'.[1] As well as the study of the village of Corsley in Wiltshire, where her family lived at Corsley House, Maud wrote a contribution to the embryonic Victoria County History on the economic & social history of Wiltshire. She was also an active member of the Fabian Society, was involved with school care committees in London, and was planning a study of the white slave traffic. Shortly before her death she was described as suffering from over work, and there were some unusual circumstances surrounding the final days of her life which will be discussed below. In the last two decades of Maud Davies's tragically short life she had demonstrated her intelligence, application and serious philanthropic concern in a variety of activities which received recognition from her colleagues and friends. She no doubt had intentions for much more which would sadly not come to fruition. This brief biographical essay introducing the Hobnob Press reprint of *Life in an English Village* is offered in acknowledgment of Maud Davies's qualities and achievements.

1   *Wiltshire News* 14 February 1913. WANHS Library Cuttings Book 13 p 99

Life in an English Village (*LEV*) was first published in the Autumn of 1909. When its author Maud Davies died just over three years later Edward Pease, Secretary of the Fabian Society, declared 'This book will be read 100 years hence, and will always remain a classic of sociological enquiry'.[2] He was right to the extent that it is widely quoted by modern historians as providing analysis of an Edwardian rural community, in parallel with the better known work of Booth, Rowntree, Bowley and Mann.

LEV has long been out of print so largely unavailable to modern readers. As will be explained, although the original print run is unknown, there was a deliberate attempt to withdraw copies from circulation, so it is not surprising that there are relatively few of the 1909 edition to be found.[3]

The years of the late 19th century and the decade before the outbreak of the First World War saw a growing interest in social conditions and the consequent development of strategies to ameliorate the worst. Physical deterioration revealed in the British army fighting in the Boer War, and the 'national efficiency' debate that followed encouraged investigation and then policies, such as infant and child welfare legislation, and national insurance and old age pensions, that are characteristic of the Edwardian period. Maud Davies carried out her study of Corsley against this background, in the footsteps of Charles Booth and Seebohm Rowntree. She had been preceded in carrying out 'a Rowntree-type survey of rural communities' by Harold Mann who had surveyed the village of Ridgmount in Bedfordshire in 1903, publishing his findings two years later.[4]

2   *Daily Express* 7 February 1913 p 1

3   The second part of the book appeared as one of the extensive collection of documents published in five volumes in 2005, with a modern editorial commentary by Mark Freeman, as *The English Rural Poor 1850-1914*, Pickering and Chatto at £450. There are now also two versions accessible on the internet from Cornell University Library.

4   Freeman, M , 2003, *Social Investigation and Rural England 1870 – 1914*. Boydell

Maud Davies's results and the analysis she provided are of continuing interest, and her work is still quoted widely.[5] A comprehensive critical discussion of *LEV* in the context of her contemporary investigators is to be found in Mark Freeman's *Social Investigation and Rural England 1870-1914*.[6] He notes her application of the distinction initiated by Rowntree between 'primary' and 'secondary' poverty; adding '[s]he has one claim to conceptual and methodological innovation ... she included in her secondary poverty category those households with a margin of less than 1s above the primary poverty line'.[7] The project demonstrated her use of a variety of methods – including questionnaires, budget diaries, information and comment from authority figures such as clergy and schoolteachers, and personal observation.

Despite good intentions of approaching research such as this with scientific objectivity, it was inevitable that the investigator 'was ultimately unable to operate outside either the cultural framework that surrounded the English countryside or the moral structures that conditioned middle-class responses to working-class behavioural norms';[8] as Freeman has put it somewhat harshly 'she swept into her own working-class backyard inquiring into the habits of the poor with an air of moral judgementalism . . . '.[9] Maud Davies herself was indeed aware of both the limitations of the statistics she collected 'all these sources of information were liable to more or less error',[10] and of the moral difficulties of accepting evidence from neighbours and others, as she explained when discussing the skills required for the

---

for The Royal Historical Society

5   See pages 308-9 below for some examples

6   Freeman, 2003, ch 4

7   ibid p 119, *LEV* p 145

8   ibid p 132

9   ibid p 127

10 *LEV* p 102

operations of school care committees.

Social scientific investigations in the early years of the twentieth century reflected both the stage of development of the subject and the backgrounds of those in a position to carry them out. But the efforts of people like Maud Davies, however flawed, revealed poverty as widespread in rural districts as in York and London, and contributed 'to a greater awareness of rural social problems, and fed their concerns for the present into a development contemporary interest in the problems of the English rural past'.[11]

Not only does Maud Davies's work retain interest in itself but the information about Corsley in *LEV* can be used as the basis of comparative studies on rural life based on other contemporary or near-contemporary sources. Reprinted in this volume is the case study by Brian Short employing the Field Books produced by the Valuation Office Survey 1910-15.[12] Amongst the proposals of Lloyd George's 1909 Budget was an increment value duty on land. For this it was necessary to undertake a survey of all property to establish a base line from which increases in value could be calculated, and the difference taxed. The enormous exercise of making the valuation survey was carried out, at a cost of over two million pounds; then the duty was repealed by the 1920 Finance Act. 'But this fiscal white elephant resulted in the creation of a detailed archive which provides a wealth of information about the population of Britain, their homes and workplaces, just before the immense social changes that followed the First World War'.[13] It is this archive that Professor Short has exploited to our advantage.

More recently, further possibilities are opened by the availability of the household schedules in the census enumerators'

11 Freeman, 2003, p 124, 126

12 Short, B 1997, *Land and Society in Edwardian Britain*, Cambridge University Press, pp 273 – 282, and pages 295-305 here

13 Beech, G and Mitchell, R , 2004, *Maps for Family and Local History*, The National Archives pp 36-68, quote from p 37

books completed in 1911. These would provide an opportunity, as yet untapped, for another detailed study of Corsley linking the family details from the census (both 1901 and 1911) to the original analysis carried out for *LEV* and to characteristics such as the physical surroundings and property relationships within the village from the Field Books. This project awaits a local historian.

Maud Davies herself was representative of the women who were attempting to break out of the orthodox lifestyle expected of an upper middle class female. She studied new subjects and learnt new skills in an education that led her away from the traditional obligations of the wives and daughters of prominent families in a small community, and towards a modern social-scientific approach to relationships between social classes that for some would become the basis of a professional career. Living an independent life was not always easy, and practical and emotional difficulties may have contributed to Maud's untimely and unexplained death.

It has to be assumed that Maud's family provided her with an income which was normally sufficient to support her independence.[14] She did not, apparently, take the route of seeking full-time paid employment and it is not known whether she would have preferred this option. She often resided with other members of the family, though did rent her own small flat near Euston. On completion of her text for the Victoria County History she then had to ask for an interim payment as she was in need of funds, so perhaps she was not always financially secure. After her death, Maud was described as 'a woman of means' who 'gave much money away quietly and unostentatiously'.[15]

Between 1901 when she first enrolled at the London School of Economics and 1913 when she died, Maud was involved in a variety of activities all based in either or both of her main interests. Her

14 She held shares in the GWR. Great Western Railway Shareholders 1835-1932 findmypast.co.uk

15 *Wiltshire News* 14 February 1913. WANHS Library Cuttings Book 13 p 99

studies taught her historical scholarship that she applied to her work for the VCH, and on *LEV*. The particular scientific approach, and the belief that policy change should be based on factual research, came from her association with the major thinkers at both LSE and the Fabian Society, and informed her investigations into contemporary Corsley, her interest in conditions amongst London school children, her chapter in *Married Women's Work*, and would have contributed similarly to her intended exploration of white slave traffic.

Maud Davies was connected to a network of intellectual, literary and artistic friends and colleagues, many of whom would probably not have been accepted with any enthusiasm in her home and family circle. She developed her own interests as an academic historian amongst archives, and as a practical social investigator amongst the poorer population of both Wiltshire and London. Her analysis was inevitably coloured by her upbringing and by her gender. Joan Thirsk has described *LEV* as 'a classic local history, structured in accordance with women's preferences, and building up a picture of both landscape and people viewed from many angles'.[16]

Family

MAUD FRANCES DAVIES was born in London on 18 January 1876. Little is known of her early life but she lived with her parents Byam Martin Davies and Frances Ann Davies (formerly Conant) at various addresses in the home counties during her childhood. These included Mitchen Hall near Godalming, Surrey and Broughton Grange near Banbury, Oxfordshire.[17] They first rented Corsley House in 1894, and then purchased the property

16 Thirsk in Hey, D, ed, 1996, *The Oxford Companion to Local and Family History*, OUP p 501.

17 1881 and 1891 census respectively; Mitchen Hall lease 1886 'lately occupied by Byam Martin Davies esq', Surrey History Centre 1346

for £6,000 in 1897, including 60 acres of land and a cottage.[18] Even then they do not seem to have lived there permanently, continuing to spend time at Frances Davies' family home of Waltham Place, Maidenhead.[19]

The family had a strong tradition of military service: grandfather, uncle, cousins and brothers rising to commands in the Grenadier Guards and the Rifle Brigade, including Maud's uncle General Henry Fanshawe Davies and her cousin who would become General Sir Francis John Davies. Byam Martin Davies' eldest brother Francis Byam had died in the Crimean War in 1854 of wounds received at the battle of Sebastopol. Much more immediate for Maud was the Boer War in which two of her brothers were on active duty. Warburton Edward was involved in the siege of Ladysmith and returned home safely. Sadly for the family Lt Byam Henry Ernest of the 3rd Wiltshire Regiment was killed at Winbult in the Orange River Colony, South Africa in February 1902.[20]

Ten years earlier Maud's sister Cecil Charlotte had died, aged only 15. The cause of death was given as 'Influenza, 10 days, Pleuro Pneumonia' so it is possible that in the initial stages of illness the danger to her life was not appreciated, but that her death then came swiftly making the impact on those around her more traumatic.[21] These two girls were born less than one year apart; with no direct evidence it can only be imagined how this would have distressed Maud, and her

---

18 TNA MH32/111 correspondence between Byam Davies and Local Government Board, July 1894; Hutchings p 37

19 TNA MH32/111 March 1901. It was necessary for Inspectors to obtain sanction from the Board to change addres, especially if this might necessitate an increase in expense claims.

20 Commemorated in a bronze wall plaque in the church of St Mary, White Waltham, Berksire.

21 For a discussion of attitudes to death Jalland, P, 1996, *Death in the Victorian Family*, OUP. Coincidentally one of the case studies presented by Jalland is that of Beatrice Webb's mother Lawrencina Potter in 1882, p 55

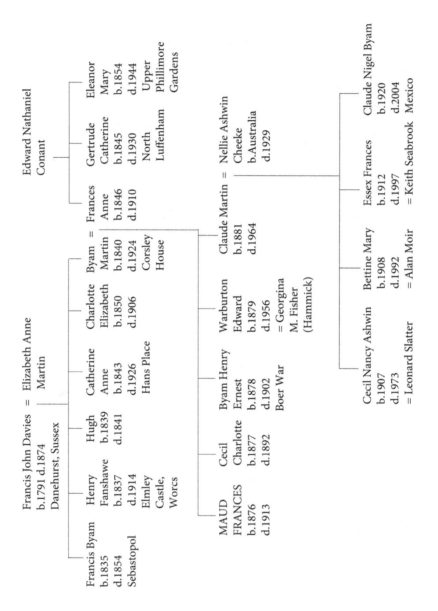

Davies and Conant family tree

parents. It is likely that the sisters were close companions through their childhood, sharing education and amusements. [22]

Maud's father did not follow his relations into the army. He attended Christ Church, Oxford University, and was called to the Bar in January 1866.[23] In the early 1880s Byam Davies became an inspector of Poor Law schools for the Local Government Board, a role he held for over 20 years.[24] Initially responsible for the 'Eastern and Midland' district, after re-arrangements in 1891 his area was extended to include most of the southern half of England, apart from London. Although this inevitably involved a great deal of travelling, the number of schools to be visited declined over the period as children living in workhouses increasingly attended the local elementary school. That the children would benefit greatly from not spending their whole life in the workhouse was an argument he put forward in some of his earliest reports. In his final report, in 1904, Byam Davies was in reflective mood, and commented on other developments he had witnessed, emphasising improvements in the quality of teachers in workhouse schools and in the service provided for vocational training.

As Maud grew up it is highly likely that she and her father discussed his work, and from this came her interest in the social issues that were to become so important to her. It could also have been the stimulus for her to take the next steps towards learning the approach to analysing and understanding the investigations she would subsequently put into print. Without his support, the process of breaking away from the expectations of an apparently otherwise conventional upbringing, leaving a comfortable home and setting out into a new independent way of life would have been even harder.

22 Although nothing is known of Maud's (henceforth MFD in notes) early education, there was a 'school room maid' listed in the 1891 census at Broughton Grange.

23 Foster, J, 1885, *Men-at-the-Bar: a biographical handlist of the members of the various Inns of Court*, Hazel, Watson & Viney, (ebook)

24 This section based on correspondence in TNA MH32/111.

Frances Davies, Maud's mother, 'took a leading part in promoting charitable movements' and 'her thought for the poor was constant' as the writer of her obituary expressed it.[25] Although this was doing no more than would be expected of the lady of the big house in a small community, and her daughter would have been expected to accompany her and follow in her footsteps, it was another opportunity for Maud to begin to understand how other sections of society lived.

Amongst her many relations Maud had maiden aunts, Catherine Anne Davies on her father's, and Gertrude Catherine Conant and Eleanor Mary Conant on her mother's side of the family, who may have provided role models of independent women, as property owners and voters. They had London homes, where Maud is known to have stayed with Eleanor Conant and with Catherine Davies;[26] and Gertrude Conant also lived in Rutland where Maud visited her in 1907.[27] Indeed, at times in her life Maud appears to have been almost nomadic. While working on the economic & social history of Wiltshire for the Victoria County History, she corresponded from eleven different addresses, several but not all identified as belonging to members of the family.

London School of Economics

THE LONDON SCHOOL of Economics held its first classes in October 1895; in 1900 it was recognised as a faculty in the newly-constituted University of London and two years later the School moved to its present site, in Clare Market and Houghton Street, off

25   *Warminster Journal* 15 July 1910 p 8

26   When working for VCH (letter 13 Nov 1906), and probably when she was serving on a School Care Committee, see below

27   When working for VCH (letters 4 April and 23 May 1907). The Pastures, North Luffenham was built for Gertrude Conant by the Arts & Crafts architect C F A Voysey.

the Aldwych. Sidney and Beatrice Webb, together with Graham Wallas and George Bernard Shaw, had put into effect their ideas for 'a centre not only of lectures on special subjects but an association of students who would be directed and supported in doing original work'.[28] Of particular relevance here was Beatrice Webb's observation 'such history as will be taught at the School will be the history of social institutions discovered from documents, statistics and the observation of the actual structure and working of living organizations'.[29]

Maud Davies first enrolled at the LSE in 1901, and then was a student intermittently until she kept whole years of 1905-6 and 1906-7, and she matriculated BSc (London).[30] It seems she had already embarked on an independent life by early 1901, perhaps in preparation for becoming a student, as at the time of the census that year she was living as a boarder in a lodging house in Pimlico, working as a commercial clerk.[31] Whether she had any training for this, and if so how and where, is unknown. Clerical work by this time was seen as a respectable opportunity for women in need of earning a living and 'schools' had been established to teach shorthand and typewriting.[32]

The preface to *LEV* began as follows

In 1905, when a student at the London School of Economics, it was suggested to me by Mr and Mrs Webb that I should pursue my studies of economic history and social science by making an investigation into the history and present conditions of the parish in which I was living ... [t]o Mr and Mrs Webb ... I owe the most valuable advice

28 LSE website

29 MacKenzie, N and J, eds, 1983, *The Diary of Beatrice Webb* Volume Two 1892-1905, Virago and LSE, p 171

30 LSE 19/4/16, pp 54, 182

31 1901 census RG 13/86

32 Holcombe, L, 1973 *Victorian Ladies at Work*, Archon Books, ch 6, and Jordan, E, 1999, *The Women's Movement and Women's Employment in Nineteenth Century Britain*, Routledge, particularly ch 9.

on how to investigate and where to look for possible sources of information, historical or otherwise.[33]

Thanks expressed to members of staff at the LSE provide names of other academics who were a particular influence on her work. In 1904 Lilian Knowles had been appointed the first full-time teacher of economic history at any British university, becoming reader at the University of London in 1907.[34] Not only was she a pioneer in a new discipline; '[h]er teaching was vigorous and wide in scope, but also attentive to original sources. To her, LSE was a place to which people came to be taught, and she threw her soul into teaching'.[35] A new student would not find it hard to catch this infectious enthusiasm.

Hubert Hall was a professional archivist who worked at the Public Record Office and 'spent his leisure in research on medieval history'.[36] Another strong supporter of the LSE, between 1896 and 1919 he taught palaeography, diplomatic and economic history there, and collaborated with the Webbs on their history of English Local Government. Hall also trained researchers who contributed to the Victoria County Histories.

The establishment of a Library at LSE was seen as a crucial part of the School. After an energetic appeal for funds, the British Library

33   *LEV* vii

34   A student at Girton College, Cambridge, although gaining a first class in the history tripos in 1893 and the first woman to achieve a first in the law tripos the following year, Lilian Tomn as she was then could not receive a degree, as Cambridge University did not grant degrees to women until 1948. In 1905 she took DLitt at Trinity College, Dublin. ODNB this paragraph

35   Although MFD does not provide a bibliography of secondary sources consulted for LEV, a fn on p 8 refers to the work of F W Maitland, an influential figure at Cambridge when Knowles was there.

36   ODNB this para. For much more on Hall's life, including his approach to history, use of original records, and relationships with students (particularly his encouragement of women)   see Procter, M, 2012, 'Hubert Hall (1857-1944):Archival endeavour and the promotion of historical enterprise', unpublished PhD thesis, University of Liverpool.

of Political Science was opened in 1896, under John McKillop, who had originally been appointed as Secretary to the School's Director. McKillop was the third person mentioned in the *LEV* preface. A library would not have been a novelty to someone with Maud's upbringing; even late in the 19th century middle-class girls took their education into their own hands by making use of their family collections of books, an essential part of a gentleman's household. The directed reading and specialist resources available at LSE provided both ideas and the means to carry out her intentions to become an active researcher.

But it was Sidney and Beatrice Webb who provided the inspiration. In the introduction to the second volume of Beatrice's published diaries it is said that she made up her mind to be part of the 'working sisterhood of celibate professional women and pursue her vocation as a social investigator'.[37] Although she subsequently did marry, this ambition to lead a useful life with like-minded people would serve as an example to many young women with whom the Webbs came into contact, such as Maud Davies.

Victoria County History

O NE OUTLET FOR the historical skills students at LSE were acquiring was with the Victoria History of the Counties of England, commenced in 1899 under the editorship of Arthur Doubleday of the publishers Constable. During the years preceding its financial difficulties from 1908, the VCH employed numerous educated women as researchers and authors; they listed records from Public Record Office catalogues, drafted manorial histories, and wrote some of the general essays.[38] Recruitment to this work seems to

37 MacKenzie N and J, eds, 1983 p 5

38 Beckett J, 2013. 'Women Writers and the Victoria County History, forthcoming. Joan Thirsk recognises this contribution her essay 'women local and family

have used existing networks of association between suitable women at the time. Contacts at Oxford, and to a lesser extent Cambridge, identified candidates amongst the history students and staff, and 'the recruits themselves happily recommended their own friends and colleagues'.[39] Hubert Hall at LSE suggested potential authors from among the students there. It is likely there were also links between people working on the same or related material. So Maud's research for her Corsley study would have brought her into contact with Miss Moffat and Miss Simkins working on Wiltshire, and also with Miss MMC Calthrop, one of the women on the VCH staff from 1904.[40]

Preparations for various volumes of Wiltshire VCH had been underway from the beginning.[41] Elsbeth Philipps had written to Doubleday with a list of suggested names against the key subject areas. Rev Christopher Wordsworth, for example, became involved with work on Ecclesiastical History and Religious Houses. In 1905 William Page, then general editor, wrote to Miss Philipps to ask her if she would do the Social and Economic volume for Wiltshire. Now married, Mrs Marcus Dimsdale replied that she was unable to let him know for some months as she did not know her movements between Cambridge and Wiltshire. In Sept 1905 Page wrote to ask her

> would it be of any assistance to you to collaborate with another lady? A Miss Maud F Davies of Elmley Castle, Pershore, who is living at Warminster and is anxious to do some work on the later part of the social and economic history of Wiltshire? She was recommended to

historians' in Hey, D, ed, 1996

39 Beckett J, 2013, p 14

40 Beckett J, 2013, p 7. Corsley and Longleat sources used in LEV re-appear in the VCH manuscript. Miss M Calthrop was thanked for 'information, advice or loan of documents' in the Preface to *LEV*.

41 VCH Archive Box A19 package 1506 'Wilts early correspondence' contains letters exchanged between the central office and Wiltshire contributors, including Maud Davies, on which this section is based.

me by Mr Hubert Hall of the Record Office [TNA] who writes that she is one of his promising postgraduate students at the school of economics. I do not think she would be quite up to undertake the earlier part of the work as I understand her Latin is not good.

Elsbeth Dimsdale replied promptly that she herself would not do the work 'but I know Miss Maud Davies very well, and I know that she is a careful, conscientious and thorough worker. I believe if she undertook it, she would be quite capable of doing the whole article very well indeed'. She continued, and this throws interesting light on local historical research in days before the establishment of county record offices, '. . . [Miss Davies] knows so many people in the county well that she would have no difficulty in getting access to any of the libraries or assistance from any of the county antiquarians – and I am sure the Longleat papers would be easily at her disposal'.[42]

Page sent Maud a copy of the Guide that had been prepared for contributors, and she prepared a plan for the article. Despite Mrs Dimsdale's reassurance, and Maud's acknowledgment that she did not have the requisite Latin though would be willing to work from secondary sources and published transcriptions, Page continued to worry about the earlier history. He again consulted Hall who suggested Miss Moffat 'who works under him at the school of economics' to

42 Elsbeth Philipps (1871-1949) was the daughter of Rev Canon Sir James Erasmus Philipps, vicar of Warminster; she read history at Somerville, Oxford and held a Research Fellowship at Newnham College Cambridge. Her article 'A List of printed Churchwardens' Accounts', *English Historical Review* April 1900, still appears in modern bibliographies (eg www.churchguides.co.uk/how-to.php). She turned to social and political work, becoming a county councillor, poor law guardian, and a member of the Ministry of Health Consultative Committee on Local Government, among many public roles. All the large houses in the county would have had private libraries, and that of the Wiltshire Archaeological and Natural History Society in Devizes held a considerable collection. Access to non-members was permitted at the discretion of the Librarian in January 1906. Thomas J H (ed), 2003, *Wiltshire Archaeological & Natural History Society: the first 150 years,* WANHS, ch 6

London in the spring.
If you cannot
give me Wiltshire
I would prefer not
to undertake anything
else at present,
but if in about a
year's time you still
had Worcestershire,
or perhaps Rutland
unallotted I should
probably be very glad
to undertake it.
I should be glad to
know, if you give me
the work, what the
remuneration will be —

[Yours truly   Maud F. Davies]

ELMLEY CASTLE,
PERSHORE,
WORCESTERSHIRE.

Sept 26th 1905

Dear Mr Page
    In accordance with
your suggestion I
am sending you
a sketch of what I
should propose to do
should you give me
a chapter on the
Social & Economic
history of a county

to write —
Of course I should
like to be free to
vary my scheme
should a study of
the available materials
suggest improvements.
If you could give
me the chapter in
the Wiltshire history
I should be very
much pleased to
undertake it now —

as I am going to
spend the next 4
months in the
county at
Corsley House
Warminster
studying parish history
and I might at
the same time make
investigations for
the history of
the county — and
could then carry on
my researches in

facing page: Letter written by Maud Davies to William Page from Elmley Castle, Worcs., in 1905, concerning work she might undertake for the Victoria County History project. Both spreads of a folded sheet are reproduced, so the letter reads: top right, bottom left and right, top left. (VCH Archives, Matthew Bristow)

---

collaborate. They settled to this arrangement, working through 1906, using the social and economic chapter for Essex as an exemplar, asking for extensions of deadlines, reading and commenting on each other's text, having pages posted around the country. The result of their combined efforts is no doubt the typescript that now resides at WSA. Maud was concerned that they had exceeded the agreed word limit 'I paid for typing 32,000 [words]' but Page replied that they could have up to 40,000 as 'I am not so hampered with space in the Wiltshire volume . . .'[43]

Maud was becoming an increasingly confident historian, no doubt benefiting from the experience she was gaining with the VCH, in parallel with her work on *LEV*. In March 1907 she asked Page to return her manuscript 'to show to Dr Cunningham, he is bringing out a new edition of his Economic History and will probably refer to my article in the Victoria County History and to some of the facts I have given in it'.[44]

There were no Wiltshire VCH proofs during the summer of 1907, and it would appear that decisions were already being made centrally about priorities of production. Writing continued, and Page offered Maud more work, which she declined on the grounds 'that kind of research work is rather too trying for my eyesight at present'.

The VCH standard rate of remuneration was one guinea per thousand words, and the normal practice was not to pay until the volume containing the relevant article was printed. At the end of

43 The typing was done at The Women's Institute Typing Bureau, 92 Victoria St, London SW. WSA 146A/1/1

44 Cunningham, W, 1907, *The Growth of English industry and Commerce in Modern Times*, CUP. Preface to the Fourth Edition concludes 'I am indebted for suggestions and assistance to . . . Miss M F Davies'.

1907 Maud wrote to Page asking for some payment: 'I counted on this money to meet certain expenses which I find have to be settled now, and I was of course a good deal out of pocket when I did the work'. £20 was agreed and paid.

A year later there was still no sign of the Wiltshire volume containing Maud's work appearing in print.[45] But meanwhile she was making progress on *LEV*, and her correspondence with Page turned to that. He had given her an introduction to Constables, who declined to publish *LEV*, and had read the work himself. 'I had a look at your monograph on a Wiltshire parish, and I liked a great part of it. . . . I cannot do more than offer you advice about it but I like to see such careful work and if you think a little friendly criticism of any value I shall be glad to give it'. It would be most interesting to know the nature of that criticism. Whether or not Maud accepted Page's advice, she completed the volume, found a publisher, and launched the work for which she is still remembered.

Life in an English Village

*L*EV, DESCRIBED BY one reviewer, 'is a stout volume on good paper, well printed, and its scope may be judged of from the proportionate lengths of the two parts into which it is divided; Part I 'Corsley in the past' occupying pp 4 – 96, whilst 'Corsley in the present' fills pp 99-290'.[46] The first, historical, section contains eight chapters. Moving swiftly through a brief description of the area's geography, and its early history, Maud used two chapters to examine the early modern period, particularly the cloth industry in Corsley.

45 In June 1910 the Secretary of the County History Syndicate Ltd wrote to say that Wiltshire was not one of the counties being completed, and sent £8 to close the account. Maud returned the manuscript with corrected notes to Page in October 1910, and that was presumably transferred to Chippenham as WSA 1946A.

46 *WANHM* Vol 361909-10, p 340

Her parallel work on the social and economic history of the county probably helped the chapter on Industry and Agriculture 1760-1837, and the influence of the Webbs can be clearly seen in her concern with the operation of the poor laws, and the impact of enclosure. Finally in the first section she considered 'Corsley in the Nineteenth Century', looking at trends such as declining population, and changes in education, transport and increased 'accommodation for religious services', concluding that people 'may find that this parish, with its healthy climate and its singularly beautiful scenery is, after all, a good place to live in'.[47]

The second part of *LEV* sets out the results of Maud Davies's comprehensive social survey of the parish that constitutes 'perhaps the most detailed account of the life of a single English rural community in this period'.[48] She began by describing how she carried out the work, using a house-to-enquiry to complete a questionnaire for every household during the winter months of 1905-6. She also sought reports 'as to the characteristics of the various households' and information on incomes, that she admitted 'was somewhat difficult' and took more time.[49] This was the approach most likely to fall foul of subjective description, though she thought she took care to consult people with 'no personal interest in concealing or exaggerating the facts'. The identity of 'a person who knew the parish intimately' is unknown, possibly Rev Kershaw the rector, or Mr Leatham the schoolmaster.[50] 'The authorities at Corsley and Chapmanslade schools' provided her

47 *LEV* p 89

48 Freeman M, 2005

49 *LEV* p 100-4

50 WSA F8/500/84/1/1 Corsley C E School log book. Albert Leatham was appointed in March 1905, so it is possible MFD made contact with his predecessor Miss Robinson. She made one official visit, recorded in the log book in January 1904. Later, it was said, 'she frequently visited the village school and took a great interest in the work carried on there by Mr and Mrs Leatham'. *Wiltshire News* 7 February 1913 WANHS Library Cuttings Book 13 p 99

with reports on the children and their families.[51]

Family budgets and diaries of food were collected during 1906-7; during the first winter Maud also gathered information on religion, friendly societies, insurance, and amusements; then a year later on women's earnings, medical attendance and rents. From the start she determined to ensure the anonymity of her respondents, numbering the households in some sort of random order, and grouping them under occupation. Names were indeed treated confidentially, and Maud reassured her informants that this would be so, with the result that she felt they answered her questions willingly. However, as will be seen, once people who knew the parish got hold of copies it proved only too easy to identify the subjects.

Readers can discover the details of the lives of the villagers of Corsley between 1905 and 1907 by reading Maud's own words. The population was concentrated in a number of small centres scattered through the parish, so despite the title of the book, it was not a typical 'village'. It had a relatively broad occupational structure, and supplementary incomes were important for many families. There was indeed poverty, with more households experiencing secondary than primary poverty. The main causes of the latter were low wages and large families; contributing to the former was 'drink, or other wasteful expenditure, or bad management'.[52] In her conclusion Maud admitted that some of her discoveries 'were entirely at variance with the preconceived notions she had formed'. The commonly held assumption that labourers in Wiltshire and Dorset were the most poverty-stricken class in rural England was found to be wrong, as the majority of the inhabitants in Corsley were found 'in quite affluent circumstances' due largely to the availability of gardens and allotments, combined with relatively small numbers of children.[53]

51 *LEV* p 151-2

52 *LEV* ch XII

53 *LEV* pp 285-6

Publication and reception

L EV RECEIVED FAVOURABLE reviews in a number of publications, and others that contained an element of criticism. In the *Wiltshire Archaeological & Natural History Magazine* of December 1909, the reviewer (probably the editor Canon E H Goddard) concluded '[t]his book is a monument of scientific industry and accuracy . . . It is and will always remain a standard authority for present day conditions in the life of a somewhat favourably-situated Wiltshire village'.[54] The reviewer's particular interest in the historical sections was clear, and it is there he gave the most detailed account, and offered compliments on the author's use of sources: 'the parish registers for the eighteenth century are carefully analysed', though he regretted that '[t]he early and medieval history of the place is only touched upon in the lightest way'. Despite his personal preferences Goddard recognised that '[t]he real pith and kernel of the book' was the 'picture of Corsley in 1905-6'.

Two less friendly reviews were pasted into the Wiltshire Natural History & Archaeological Society Library cuttings book by Goddard. Readers of the *Standard* of 7 February 1910 were recommended to question Maud's interpretation of the impact of the Old Poor Law and of enclosures, though the conclusion remarked 'Miss Davies has evidently spared no pains to get at the truth about the home life of the labourer'.[55] A month earlier a review by T E Kebbel had appeared in the *Guardian*. Although beginning 'In this very interesting volume . . . ' Kebbel reminded his readers that he had published on the same subject[56] and went on to point out, somewhat unfairly, what he saw

54 *WANHM* Vol 361909-10, pp 340-343

55 *Standard* 7 February 1910 WANHS Library Cuttings Book 13 p 69

56 Kebbel, T E, various editions 1870 -1907 *The agricultural labourer: a short summary of his position*

as omissions on Maud's part: 'Miss Davies takes no account of the old village festivals . . . I should have liked to hear something about the Harvest Home'.[57]

One of Maud's colleagues working at the VCH reviewed *LEV* for *Fabian News*, using her initials M M C C. Miss Muriel Calthrop wrote at length and in sympathetic tone, if without excessive enthusiasm. She too acknowledged the skill of Miss Davies's approach to the second part of the book where 'the author in a succession of delicate touches shows us the assortment of elements which compose the village life of today'. Miss Calthrop would have liked, in the section on budgets, information on one of the gentlemen's families for comparison. She concluded '[t]hroughout the book the author maintains a decent attitude of keeping herself to herself. Her villagers examine themselves, unfold themselves, judge, condemn and commend themselves automatically, as it were, under her tests. This admirable modesty constrains us therefore the more to attend the conclusions with which she steps forward at the close'.[58]

The reviewer in the *Economic Journal* was Norman B Dearle (1882-1961). He noted '[t]he work, which is admirably done, is typical of the aims of modern sociology, which endeavours above all things to get knowledge, and seeks to know before it attempts to reform'. Maud received plaudits: 'To her task Miss Davies has brought many admirable qualifications. To a knowledge of, and sympathy with, the people . . . she has added considerable acquaintance with urban conditions, a grasp of economic principles and of historical facts'. Dearle agreed with others that the 'main interest and merit' lay in the second section of the book, and he considered 'the analysis of character in relation to poverty is extraordinarily good', and pointed out the 'thoroughness and impartiality of the author'.[59]

57 *Guardian* 7 January 1910 WANHS Library Cuttings Book 13 p 69

58 *Fabian News* XXI No 4, March 1910 pp 29-30

59 *Economic Journal* Vol 20 No 80 Dec 1910 pp 609-12

There was no impartiality or detachment demonstrated at the reception of *LEV* in Corsley itself. The parish council was made aware of the book by a local farmer and parish councillor Mr A B White who raised the matter at a meeting on 3 January 1910. White felt that much of the book was interesting but certain portions describing the characters of individual residents might be considered 'a slander on the poor'. Although Maud had thought her methods would retain the anonymity of her respondents, councillors felt there was sufficient particular detail in the book that people could be identified by those familiar with the village.

Most of the council members agreed with Mr White, and a resolution was carried unanimously 'that Miss Davies be requested to consider whether she could see her way to withdraw the book . . . from circulation in the parish and neighbourhood'.[60] In the local press the meeting was reported under the headline 'Slandering the Poor':

> the villagers are indignant in regard to certain pages in what is otherwise admitted to be a highly interesting and readable volume. . . Rev J T Kershaw [vicar of Corsley] said that Miss Davies had seen him and expressed regret that she should have hurt anyone's feelings, adding that she thought the characters would not be recognized. The reverend gentleman agreed that anybody who knew the parish had no difficulty in recognizing the characters and remarked that he could recognize them himself.[61]

Maud's purpose in the book had been to better the lot of the poor by exposing and analysing their poverty, while the councillors considered they were defending the poor of the parish against criticism. Also of interest is that they requested not complete withdrawal of the book, only from local circulation. Presumably news of the book had

60 Corsley Parish Council Minute Book WSA 1097/20

61 *Warminster & Westbury Journal* 7 January 1910 p 8

filtered through the community from the more educated residents, farmers or tradesmen. Indeed it might have even have been promoted by Byam Davies expressing pride in his daughter's achievement. Was it available in Alfred Coates' bookshop and circulating library in Warminster Market Place? Maud herself presented a copy to the WANHS library in Devizes.[62]

In his book on Corsley House, Hugh Grice stated that, as described to him by a member of the family, 'this absolute furore' caused 'her father to buy up all the copies of the book he could lay his hands on', a reaction that is reported in subsequent descriptions of the village without more detailed attribution.[63] This is said to account for the relative rarity of copies of the original edition today.

Where should blame for this difficult situation in Corsley be placed? Was it naive on Maud's part to believe that the leaders of the local community would have accepted her approach and understood her motives? What academic support and supervision of her work did she receive from LSE staff, who perhaps should have warned her at an early stage that her methods were in danger of alienating the very people she was attempting to study sympathetically? Might this have been one of the 'friendly criticisms' offered by William Page?

Did this seriously undermine either the position of the Davies in the village or the relationship between Maud and her family? Grice goes further 'he [Byam Davies] was doubtless held responsible for this breach of trust by his daughter, or for repeating gossip he acquired as a magistrate, and was then slighted by those whose favourable opinions he would have preferred to cultivate' and speculates that the furore may have affected Maud's mother's health and her own state of mind that resulted in suicide.[64]

62 *WANHM* Vol 36 1909-10 p 358

63 Grice, H, 1999, p 35, Hutchings,V, 2000, p 37, and Wiltshire Community History website on Corsley

64 Grice, H,1999, p 36

The obituaries published on the deaths of Frances Davies later in 1910 and Byam Davies in 1924 emphasised the affection with which the family was held: 'Mr and Mrs Davies have resided at Corsley during about the last sixteen years, and endeared themselves to the inhabitants of the village and surrounding neighbourhood by their generosity and thoughtfulness'.[65] 'Mr Byam Davies commanded the highest esteem of all classes in the neighbourhood, and there was general regret when he left the district about six years ago'.[66] If there was resentment it had faded quickly, or was not focused on Maud's parents. When she herself died, the news 'was received at Corsley with deep regret and much sympathy'[67] so perhaps she too was forgiven. Maud went on to other projects, and continued to return to Corsley House as one of the places she lived.

Fabian Society

A S WELL AS completing her studies in 1907, and also no doubt under the influence of the Webbs and fellow LSE students, Maud became a member of the Fabian Society.[68] Her somewhat erratic involvement was focused on the Fabian Women's Group (FWG) which first met in early 1908 at the London home of Maud Pember Reeves. These women felt they had not made their presence felt sufficiently strongly, so saw the need for a separate sub-group to 'link two vital movements of their time – socialism and women's emancipation'.[69] They were, like their male counterparts, writers, journalists, lecturers, teachers, and also members of newer professions such as

65 *Warminster & Westbury Journal* 15 July 1910 p 8

66 *Warminster & Westbury Journal* 17 Oct 1924 p 5

67 *Wiltshire News* 7 February 1913 WANHS Library Cuttings Book 13 p 99

68 *Fabian News* March 1907 p 32 Candidates for election included Miss Maud F Davies, Waltham Place, Maidenhead.

69 Alexander S, ed, 1988 *Women's Fabian Tracts*, Routledge p 5-6

doctors, nurses, local government officers, sanitary inspectors and unemployment officers.

Maud Davies' name appears in three or four main areas of activity. She attended FWG meetings spasmodically.[70] In addition to the formal contributions mentioned below she supported a resolution from the Society of Authors to the House of Commons standing committee on the Copyright Bill in May 1911 whereby a married woman, when joint author with her husband, would have her interest in the work considered as if she were *femme sole*. And later that year she suggested that a list of defaulters on subscriptions be hung up at meetings for all to see![71]

Maud's interest and experience as an economic historian and as a social investigator was put to good use in this context. In 1911 she presented two papers at FWG meetings: 'Women Workers in Village Life' in March, and 'Women in Agriculture after the break-up of the Manorial System' in May.[72] The latter was one in a series of historical papers under the overall title of 'Women as productive workers and as consumers in the past'.

She went to two Fabian Summer Schools, in 1911 in Switzerland and 1912 in Keswick. These events became landmarks in the Fabian calendar even though they did not always conform to the Webbs' objectives of 'a compromise between studiousness and a certain amount of carefully devised entertainment'.[73]

70 LSE Fabian Archive H27 Fabian Women's Group Attendance List 1909-1921. MFD attended in May, July and November 1909, March April May June and October 1911, and January and October 1912

71 H25 Fabian Women's Group Meetings 1908-1914

72 Fabian Women's Group *Three Years Work*, p14 and 15, reprinted in Alexander 1988 p159 -160

73 Beatrice Webb reflecting on the six weeks she and Sidney had spent at the 1910 summer school set out the criteria for improvement in future years. The Webbs were out of the country in 1911 and only just returned in 1912 for the two summer schools, attended by Maud, so sadly there are no comments from that source. BW diary 4 September 1910. LSE Digital Library

The Fabian Society published lists of their members who were prepared to give lectures around the country. On the list of July 1912 Maud F Davies offered a selection of topics which, with one exception, represented her interests and expertise revealed in her range of other activities.[74] 'Care of Schoolchildren', 'Rural Revival', 'Women in Local Government', 'Sweated industries in the Rural Districts', and 'Woman's Suffrage'. The last title is something of a surprise, as no other evidence has been found of her direct involvement in the suffrage movement. Within the FWG, the parliamentary franchise was the concern of the Suffrage Committee, of which Maud was not a member. She did sit on the Citizenship Sub-Committee, which was concerned with women in local government. The terms of reference of this committee focussed on promoting women as candidates and 'to educate women electors in their responsibilities and opportunities'.[75] Even if she herself did not wish to stand for election there would have been plenty to do as a canvasser or organiser. Maud's father's experience with the Poor Law Board, and perhaps even her own brush with the Parish Council in Corsley might have stimulated this interest.

Maud Davies also sat on the 'Women's Right to Work' sub-committee.[76] This group had a wide remit watching regulation affecting women's work, identifying opportunities for women's work, and advocating equal pay for equal work. Maud's involvement with this topic would have been based partly on her own experience, but also she was able to develop the work she had done for *LEV*, which appeared in two posthumous publications.

Married Women's Work edited by Clementina Black was first published in 1915. It was 'the report of an enquiry undertaken by

---

74 Fabian Archives C62/1 ff177

75 FWG Fifth Annual Report published as supplement to *Fabian News* February 1913 p 4

76 ibid p 2

the Women's Industrial Council'.[77] The WIC had been established in 1894 with a very broad interest in women's work, its members were 'social activists as well as social investigators' and its commitment to investigation as a tool for understanding social problems and bringing about change would have reflected what Maud had learnt from the Webbs and others at LSE and which she had aimed to achieve with *LEV*. The women involved with this project were given a booklet of suggestions *Hints to Investigators,* and charged with obtaining a substantial quantity of information about the women they interviewed, their family and working lives, and the economic context of their community.[78] Maud wrote the chapter on Rural Districts. For this she worked from her familiarity with west Wiltshire, contrasting the working lives of married women who took in hand stitching for the gloving industry with those who worked outside the home, concluding '[c]ertainly the Wiltshire cottage woman who goes out to work is a healthier, happier person, a better mother, and, presumably, a better mate than her home-keeping sister'. Studies by Maud of tailoresses in an area of rural Essex, and agricultural workers in west Worcestershire, permitted comparisons to be made which reinforced her favourable view of married women who worked outside the home. Given the reaction in Corsley to the publication of *LEV*, it is interesting that she felt able to return only a few years later to a district not far distant to carry out a detailed, and what might be considered equally intrusive investigation. However, the results, though not always uncritical, were couched in a format less likely to permit the identification of individuals, and of course by the time they were published Maud was dead.

77 Black, C, 1915 *Married Women's Work*, G Bell, reprinted Virago Press 1983 with new introduction by E F Mappen, on which this paragraph is based. MFD's chapter has footnote 'the articles about rural workers had not received their final revision at the time of the author's death, and might have been altered in a few particulars'. Virago edn p 230

78 The 'schedule of enquiry employed' is included as Appendix 1, Virago edn p 254

The obituary for Maud Davies carried in *Fabian News* states '[s]he took part in our Rural Enquiry, which has been sitting during the autumn, and was intending to devote her time to rural reform on her return ...'.[79] In August 1913 a special supplement appeared in *The New Statesman* which contained the 'Draft Report of the Chairman of the Land and Rural Problems Committee of the Fabian Society, which for the past year has been investigating the subject'.[80] To illustrate 'the poverty of the labourer' data from *LEV* was quoted, in complimentary terms to its author: 'in her clever book', and 'the best authorities [on budgets] are again Miss Davies and Mr Mann'. There would have been plenty for her to do campaigning for rural reform based on the extensive recommendations in the report, including amongst the nearly 20 clauses a minimum wage for agricultural labourers, the abolition of the Poor Law, the establishment of experimental farms by local authorities and the nationalisation of the railways.

As a final contribution to the Fabian Society, Maud had left a note amongst her papers saying that 'if she made a will she would have left £100 to Mr Pease and Mr Sidney Webb to be used for any purposes they thought fit, such as the Enquiry on Industrial Organisation. Her family have taken the view that her wishes in this matter should be respected, and have forwarded a cheque for the amount, an action on their part which will, we are sure, be appreciated by all concerned'.[81] Without knowing when the note was written, did this indicate simple common sense rather than a premonition on Maud's part when she set off on her final travels? And on the assumption that Maud's family would have had no sympathy with the objectives of the Fabian Society, the respect for her wishes is significant.

79 *Fabian News* Vol XXIV No 4 March 1913 p 28

80 *New Statesman*, Vol 17 Saturday 2 August 1913, additional pages not numbered

81 *Fabian News* Vol XXIV No 7 June 1913

School Care Committees

M AUD DAVIES' SECOND known published work is also dated
1909. *School Care Committees. A guide to their work* was based
on her experience in this specialised area of social welfare in London,
which again reflected her fundamental belief in the importance of
understanding the causes of poverty. The pioneer in this field was
Margaret Frere who, as a school manager in a very poor district of the
capital in the late 1890s, set out to discover *why* children continued to
come to school underfed and wearing little but rags despite generous
charitable schemes providing meals, boots and clothing. At her school
she established a Charitable Funds Committee 'to concern itself with
everything affecting the welfare of the children. They [the committee
members] visited families in connection with boots and clothing,
physical defects, holidays and employment on leaving school'.[82] In
1902 this became the first Children's Care Committee and was used
as an exemplar when the London County Council took over from
the London School Board in 1904 and looked in more detail at the
welfare of schoolchildren. Their responsibilities were extended under
the Education (Provision of Meals) Act of 1906 and in the following
year the Education (Administrative Provisions) Act that provided for
the medical inspection of children at school. Margaret Frere herself,
by then a member of LCC Education Committee, wrote *Children's
Care Committees. How to work them in public elementary schools,* also
published in 1909, and giving the impression of taking the 'official'
line on the operation of care committees. 'School and home,' she
insisted, 'must be much more firmly linked together in the new order
of things than they were in the old'. [83]

82 Quoted in Williams, A S, Ivin, P and Mores, C, 2001, *The Children of London,*
    Institute of Education, of which ch 3 is the main source for this section. See
    also Willmott, P, 2004, 'London's School Care Committee Service 1908-1989,'
    Voluntary Action Vol 6, No 2

83 Quoted in Williams et al, 2001, p 46

Maud's substantial booklet is a very practical handbook, emphasising the delicate but vital role of the women volunteers who performed the fundamental work of the committees in visiting children's homes.

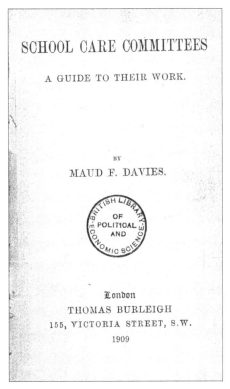

The work affords scope therefore for ability and experience of a high degree, and of very varied nature, and it is to be anticipated that it will appeal most strongly to capable women of leisure, who by co-operation with school medical officers, and other public officials, will find an unlimited field for effectual work, yielding rapid and gratifying returns, in the visible improvement of the children.[84]

SCHOOL CARE COMMITTEES

A GUIDE TO THEIR WORK.

BY

MAUD F. DAVIES.

London

THOMAS BURLEIGH

155, VICTORIA STREET, S.W.

1909

*Title page of School Care Committees
(copy in British Library of Political and
Economic Science)*

'Capable women of leisure' meant those like herself and older, some married, some not, who had time to spare and the inclination to seek a purposeful role in society. Care committees provided a hierarchical structure that also gave valuable experience on which women who subsequently sought a professional career could build. [85] The recruitment, training and deployment of the women volunteers

84 Davies, M F, 1909a, p 8

85 Willmott , 2004

was essential to running an effective service and Maud Davies was critical of some aspects of the official approach that failed in this respect. Emphasis on close examination of 'deserving cases' held, she felt, a mistaken echo of the Poor Law; the distinction between 'visiting' and 'investigation' was unhelpful, and was required by concern for 'the proper expenditure of the rate-payers' money'. [86]

Her criticisms were taken further in a paper given by Maud Davies at the National Conference on the Prevention of Destitution held in London in the summer of 1911. On the morning of the third day, the first of six papers was 'The Work and Organisation of a Care Committee' by Miss Maud E (sic) Davies. [87] In her opening remarks she commented '. . . as a bold experiment in employing voluntary help in the public service failure is no less instructive than success, and from this point of view it [LCC Children's Care Committees as at present constituted] offers most valuable lessons'.[88]   In turn she analysed the 'various types' of *personelle* , as she put it, who are 'thrown, more or less haphazard . . . into separate committees attached to each school'. Many might indeed be effectively deployed but she found voluntary workers 'are not being given the right things to do and are turning away in disgust', while there is ' little regular, smoothly working routine connected with this somewhat imperfect and inadequate machinery'.[89] After expounding at length on the difficulties and inadequacies she had noticed, she ended on a slightly more positive note:

86   Davies, M F, 1909a, p 11

87   Report of the Proceedings of the National Conference on the Prevention of Destitution held at Caxton Hall, Westminster on May 30th and 31st, and June 1st and 2nd 1911. University of California Library digital copy online at www.archive.org/details/reportofproceedioonatiiala. The papers were circulated beforehand and taken as read, each paper reader was allowed 10 minutes at the beginning of the discussion to give a brief summary.

88   ibid p 308

89   ibid p 310

To conclude, while all investigation, registration and routine should be in the hands of paid officers, who would provide a headquarters for organisation and information to parents and children on the one hand and voluntary workers on the other, volunteers can find full scope – *Firstly* in home visiting, either for definite purposes such as after-care, or for permanent and periodical supervision and friendly visiting of particular families; *secondly* in help at boys' and girls' clubs, play centres, happy evenings etc; and *thirdly* in inaugurating new and as yet unthought-of schemes for the social betterment of children.[90]

Maud was followed in the programme by London County Council's Organiser of Care Committees, Douglas Pepler, and it did not escape the notice of the audience that the voluntary worker was critical of her fellow volunteers, and Mr Pepler was critical of aspects of the work of the officials in the scheme. [91]

While Maud Davies was clearly writing with passion and from experience, it is difficult to ascertain the details of her personal involvement. The emphasis she placed on the role of the volunteer as a visitor being a sympathetic listener, who will discover 'a great deal of information will be poured into her willing ears . . . and after a period of observation . . . she will be in a position to make tactful suggestions'; 'she can at least exert a beneficial effect by merely being a soothing or civilising influence in the home',[92] suggest that this was where she found most satisfaction and impact in her own work.

In 1909 Miss Davies was a member of the School Care Committee at Upper Kensington Lane School, and Vauxhall Street School. Her address was given as 28 Hans Place, SW. This was where Maud's aunt Catherine Anne Davies lived, so the interpretation has to be either

90   ibid p 315

91   ibid p 352

92   Davies, M F, 1909a p 10-11

that Maud was staying with her or that Catherine Davies herself was a Care Committee Volunteer, in the latter case she would have been able to share her knowledge with Maud. Later in the same year and into 1910-11, Miss Davies at 23 Hogarth Road, Earl's Court SW, was on the committee for a group of schools in Camberwell. Confirmation that this was Maud herself comes from a note in *Fabian News* when she was the contact for a proposed 'Care Committee Guild' to consist of 'members of Children's Care Committees who are anxious to carry out efficiently and to extend the work entrusted to them . . .'.[93]

The respect paid by her mentors to Maud's publication on care committees might perhaps be measured by its inclusion in the list of books requested by Beatrice Webb writing to members and friends of the National Committee for the Prevention of Destitution on the lines of the Minority Report of the Poor Law Commission for the new library (*LEV* was there too), and in the reading list for the same organisation's course of study on the prevention of destitution.[94]

The white slave trade

THIS EMOTIVE SUBJECT, involving the luring, sometimes kidnapping, of women for sale into prostitution across international boundaries, was current from the later-19th century but popular interest in the subject came to a head in the years immediately preceding the First World War.[95] The traffic took a number of routes, the most notorious being from eastern Europe to north and south America, some through major UK ports. Rescue

93 *Fabian News* Vol XXI No 2 January 1910 p 13

94 LES archives COLL MISC 0862. It also appears in the bibliography of *What an Education Committee Can Do (Elementary Schools)*, Fabian Tract No 156 published in 1911

95 Bristow E J, 1977 *Vice and vigilance: purity movements in Britain since 1700*, Gill & Macmillan

for these vulnerable, often very young, victims became an important philanthropic objective for various bodies, particularly the National Vigilance Association founded in 1885, and others developed by specific religious groups.

Fighting the Traffic in Young Girls or War on the White Slave Trade was published in 1910, edited by Ernest A Bell, secretary of the Illinois Vigilance Association and Superintendent of Midnight Missions. It claimed to be

> a complete and detailed account of the shameless traffic in young girls, the methods by which the procurers and panders lure innocent young girls away from home and sell them to keepers of dives . . . How to combat this hideous monster . . . What you can do to help wipe out this curse of humanity . . .,

and included 32 pages of 'striking pictures showing the workings of the blackest slavery that has ever stained the human race'.[96] William A Coote, secretary of the 'NVA for the suppression of white slave traffic', London, England, contributed a chapter that set out the long history of the trade and described his investigations around Europe. In 1902 the French government had taken the initiative to call together representatives of 16 countries that resulted in an International Agreement which 'if adopted by all civilised countries' would protect legitimate female travellers and contribute to stamping out the trade. In Britain, the Criminal Law Amendment Act (White Slave Traffic) came into effect in 1913. Campaigning for the Bill through 1912 had brought the topic to public attention that built on the propaganda in publications such as Bell's.

While full of racial and social stereotypes typical of the age, the descriptions in Bell's book of both the experiences of victims and the diligence of rescuers, set out the context within which someone

96 Bell, E A , 1910, *Fighting the Traffic in Young Girls*, G S Bell, title page

like Maud Davies might have become involved. Although her name does not appear amongst the ladies recruited for patrolling railway stations and ports, that would indeed have been one practical role. At the inquest following her death Maud's brother reported 'she was keenly interested in social problems and had lately been carrying out investigations into the white slave trade'.[97] With no further information it is only possible to speculate what this might have involved. Was the journey she undertook in the last weeks of her life part of these investigations?

The Writers' Club, Whitehall Hotel, and Wellesley Buildings

WITH THE INCREASE in opportunities in the later decades of the 19th and beginning of the 20th centuries for middle class women to take respectable employment there grew a demand from them for accommodation and for places to meet socially and safely. As a commentator wrote in 1899

> The modern professional woman, be she artist, journalist, clerk, doctor, teacher or nurse, living as she often does in rooms in the suburbs, needs some fairly central haven of refuge where she can drop in, when she has a spare hour, for a rest, cup of tea, and a glance at the newspapers.[98]

Maud Davies was a member of the Writers' Club, opened in 1892 'to provide a social and working centre for women authors and journalists'.[99] Despite its somewhat austere facilities and premises

97 *Daily Express* 14 February 1913 p 6

98 Dora Jones, quoted in Doughan D & Gordan P, 2006, *Women, Clubs and Associations in Britain,* Routledge London p 47

99 Crawford E, 'Rooms of their own' in *Ancestors* July 2007 pp36 - 41

Wellesley Buildings, Euston, London, where Maud rented a London C.C. flat

in Norfolk Street off the Strand, and its reputation for indifferent catering, the Friday house-teas came 'to rank among the most interesting gatherings in literary London'.[100] Amongst the members were eminent women writers of the time; it is pleasant to imagine Maud in their company, perhaps participating in discussion on issues of the day. It was said that she was 'an almost daily visitor' in 1912.[101] She used the Club as her postal address for a number of her activities, including registration for Fabian Summer Schools.[102]

Wellesley Buildings near Euston, and the Whitehall Hotel, Coram Street, were the two other contrasting addresses associated with Maud towards the end of her life. She apparently had the means to be comfortable, and spent much of November 1912 at the Whitehall

100 Dora Jones, Doughan & Gordon p 52, Crawford p 40.

101 *Daily Express* 6 February 1913 p 1

102 LSE archives G9 Fabian Summer School Visitors' Book 1907-1912

Hotel. The manageress there, speaking to a newspaper reporter after Maud's death, said Maud had said she would stay there again 'on a future visit to London'. It was also said 'she had many lady friends to see her here'.[103]

At the same time Maud held the tenancy of an LCC flat close to Euston station. Wellesley Buildings had been constructed as part of a slum-clearance scheme developed from 1901, with the objective of providing improved accommodation for London's working class families.[104] Quite why Maud rented this flat is unclear. It was said that she had lived there 'for some considerable time', renting 'a small top flat at 7s 6d so that she might live in the social surroundings of which she wrote', as 'she believed in studying conditions at first hand'.[105] However, financial constraints on the development meant that rents were at the top end for the nature of the housing, so Maud would not have encountered particularly needy people.[106] That she intended to continue with this arrangement was indicated by payment in advance of the rent, and also she left money with a neighbour 'to keep her doorstep and knocker clean'. When she was staying at the Whitehall Hotel from 28 October 1912, she 'used the flat as a warehouse for her furniture and as an office'.[107]

Final weeks

MOST OF THE information available about the last months of Maud Davies's life comes from press reports of evidence supplied at her inquest or from journalists who questioned her friends

---

103 *Kensington News & West London Times* 7 February 1913 p 5

104 Stillwell, M, 2011 'Housing the workers: early London County Council housing 1889-1914', *The Local Historian* Vol 41 No 4 November 2011 pp 308 - 320

105 *Daily Express* 7 February 1913 p 1

106 Stilwell p 319

107 ibid

and associates. Overall the events are reported consistently, with only minor variations, so it is possible to set out the facts as follows.

On 3 December she sailed from Southampton on board the *Arcadian*.[108] Towards the end of 1912 Maud was said to be 'run down by overwork', and decided to travel round the world.[109] She had stayed at the Whitehall Residential Hotel, Coram Street, in London from 28 October to 29 November, and told them she was going to the seaside.[110] The *Arcadian* was bound for the West Indies and New York. 138 people joined the ship at Southampton, with destinations of Madeira, Bermuda, Trinidad, Jamaica and New York. Maud was 'contracted to land' at Jamaica.[111]

Six weeks later she left Kingston, Jamaica, on 16 January 1913 on *SS Prinz August Wilhelm*[112] bound for New York. She kept in touch with her family in 'cheerful' letters. Her brother described how the last letter he received from her was dated 19 January and set out her intention of returning on the *Majestic*, due in Liverpool on 25 January. Plans seem to have changed, for Maud travelled back to the UK on the *Baltic* that docked in Liverpool overnight of 31 January-1 February. On Saturday 1 February Maud and other passengers took the boat

108 TNA BT/27/784

109 *Kensington News & West London Times* 7 February 1913 p 5. Evidence from Capt [Claude] Martin Davies (brother)

110 *Daily Express* 6 February 1913, p 1, the hotel manageress talking to an 'Express representative'.

111 She held contract ticket number 2. Ticket 1 belonged to Mr and Mrs D Urwick, also travelling to Jamaica. Hugh Grice has speculated whether Maud Davies was travelling with the Urwicks (their tickets having been purchased together), as there was a Professor E J Urwick (1867-1945) a sociolgist at LSE (personal communication to John Chandler). I can find no connection between Prof Urwick and Douglas Ridsdale Urwick, who came from a long line of London wine merchants and travelled abroad frequently (often to Portugal where his wife was born). Mr and Mrs D Urwick returned to Southampton on the *Oruba* on 3 February and were not called at the inquest.

112 Ancestry, passenger list

train to London, where it arrived at Euston at 2.30 pm.[113] Her luggage was left at the station, all labelled 'Miss Davies room 173 SS Baltic', despite the proximity of her flat in Wellesley Buildings. She travelled to High Street, Kensington, (one underground ticket was issued to that station from Euston that day), where at 4.45pm she purchased a ticket to Notting Hill Gate. Her decapitated body was found in the tunnel in the early hours of the following morning, on the line some 70 yards from the station.

Nothing is known about Maud's time in Jamaica, or the days she spent in New York. And there are several strange facets of her homeward journey on the *Baltic*. When Hugh Grice wrote *Corsley House: a history* in 1999 he consulted the relevant passenger list for the incoming voyage at the then Public Record Office, only to find no one with the name Maud Davies. There was a Muriel Davies, aged 37, travelling 2nd class and described as a 'Domestic', whose name appeared amongst a group of unaccompanied men.[114] This class of record has now been transferred to the 'Ancestry' website, but that particular sailing is missing, and the original can no longer be located.[115] 'Domestic' was a vague term, but with distinct social connotations in the early twentieth century. However, second class accommodation on the *Baltic* was advertised for travellers who 'wish for the highest modicum of comfort in keeping with a reasonable rate of passage'[116] and so might not have prevented acquaintance with other women passengers likely to propose a debate on women's franchise.[117] Passports were not mandatory for overseas travel before 1914, so matching of

---

113 Newspaper reports differ on the time, some say 2, others 2.30.

114 Grice 1999, p 38; BT26/556

115 Appendix 6 in Grice 1999 is a photocopy of the page containing the entry for Muriel Davies; it is no longer possible to check the entire passenger list.

116 1907 White Star Line brochure www.gjenvick.com; it would appear that MFD cabin number 173 was located in second class accommodation www.norwayheritage.com/p_ship.asp?sh-balt2

117 As reported by Mrs Margaret Davies *Daily Express* 14 Feb p 6

name on ticket and name on passport was not an issue.

The only passenger from the voyage who gave evidence at the inquest was Mrs Margaret Davies (no relation to Maud) who had travelled to England with her husband and son, and reported shipboard conversations which suggested that Maud was physically unwell ('her face was blue and her teeth were chattering') but also 'gave suspicions of her mental condition' when Maud said she thought 'the boat is full of spies'.[118] Margaret Davies and Maud travelled from Liverpool to London together. Maud asked for Mrs Davies's address before they parted, and it is possible that this was how Mrs Davies was located to attend the inquest.

According to the *Daily Express*, the Baltic's medical officer 'had, it was said, reported that while on the boat Miss Davies had been ill, and 'subject to delusions" but he does not seem to have given evidence directly.[119] Dr Townsend, the police surgeon, did attend the inquest and stated that Miss Davies appeared to be in the early stages of pneumonia which 'always upsets the nervous system'. More dramatically, he also described finding 'over the heart a number of small puncture wounds. All of them had penetrated the muscles of the chest . . . and one of them had penetrated into the heart. The wounds were caused during life with some sharp instrument such as possibly a hatpin. They were not sufficient to have had any part in causing death . . . [but] they had been caused within a few hours of death'. [120] On further questioning he said it was 'impossible to say positively' if the stabs had been self-inflicted. Curious findings on the boat train from Liverpool were mentioned at the inquest: 'a search later showed thirty or forty blood stains on the lavatory, and blood marks on the basin, of which the brass spring had been pulled out

118 *Warminster & Westbury Journal* 7 February 1913, p 4

119 *Daily Express* 14 February 1913 p 6

120 *Daily Express* 6 Feb; on 8 Feb this had become a headline 'Fifteen Stabs'

straight' but with no direct evidence to connect this to Maud.[121] The broken top of a hat pin was eventually discovered in the tunnel, after several searches, again not necessarily linked.

William Clark, a ganger for the Metropolitan Railway, discovered Maud's body at 2 am, and reported that the last train would have passed at about a quarter to one. However, Maud's broken watch had stopped at 4.50, and in Dr Townsend's opinion death had occurred some hours before she was found. The body was lying between the rails of the up line, so the hundreds of trains passing by between 5 pm and 2 am would not have disturbed it. A search 'was most carefully and systematically conducted, every inch of ground being examined with lamps . . . there were no marks on the tunnel wall . . . and so sign of any struggle'.[122]

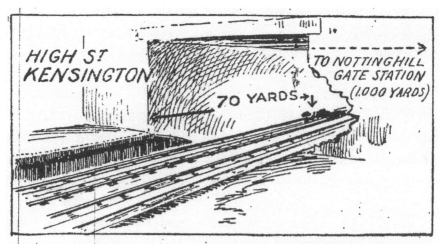

Scene of the discovery of the decapitated body of Miss Maud Davies, who had been stabbed before her death.

Sketch of the scene of Maud's death, published in the Daily Express, 6 February, 1913

An *Express* representative, as it was put by the paper, visited the scene and described 'a tunnel as black as pitch', considered that it

121 *Daily Express* 14 Feb p 6

122 *Daily Express* 7 Feb p1

would be improbable for someone to be thrown, fall (or indeed jump) out of a carriage without being seen, though at the 'usually deserted' end of the platform, a 'steep incline . . . runs down into the darkness of the tunnel and it would be possible for any person to walk down and disappear unobserved'.[123]

The inquest jury 'who met in the little coroner's court behind Kensington Town Hall, almost over the tunnel in which Miss Davies was found dead', returned an open verdict, stating that 'the evidence was not sufficient to show how she came to be in the tunnel, or how she received the many puncture wounds . . . They expressed themselves satisfied, however, that there was no evidence in support of the suggestion of murder'.[124] Local press speculation included that Maud could have been 'lured into the tunnel . . . and have then been attacked and murdered' though against that was she appeared not to have been robbed.[125] But they also took the opportunity to say 'it is trusted that the tragedy will still more forcibly direct the attention of the railway companies to the wide sliding doors, which are far from satisfactory. We ourselves have on several occasions observed them partly and even wide open after the trains have left the station'.

Many questions remain unanswered. If Maud was not murdered, did she die by accident or by her own hand? Maud's friend the stained-glass artist Caroline Townshend said she was 'absolutely satisfied that there was no foul play in this case, being convinced it was an accident'. [126] Was Maud unwell enough to be unable to prevent herself wandering off the platform, or falling from a train? Or was she sufficiently mentally ill to wish to take her own life? If so, were the puncture wounds part of this attempt, or signs of self-harm of a

123 *Daily Express* 6 Feb p 1

124 *Daily Express* 14 Feb p 6. There is no evidence from Metropolitan Police archives that her death was investigated by them as murder. MEPO 20/1

125 *Kensington News & West London Times* 7 Feb 1913 p 5

126 *West London Press* 7 Feb 1913

different order?

If Maud's original intention had indeed been to make a world tour, as stated by her brother at the inquest, why did she curtail the journey? Why did she travel from New York using a different first name? If she was becoming short of money that might account for the second class ticket, and indeed fit with the disappearance of a necklace and cross that her brother stated she intended to take with her. Captain Davies also told the coroner that Maud had had a love affair 'not so long ago' but 'she had determined not to marry the man'. Was this person persisting in his unwanted attentions? Or had Maud crossed some ruthless elements in the white slave trade she had been researching? Or perhaps was she even travelling incognito as part of this investigation?

Comments from Maud's brother and her friends were consistent in believing that she was most unlikely to commit suicide.[127] Miss C S MacTaggart, the registrar at the London School of Economics, had known her for 14 years and summed up the general view: 'I knew her well enough to be able to state confidently that she was a sane, sedate, clear-brained, level-headed, refined gentle woman of the best type, and incidentally with the most charming manners. Behind these delightful manners, however, lay a quiet determination. She was a woman who preferred philanthropy and the study of social conditions to the easy life of luxury, of golfing all day and dancing all night'.

How supportive were Maud's family of her desire to study at LSE, to undertake social research and to publish the results of her investigations? There is no evidence that she was prevented from making her own decisions about her life, but it had caused them some trouble such as the local furore over *LEV*. Just because she was

---

127 As well as the social stigma associated with suicide, it must be remembered that it was not decriminalised until 1961. Juries often interpreted the law mercifully, for the sake of families, by recording verdicts of 'temporary insanity' rather than the crime of '*felo de se*' with the consequent loss of property and, before 1882, shameful burial.

not actively opposed, did not mean she received any encouragement. The many different places she stayed, both in London and around the country, perhaps suggest she felt she had no settled home to call her own. Would having friends who led unconventional lifestyles have met with disapproval from the members of her family who held traditional social values to be of great importance? Did this make her life intolerably difficult?

What had been Maud's relationship with her mother? How did Frances Davies' death in the summer of 1910 affect her daughter? In the mid-1890s Mrs Davies had had surgery for breast cancer, and presumably recovered her health.[128] Her death certificate states that the carcinoma had appeared in her lung some 3 to 5 months earlier, and she had suffered from pleurisy for the final ten days of her life. It is not known if Maud was with her. The death was registered by her son Claude Martin Davies.

Also unknown is Maud's father's state of health; he lived until 1924 but was presumably also affected by his wife's death, and he might not have been sufficiently well to be a positive support to his daughter. Shortly after Maud's death Byam Davies undertook a tour of European cities with George Atwood, rector of Bishopstrow. Rev Atwood kept a diary in which he recorded their journey but made no comment about the health of his companion beyond both their tendencies to catch colds. Atwood was the more confident traveller, but both appear to have enjoyed the holiday.[129]

At the time it would have still been expected that an unmarried daughter remain in the family home at the disposal of her parents. Maud had already left before her mother's final illness, and although

128 She was visiting the local school in the first decade of the 20th century. Eg January 23 1905 'Mrs Davis (sic) visited the school and gave a present to each child in the Infant Department'. Corsley School Log Book. WSA F8/500/84/1/1

129 WSA 1229/1. Atwood expressed views that were vehemently anti-women's suffrage, so may also have been out of sympathy with Davies' support of his daughter.

her father was well enough to travel, and lived for another decade, he was not a young man. Did her brothers express their disapproval of her failure to conform to orthodox expectations, leaving them to take responsibility for their parents? Claude and Warburton dealt with Maud's affairs after her death[130]; Claude and his father superintended the erection of her gravestone[131] but that did not mean they had not put intolerable pressure on her over the years to change her life back to being simply a dutiful daughter.

Against these negative forces, Maud was held in high regard by associates and friends in her many activities in London. As has been demonstrated in the sections above examining the varied work with which she became involved, as well as comments made after her death, Maud was building a reputation for herself. This might have encouraged her to hold a more optimistic view of the future, but was perhaps not powerful enough.

'An astonishing mystery [is left] a mystery still' was how both the *Wiltshire News* and the *Daily Express* closed their final reports.[132] Maud Davies's death remains unexplained to this day.

130 Claude gave evidence at the inquest; Warburton as executor dealt with her GWR shares.

131 WSA 1229/1 Rev Atwood's diary 18 November 1913

132 *Wiltshire News* 27 Feb 1913 WANHS Library Cuttings Book 13 p 95 ; *Daily Express* 14 Feb 1913 p 6. In their first report the comment was made 'Even the apparently insoluble *Mystery of the Yellow Room* presented a problem little more difficult than this' 6 February 1913 p 1. Written by Gaston Leroux, better known as the author of *The Phantom of the Opera*, this was one of the earliest 'locked room mystery' crime fiction novels. It was first published in 1908, having previously appeared in instalments in the periodical *L'Illustration* . It is said that 'the emphasis of the story is firmly on the intellectual challenge to the reader' (Wikipedia). *Mystery of the Yellow Room* is available as a free ebook from Project Gutenburg for readers who might wish to follow up the analogy.

LIFE IN AN ENGLISH VILLAGE

PART ONE

CORSLEY IN THE PAST

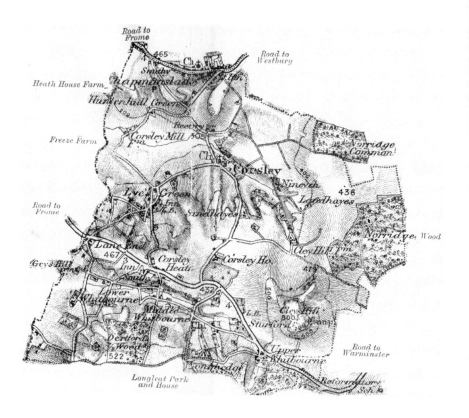

Corsley parish, from Ordnance Survey mapping, c. 1890

I

The Parish under Cley Hill

BEYOND THE FAR western border of Salisbury Plain, dividing the chalk Downs, which descend to it with a sweeping curve, from the rich, wooded vales of Somersetshire, lies a shelf or plateau, some four hundred feet below the Downs, and midway between their summits and the sea, but with a wide view over the yet lower lying valley to the west.

On this shelf, which is composed of a rich and fertile sandy soil, the parish of Corsley is situated, extending over an area of 4 ¾ square miles.[1]

Towards the eastern margin of the parish an oval-shaped hill rises abruptly from the plain, and stands, facing the downs, two miles distant, resembling them in every feature of substance and form, an isolated fragment, which has somehow been separated from the main body and left stranded on a foreign soil.

The eastern boundary of Corsley parish passes over this hill, whose name, Cley Hill, is probably a Celtic and Saxon reduplication, and from its summit we may obtain a wide view of the environments, while the parish itself lies spread below us to the west.

Facing eastward we see the rolling Downs, extending line beyond line to the far horizon. Through their centre the River Wylie has cut a broad valley, down which it finds its way to meet the southern

---

1 The exact area is 3,056 statute acres. At the census of 1881 the area was 2,580 statute acres, or 4 square miles; but between 1881 and 1891 part of Norton Bavant was transferred to Corsley parish (*Census Report, 1891*, vol. ii. p. 394).

Avon, a valley now traversed by the high-road and the line of the Great Western Railway from Warminster to Salisbury.

Near at hand, in the mouth of the valley, with a background of green hills and woods, lies Warminster, plainly distinguishable, with its churches, while to the left lime-quarriers have cut the Down into perpendicular white cliffs. This little town, about two miles distant as the crow flies, was formerly the principal corn-market of the West of England, and is one of the four places where the Wiltshire Quarter Sessions are held. The level land between Cley Hill and the Downs, to the north-east, is occupied by Norridge Wood.

Round Cley Hill the high ground forms a rough semicircle from north and east to south, where, divided from us, as we stand on the hilltop, by a narrow gap, through which the roadway from Frome to Warminster passes, the land rises fully to the height of the neighbouring grassy Downs, its true relationship to the latter being veiled by a rich covering of pines and deciduous trees, of rhododendron and azalea; for the whole tract to the south of Corsley belongs to the famous park and woods of Longleat, once within the bounds of the ancient Forest of Selwood, the beauty of its splendid timber and rich pastures being wonderfully enhanced by the broken and hilly character of the ground, which lends itself to their full display, besides affording more distant views of surprising beauty.

Turning back to the north, we see at the foot of the Downs, four miles away, the market town of Westbury, with red smoke emerging from the chimneys of the iron-works. The main line of the Great Western Railway to Weymouth and Cornwall passes through Westbury, thence running on into Somersetshire, where it touches Frome.

This latter picturesque old town lies for the most part buried from our sight in a cuplike valley four miles distant to the west, those dwellings only which are situated on the hilltops around it meeting the eye from where we stand. Midway between Frome and Cley Hill runs the line of division between Wiltshire and Somersetshire, this line coinciding with the western boundary of Corsley parish.

Beyond Frome, across the broad valley of the Bristol Avon, is a line of low hills, bounding the view on the western horizon. Behind these lie the coal-mines of Radstock, important to the parish of Corsley on account of the considerable business which is carried on by the inhabitants in transporting timber thither and returning with coal, timber having, during the nineteenth century, taken the place in this transaction of the corn from Warminster market, which for many centuries was carried at first on packhorses, later in wagons, to feed the populous cities of Bristol and Bath.

Having surveyed the environment, we may now turn our eyes downwards to the parish at our feet.

Cley Hill and the ridge in Longleat woods form part of the watershed between the rivers of the south on the one hand which flow into the English Channel, and on the other the rivers of the west flowing northwards into the Bristol Channel.

Two tiny streams rise and flow westward through Corsley. Small as they are, these little brooks serve to feed the rich and valuable water meadows which lie along their margin.

Between these streams, which run near the northern and southern borders of the parish, the land falls gently from the foot of the steep chalk hills, for Cley Hill has a diminutive companion to the north. Round the hills is a belt of arable land;[1] next to this a fine pasture, with here and there an arable field, extending westward for a mile or so, intersected by well-timbered hedgerows and small copses; then, beyond, the ground falls out of sight in broken valleys, which verge on the Somersetshire country.

The visitor who climbs to the summit of the hill usually inquires, after a survey, 'Where is the village?' – the remarkable fact being that, with a population of from seven hundred to eight hundred, there is no village, properly speaking. The dwellings lie scattered over the area, in hamlets, in groups of two or three, or in solitary houses.

1   Part of this was laid down to grass in 1907.

One group is formed by the parish church, a farmhouse, once the manor-house, and the parish school, no other dwellings being found here.

Sturford Mead, one of the larger houses of the parish, forms the nucleus to a group of houses and cottages, as well as being in close vicinity to Whitbourne Springs and other hamlets.

Corsley House, and the smaller residence of Sandhayes, on the other hand, form isolated groups in central Corsley, with a few cottages only in their neighbourhood.

The numerous farmhouses lie scattered over the parish, some isolated, as Cley Hill Farm, one of the historical houses of the parish; others in the midst the hamlets; others, again, near the hamlets, or with a few cottages grouped round them.

The bulk of the cottage population is distributed in, roughly speaking, nine principal hamlets, besides several smaller ones, and many quite isolated pairs of cottages, or even single dwellings. These hamlets are sometimes fairly compact groups, such as Corsley Heath or Leighs Green; sometimes they are a collection of scattered or straggling dwellings, such as Dartford or Whitbourne Moor. None deserves the name of a village. There is, however, one village, situated on high ground to the north of the parish, named Chapmanslade. Curiously enough this typical village, consisting mainly of a long row of houses on either side of the village street, is not a distinct parish at all, but is divided up among three or four neighbouring parishes. The street runs east and west, and the houses to the south of the street belong to Corsley. This village, though without separate parochial rights, forms a distinct centre of social life. It has its own church, its own chapels, its school, and its police-constable, all, however, situated or resident on the northern side, and, therefore, not in our parish. It has also three public-houses, two of these being on the Corsley side of the street.

In Corsley there is no such nucleus, the parish church and school being situated in one hamlet, the Church of St. Mary and the

Baptist chapel in a second at Temple, the post-office, police-constable, and a public-house in a third at Corsley Heath, a Wesleyan chapel and a public-house in a fourth at Lane End, and another public-house in a fifth hamlet at Leighs Green.

For the position of the various hamlets and houses in Corsley the reader must be referred to the map. Speaking broadly, the population is collected along the western and southern borders, extending from Chapmanslade in the north-west, southward in the hamlets of Huntley, Leighs Green, Lane End, and Dartford, then passing east from the two latter, in Corsley Heath, Whitbourne Moor, Temple, Longhedge, and Whitbourne Springs.

No large hamlets lie in the north-easterly and central portion of the parish, and this distribution of the population dates back to feudal times, when the three great common fields lay under Cley Hill and to the north, while the hill itself was doubtless a sheepwalk, as it is to-day, and the homesteads belonging to the several manors which shared the common fields were distributed in the more sheltered nooks of the westward and southern districts. For all the evidence we have points to the fact that the more exposed hamlets, such as Corsley Heath and Longhedge, are of much more recent origin than those in the cups of the valleys like Whitbourne, Temple, and Leighs Green.

It is tempting, though perhaps somewhat rash, to speculate how it was that the dwellings of Corsley came to be scattered over its area in a fashion dissimilar to that of neighbouring parishes.

Professor Maitland, in *Domesday Book and Beyond*, describes two main types of parishes, the nucleated village and the parish of scattered hamlets and homesteads, and he suggests that the village of nucleated type may have been founded by Germanic settlers, while the scattered village owes its characteristics to a Celtic origin. [1]

Again, he throws out a hint that where within historical times large tracts of forest land have existed hamlets rather than villages

1   F.W. Maitland, *Domesday Book and Beyond*, p. 15.

may be found.[1]

The peculiar distribution of the dwellings in Corsley may be due to either or both of these causes.

There was, in olden times, a Celtic settlement upon the summit of Cley Hill,[2] which is still surrounded by the lines of its entrenchments, and crowned by two barrows, one of which was anciently used for sepulchral purposes.[3]

It is for antiquaries to discuss the probability of this Celtic settlement having extended into the valleys at the foot of the hill, and the ancient Britons having thus been, as Professor Maitland suggests, the originators of a type of parish which appears to be unique in the district.

This view is given colour by the fact that when the common fields were enclosed in the eighteenth century the award map shows that these were divided up into irregular strips and patches, quite unlike the regular rectangular strips of other common fields of the district. This would appear to be an indication of Celtic origin.

But whether or no the Celts in this district forsook the hilltops for the plain, the second cause suggested by Professor Maitland must undoubtedly have played a part in shaping the form of Corsley, which was within the bounds of the ancient royal forest of Selwood until the seventeenth century.[4] In the reign of King Edward I the office of bailiff or forester of the forest was granted at a rent of £10 per annum to Sir Reginald de Kingston, whose family are affirmed by Canon Jackson to have resided in Corsley itself.[5] Sir Reginald, in the following reign, petitioned for a reduction of his rent, as the extent of the forest had

1   Ibid. p. 16.

2   Sir Richard Colt Hoare, *History of Ancient Wilts: Hundred of Warminster*, p. 51.

3   Ibid.

4   *Wilts Archaeol. Mag.* xxiii. p. 289. Depositions as to the extent of Selwood Forest, taken about A.D. 1620-30.

5   *Wilts Archaeol. Mag.* xxiii. p. 286.

been so reduced as to result in a loss instead of a profit to the bailiff. An inquisition held at Longbridge Deverel found that the £10 had been raised only by violent acts of extortion and by seizing the grain of poor people;[1] the rent was accordingly reduced to one mark per annum, and all arrears remitted, without, however, any subsequent benefit to the oppressed inhabitants. [2]

The vill of Corsley was, in mediaeval times, divided into several distinct manors, and at the present day the parish contains no less than seven, four completely, three more only in part.[3] In each manor a small nucleus of homesteads was naturally formed round the demesne farm. Then, later, upon the waste lands which abounded in Corsley new hamlets of squatters grew up. The names of the hamlets of Corsley Heath, Whitbourne Moor, and Leighs Green, seem to imply this origin, and tradition ascribes it to others, such as Longhedge.

We do not know when squatting on the wastes commenced in Corsley, but some of these new hamlets arose not long since, when the development of the cloth trade in the seventeenth and eighteenth centuries brought new immigrants. To take an example, the cluster of houses at Corsley Heath appears to have sprung up mainly after the enclosure and allotment of the main part of this common in 1742,[4] though a few cottages existed here previously.[5] Most of the houses were probably built on a piece of waste ground left unallotted at the time the inclosure was made, this being at a nodal position where lanes cross the high-road from Frome to Warminster. One small triangle of grass,

1 Ibid. p. 287. Inquisition at Longbridge Deverel, Michaelmas, 1322

2 Ibid.

3 Great Corsley, Little Corsley, Whitbourne Temple, Huntenhull, wholly in Corsley parish; Whitbourne and Bugley, partly in the parish of Warminster; Godwell and Chapmanslade, partly in Westbury parish; and Upton and Norridge, partly in Upton Scudamore.

4 See map attached to the Enclosure Agreement of 1742, in the Longleat Estate Office.

5 Corsley Survey, 1745, in the Longleat Estate Office.

with a few elms growing on it, still remains unappropriated in the centre of the hamlet, and serves as a playground for the children and a resting-place for the large trees destined to undergo transformation at the hands of the neighbouring wheelwright, or to be hauled to the Radstock coal-pits by the timber merchants. Another strip of turf here has been appropriated and enclosed into some cottage gardens within the last ten years.

Finally, after the enclosure of the common fields, when the land was for a time allotted in large farms, a new colony of labourers clustered round the principal farmhouse, where this was not already the centre of a hamlet. It was in this way that the hamlet of Chips or Landhayes grew suddenly up in a region to the north-west of Cley Hill, now again lonely as in feudal times but for the old house, once the residence of the Kington family, known as Cley Hill Farm. This hamlet sprang up rapidly with the development of corn-growing, and within the memory of living inhabitants formed the busiest centre of agricultural life, disappearing as rapidly as it rose with the agricultural depression of the latter nineteenth century and the changes from arable to pasture-farming.

Thus, while some of the hamlets of recent growth have become well established, and are more populous and important than the older groups, others, owing to the constant ebb of population which has continued since the middle of the nineteenth century, are now deserted, and remain nothing but a name and tradition, with, perhaps, a thick bed of nettles to mark where human habitations once stood.

The first description of Corsley which we have at present is found in the Domesday Survey. The vil then had its mill and its wood. There was 1 hide of land, 1 carucate being in demesne,[1] with 4 bordars. The translation of the passage runs as follows:

---

1   The expressions ('hide' and 'carucate ') are not identical, but should both correspond to the plough team. See P. Vinogradoff, *Villainage in England*, and other writings.

Azor holds 1 hide in *Corselie*. The land is 1 carucate, which is there in demesne with 4 bordars. There is a mill, paying 40 pence, and the wood is 1 furlong long and half a furlong broad. It is worth 20 shillings.[1]

We cannot here attempt to unravel the confused threads of manorial, ecclesiastical, and parochial history. Most, if not all, the lands and manors of Corsley passed in pre-Reformation days into the hands of various religious houses, and the lords and tenants of its different component manors shared in the cultivation of the three great common fields of Chedinhanger, Cley Hill, and Bickenham, while holding separate enclosed crofts, probably in the neighbourhood of their homesteads. Sheep-farming and the dairy were important branches of agriculture in mediaeval Corsley, and both horses and oxen were used to draw the plough.

In A.D. 1364 the Prior of Maiden Bradley, who was Lord of the Manor of Whitbourne, held 60½ acres of arable and meadow land in the common fields and 34 acres enclosed in crofts; he had also an acre of wood, which was used for pasture. He might keep 4 farm horses and 12 oxen, 12 cows and 250 sheep.[2]

The common fields were situated in the north-east and centre of the parish, in districts still almost uninhabited, and common-field cultivation continued until the last quarter of the eighteenth century.

Corsley is in the Hundred of Warminster,[3] and likewise in the Petty Sessional Division to which this town gives its name. It is in the parliamentary constituency of the Westbury Division of Wiltshire. The parish is situated midway on the base of a triangle formed by the

---

1   William H. Jones, *Domesday for Wilts*, p. 135

2   See extent of Whitbourne in Appendix, p. 293. ###

3   In a MS. Register at Longleat it is recorded that 'Out of Corsley Manor was paid viiis yearly to the Sheriff's Turne at *Hundred Oke*.' Tradition locates this ancient oak-tree in Southleigh Woods on the far side of Warminster. See Wilts Archaeol. Mag. xxiii. p. 284.

market towns of Warminster, Frome, and Westbury, the two former being each about 2½ miles distant from its eastern and western boundaries, while Westbury is 3½ miles from its northern extremity at Chapmanslade.

It has a main line of the Great Western Railway three miles away, with the two important stations of Frome and Westbury, the former just over, the latter just under, 100 miles from Paddington Station. From Warminster it has communication with Salisbury by a branch of the Great Western Railway, which there meets the London and South Western line.

Corsley is traversed by the main road from Frome to Warminster, which passes through or within a mile of nearly all the important hamlets. A main road from Westbury to Frome touches the northern margin of the parish, passing through the village of Chapmanslade. Good roads afford easy means of transit to Bath, Bristol, and Radstock in the west, to Trowbridge and Bradford on the north, to the towns of Somersetshire on the south, and to Salisbury on the east.

The parish itself is intersected by an intricate network of lanes and footpaths, which wind about in a manner which is often unintelligible at the present day, but which probably owe some of their unexplained turns to the position of now vanished dwellings. Some are ancient roadways sunk deep below the level of the fields they traverse, and in certain cases another roadway on the higher ground has been formed alongside them. These lanes and pathways connect up all the hamlets and scattered dwellings.

While each hamlet forms a little social group of its own, there are two main nuclei of the parish, the one at Chapmanslade, towards which Huntenhull, Huntley Green, and Gore Lane turn, the other in Corsley itself, which, though it has no definitely located centre, unless we consider the parish church and school as such, yet forms a closely connected whole for social and administrative purposes.

2

Seignorial Unification

THE REFORMATION, WHICH had such a profound and far-reaching influence on agricultural England, marks in Corsley the epoch of its unification and organisation in a form which underwent little change for over two centuries, and which retains some of its principal features at the present day. We may therefore date the modern history of Corsley from this period; and though there is much in its later life which cannot be fully understood without a reference to that earlier history of the parish which has still to be published, yet the main lines of its social, industrial, and religious development may from this time on be followed by the modern student without serious check.

The manors of Corsley, Whitbourne, and Huntenhull, hitherto held by different religious houses, more or less remotely situated, were after various vicissitudes of grant, sale, and purchase, for the first time collected into the hands of one single lord, Sir John Thynne.[1]

The other manors, partly situated in the present parish of Corsley, namely Godwell and Chapmanslade, Bugley, and Upton and Norridge, do not appear to have been acquired by the Thynne family till a later date, but Sir John Thynne purchased lands and property in these manors as well as in those where he acquired right of manorial jurisdiction, and thus the main part of the parish was for the first time since the component manors had emerged from the woodlands or had been split up into distinct tenures, brought under the influence

1   For list of purchases made by Sir John Thynne in Corsley Parish, see Appendix
    I. pp. 276-86.

and control of a single owner. Again, in ecclesiastical matters, though Corsley, with its adjoining hamlets, had during the preceding centuries gradually acquired parochial rights, other chapels beside the parish church existed within its bounds. Kington Court Chapel, the last of these, ceased to be a place of worship at the time of the Reformation, and Corsley Church became the sole centre of religious life, as it remained till the growth of a dissenting population led to the erection of chapels in the nineteenth century.

The Corsley of Sir John Thynne's day must have differed considerably in outward aspect from Corsley as we know it. It still formed part of the Forest of Selwood, which was not finally disafforested till about 1630[1] and the wild deer roamed freely over it. In Chapmanslade Wood and Dafford Wood the deer were kept by the foresters of Sir John Thynne. Corsley Woods were unenclosed, and the deer, given mast here in winter, were so tame that they would scarcely move out of the way of passers-by.[2]

Sir John Thynne is reputed to have built the Manor House, now the Manor Farm, adjacent to Corsley Church. He also impaled Corsley Park,[3] whose extent to the south of the old Manor House is still traceable in names such as Parkbarn, near Corsley House, and Deerlip, near Corsley Heath, which was, no doubt, one of the boundaries between the park and the forest, a ' deer leap ' being an arrangement to admit of wild deer entering without affording any mode of egress to them.

Round the park the land lay, for the most part, unenclosed and undivided by hedges or other division.

Near Cley Hill and in the north-easterly districts of the parish were great common fields, divided into irregular strips and patches,

1 Depositions as to the extent of Selwood Forest, taken about A.D. 1620-30, printed in the *Wilts Archeaol. Mag.* xxiii. p. 289.

2 Ibid., p. 229.

3 Ibid.

cultivated in common, according to ancient custom, by the inhabitants. Besides the three arable common fields the parish had
common meadows, where hay was made. The woods of Corsley and
the neighbouring manors were at least as extensive and important as at
the present day. A great part of the parish was waste land or common,
and on the waste lands and in the woods, as well as on the common
fields and common meadows, after the harvest was gathered, the
flocks and herds of the community pastured together, being watched
by the herdsman or shepherd of the manor. But though the main
part of the parish was unenclosed till a much later date, some fields
or 'closes' were already fenced off near the dwellings, and held by
separate owners.[1] The main feature of Corsley Heath was the 'Coney
Warren', which we find mentioned half a century later.[2] Cley Hill then,
as now, stood guard over the parish, marked with the lines of ancient
encampments, but as yet maintaining its oval shape, undefaced by
quarriers and lime-burners.

The hill in those days not only protected the parish from the east
winds, but served as a watch-tower against human enemies. At the
time when Spanish invasion was feared Mr. Carr, the elder, of Corsley,
with four men from Norridge and Bugley, and others of the 'meetest
persons', were told off 'to look after the watchman, and see that the
Beacon was well and orderly watched, and fired only on just cause, nor
without making the Justices of the Peace and constables privy thereto.'[3]
The constables of the Hundred had been instructed to provide that the
Beacon 'be well and sufficiently furnished with good and dry wood,
and a barrel in which pitch hath been, besides 5 or 6 lbs. of pitch.'[4]

1   See Appendix (Extent of the Manor of Whitbourne, 38 Ed. III.), p. 278.

2   MS. Bayliffe's Account, Corsley Manor, 1634, preserved in the Longleat Estate
Office. 'And for the warren of Connyes uppon Corsley Heath we s . . . nihil for
that the Lord keepeth the same in his owne hande and by his warrenner hath
sold the Connyes wch he is to answere for.'

3   John J. Daniell, *History of Warminster*, pp. 63, 64.

4   Ibid.

Wiltshire had long been a centre of cloth-making, but we find no record or trace of the establishment of this industry in Corsley before the Civil Wars. The population was almost entirely agricultural, and the chief inhabitants yeoman farmers. The Lye family, to whom tradition ascribes considerable importance in the parish, who presented to the benefice up to the year 1485 and who have left a permanent mark in the name of one of the most important of the hamlets which constitute the parish, appear to have died out or left the place about this time. The will of William Lye, of Corsley, husbandman, was proved in 1557, and John Lye, of Corsley, was married at Frome in 1597. His administration was granted in 1603, the occupations of the two Corsley men who were his bonds being respectively 'husbandman' and 'driver'.[1]

In the Quarter Sessions' records of the year 1599 we find mention of three inhabitants of Corsley – John Smyth, *alias* Singer, carpenter; Lambe, husbandman; and John Holloway, husbandman.[2]

Similarly, whenever we meet with an allusion to a man of Corsley, his occupation, if stated, is one belonging to a farming community, engaged in the main in tilling the soil and the care of animals, with, no doubt, a few subsidiary occupations, such as black-smith and carpenter, and perhaps also tailor and shoemaker.

An apparent exception occurs in the list of contributors to the Corsley parish stock. These include two vintners, a merchant, an upholsterer, and a victualler. If these people resided and carried on their business in Corsley, the parish was not always purely agricultural in character. But more probably these were men of Corsley abstraction, or men who came to pass their old age in this retired parish, while their working lives were spent, and their fortunes made, in one of the West of England towns.

There were some fairly well-to-do people among the farmers,

1   *The Lyes of Corsley*, by J. Henry Lea. To be published in America.
2   MS. Wilts Quarter Sessions Minutes, 1599.

Cley Hill

and probably a certain Welsh, whose house was burgled in 1606, was one of these.

The burglar confessed at Quarter Sessions that he had taken from the house 'two wastcotes, a silken scarfe, a gould ringe, a silke apron, a Holland Sheete, a Tynnyn Salte'.[1]

One of the leading families of the parish at this time were the Carrs. The head of the family was, as we have seen, appointed to superintend the Beacon in Elizabeth's reign, and a generation later, 1607-8, William Carr was one of the three freeholders of Corsley, the other two being Anthony Raxworthy and Robert Fytchne.[2]

But in 1631, Thomas Carr, in all probability a son of William, or, at any rate, another member of the family, appears to have got into financial difficulties, with the result that Cley Hill Farm, where he resided, became the property of one Hopton Haynes, who

1   *Wilts Archaeol. Mag.* xxii. p. 226.

2   List of Wilts Freeholders, *Wilts Archaeol. Mag.* xix. p. 265.

endeavoured to take possession of it.[1]

This, however, was strenuously resisted by Carr and his neighbours, 'Carr defending his possession with force of arms, and a multitude of base persons assisting him'.

Haynes petitioned for ordnance to be obtained from Bristol, and the Privy Council directed the Deputy Lieutenant of the county to assist the Sheriff with such companies of trained bands as he considered necessary. The Sheriff accordingly sent summonses to the inhabitants of Warminster and the neighbourhood, which met, however, with little attention, Sir Edward Baynton, among others, refusing to meet the Sheriff on this business, saying 'that he did not much fancy that service'. Finally, when Sir John Toppe, the Sheriff, approached the farm, he found that the men who attended him 'were totally unprovided with necessaries, and were so disinclined to the work that he felt compelled to withdraw his force, and excuse his departure by reason of the foulness of the weather and nearness of the night'. He then endeavoured to obtain gunners from Bristol, and the first gunner with difficulty procured 'behaved himself perfidiously by interleaguing with the rioters and letting fall treacherous speeches'. The people were all friendly to Carr and against Haynes, and though some of them were taken and committed to gaol, this attempt to carry out justice was a failure. Finally a gunner, John Berrow, was appointed, who carried out the service, and the property was delivered over to Haynes.[2]

This episode illustrates the close relation which existed at this time between the land and those settled on it, the rights of the latter being regarded by themselves and their neighbours as something too fundamental to be destroyed by legal enactments. It is also interesting to see what difficulties might be met with by those to whose lot it fell

1   Proc. Court of Chancery, Haynes v. Carr, Chas. I. H.H. 69,

2   See *Cal. State Papers Dom. Chas. I.* vol. 1631-33, pp. 157, 168, 170, 192,193 (3),194, 251 (2).

to execute the law, and the amount of persistence and determination which might be necessary in order to carry a decree of the courts into effect. The village community still, for the most part, lived its life in its own way, affected less by outward compulsion than by the ancient customs which it recognised as binding.

This parish does not appear to have given much trouble to the Court of Quarter Sessions. Few entries relating to it are met with in the Minutes, but in July, 1620, we find among the presentments: 'Corsley Omnia bene.'

The government was doubtless mainly carried on by the Lord of the Manor, or his steward, and the inhabitants themselves in the manorial courts. The manorial fees and rents due to the lord were paid in money or in chickens.

The rent of a cottage appears to have been 8d. and 1d. a year was the fee exacted from Robert Hooper in 1634 for 'setting his pales upon the Lordes avast' of the Manor of Huntenhull.[1]

Before the conclusion of the reign of Charles I, Selwood Forest was disafforested. Disafforestations in other parts of Wiltshire and in Dorsetshire were the cause of rebellions and riots among the people of the neighbourhood, but nothing of the kind appears to have been roused in this district, and whether any enclosure affecting the privileges of commoners took place here, or whether all went on as before in Corsley, we do not know.

Corsley possessed a stock of money arising from several charities before 1635.[2] Such stocks of money existed in nearly all

1 The following extracts from the bailiff's account show the rents of this time: Manor of Great Corsley, 1634. 'Ye rent capons and chicken of this mannor and ye Capons and chicken paid by John Hill for a coppie of licence ar to be accompted for wth the rent capons and chicken of Whitborne for all wch, for ye accompt thereof at this audite next to Whitborne.' The Manor of Huntenhull, 1634. ' And of Tho. Stephens for the rent of a Cottage wth. in this manor neere Whitborne more, viiid. And of Robert Hooper for setting his pales upon the Lordes wast of this mannor at 1d. p. annum ijd . . . . xd.'

2 *Report Charity Commission*, 1834, xxviii. p. 389.

parishes, however small, and were administered by churchwardens and overseers, after the creation of these offices. We have, however, no records of the administration of the Corsley stock before the eighteenth century.

Two tablets in the old church at Corsley formerly commemorated the various donations.[1] The donors included two of the ministers, Mr. John Cutlet, who was presented to the living in 1579, and Mr. Richard Jenkins, who was appointed in 1667. Mr. Jeremiah Hollway, merchant, made the munificent gift of £50, two vintners made donations of £5 each, an upholsterer contributed £10, and the second tablet was presented by Robert Hopkins, victualler, in 1688. But the most numerous class of benefactors were the yeomen, of whom there were five. One of these, Hugh Rogers, died in 1611, bequeathing to the parish £4, a crown of the interest to be added yearly to the stock, and the remainder to be given on the anniversary of his death to the 'parson, clark, poore, and bells'. We learn from a monumental poem, which formed an acrostic on his name, that this yeoman greatly benefited his poor neighbours during his lifetime by ministering to them as medical adviser, and freely giving them 'his salves, his plaisters, and his paynes'.

---

1   For the tablets and other monumental inscriptions, see Sir R. Colt Hoare, *History of Modern Wilts: Hundred of Warminster*, p. 66.

3

Cloth-making and its Effects in Corsley

(1660-1727)

FROM 1660 TILL the accession of George II in 1727 a systematic chronicle of what passed in the parish of Corsley is lacking; but the fragmentary evidence which exists shows plainly that shortly after the Restoration the manufacture of cloth had been introduced, and the main feature of the years which followed was the gradual transformation of a purely agricultural into a semi-industrial population.

The cloth trade had flourished in Wiltshire for at least two centuries, and was established at the neighbouring town of Westbury before the Civil Wars,[1] but in Corsley no trace of its existence before the Restoration is forthcoming, and this evidence, though negative, seems sufficient to show that at least no important industry was carried on in the parish.

At the time of the Civil Wars the Wiltshire cloth trade passed through a great cataclysm. Not only were the manufacturers subject to interference and extortion from the military forces which infested the county, but local government and trade regulations were utterly disorganised, the apprenticeship regulations broke down completely,[2]

1 See Wilts Quarter Sessions Records, in *Hist. MS. Com., various collections*, vol. i. pp. 74, 114, &c.

2 See Wilts Quarter Sessions Records, in *Hist. MS. Com., various collections*, vol. i. p. 114.

and probably the Gild regulations fared no better.

Under these circumstances it is not surprising if a capitalist clothier, when peace, but not industrial order, was restored, migrated to this out-of-the-way village, where gilds and industrial regulations had never existed, and here set up his business independently, and this is what seems to have occurred.

The first notice of the cloth trade in Corsley that we have met with is the following tradesman's token:

George Carey—The Clothworkers' arms
IN. Corsley, 1666--G.M.C.[1]

We thus find established in the parish a clothier with such a business as to make it worth his while to issue his own tokens. As to where he came from, or when he came, we know nothing. There is nothing to prove that he was not a Corsley man, who had gradually developed his trade in the parish; but the total absence of any signs of the presence of industry previous to this suggests the probability that he was a capitalist clothier who migrated with his business from some other locality.

However he may have come, he came to stay, and his family remained in the parish, first as clothiers and then as maltsters for about one hundred years. In Corsley Church is a monument with a coat of arms and Latin inscription to-

GEORGII CARY
Christiana MDCC.

In 1712 a tenement with garden, orchard, and meadow in Whitbourne,[2] closes, and 2½ acres of arable in a field near Cley

1   *Wilts Archeol. Mag.* xxvi. p. 396.
2   In the survey at the Longleat Estate Office this is noted as Sturford Mead, and

Hill were leased by the Lord of the Manor to Thomas Carey, of Corsley, clothier. In 1734 we find George Carey, of Corsley, clothier, witnessing a deed,[1] and in 1756 the tenement in Whitbourne was renewed to 'Geo. Cary of Whitborn, Maltster,' and in 1769 to 'Geo. Cary of Corsley, Maltster'. According to tradition the old house now inhabited by Mr. H. Ball was formerly a malt-house, and this was in all probability the home of the Carey family during their residence in the parish.

To return to the early history of the cloth trade in Corsley. Whenever among the scanty records of the latter half of the seventeenth century allusion is made to the occupation of inhabitants of the parish, the broadweaver and cloth-worker are henceforward found beside the yeoman and husbandman. These handicraftsmen were not, however, very numerous till after the conclusion of George I's reign, and were usually immigrants from neighbouring parishes and not of Corsley birth. In 1694 a broadweaver with his family migrated from Freshford,[2] and in 1707 a broadweaver's family from Beckington[3] came to reside here. Three other families who came from Berkley, Heytesbury, and Buckland Dinham in Somerset during the first twenty years of the eighteenth century[4] were probably likewise attracted to Corsley by opportunities of work in the clothing industry. In 1714 a boy from Frome was apprenticed to

the fact that the premises were afterwards leased to a dyer bears out this note, since the dyer, H. A. Fussell, was long a resident at Sturford Mead. It seems probable, however, that the dwelling-house was that now occupied by Mr. H. Ball. The house of Sturford Mead was not built till the nineteenth century.

1   An indenture between Thos. Wickham, yeoman, and Leonard Humphreys, blacksmith, in the possession of Mr. Seth Sparey.

2   MS. certificate in Corsley Parish Chest, from the officers of Freshford guaranteeing that Edward Twiney, broadweaver, his wife and family, shall be received back should they become chargeable.

3   Similar certificate in Corsley Parish Chest, from the officers of Beckington relating to Jeremiah Jarvis, broadweaver, his wife and children.

4   Similar MS. certificates from these parishes in Corsley Parish Chest.

a cloth-dresser of Corsley.[1]

By the early years of the eighteenth century George Carey was no longer the only capitalist clothier in the parish. William Elliott, of Boreham, clothier, leased land in Corsley in 1703, and John Hopkins, of Chapmanslade, clothier, rented a piece of ground in the Manor of Huntenhull in 1712.

Some indication of the personnel of Corsley at this time is given by the list of leases in a Survey Book of 1745,[2] but they are not sufficiently numerous before 1730 to afford much clue as to proportion and distribution of occupations.

It is notable that two or three well-to-do men from Warminster or the neighbourhood took land or tenements in the parish towards the end of the seventeenth or early in the eighteenth century. Besides those already mentioned, leases were granted to Edward Halliday, of Warminster, gentleman, in 1677, and to John Barton, of Warminster, mercer, in 1692. The occupations of other tenants are as follows:

> *From 1690 to 1699, six tenants:*
> 1 yeoman, 1 husbandman, 1 broadweaver, 1 tailor, 1 carpenter, 1 occupation unspecified.
> *From 1700 to 1709, thirteen tenants:*
> 3 yeomen, 2 husbandmen, 1 clothworker, 2 tailors, 1 blacksmith, 1 mason, 1 bricklayer, 2 occupation unspecified.
> *From 1710 to 1719, eight tenants:*
> 2 yeomen, 1 labourer, 1 gardener, 1 miller, 1 thatcher, and 2 blacksmiths.

The labourer and the gardener may, perhaps, have owed their occupations to the immigration of the moneyed townsman.

The presence of mason and bricklayer in the first decade of the

1 See MS. indenture in Corsley Parish Chest.

2 MS. Corsley Survey, 1745, in the Longleat Estate Office.

eighteenth century is an interesting indication that the population had already begun to spurt forward. An investigation of the parish registers leads one to the conclusion that the growth began with the century and continued almost steadily till about 1765. Any estimation of the population at this date must be inconclusive; but a calculation from the baptisms, deaths, and marriages recorded in the parish register gives an estimated population of seven hundred in 1691, falling to five hundred in 1701, and then rising again steadily to a little over seven hundred in 1731. If the registers were kept regularly throughout these years, there can be no doubt that this fall and rise occurred, though the absolute number must not be regarded as more than a suggestion.

The steady growth of population which went forward from the first decade of the eighteenth century was in all probability due to the development of the cloth trade, which first brought new immigrants, and later, perhaps, stimulated early marriages and a rapid rate of increase. But the records during the reign of George I. are, unfortunately, too slight to permit of very certain conclusions.

We learn from the Longleat Survey Book of 1745 that the payment of rents in kind had never wholly died out or else had been revived in this neighbourhood, and the system lingered on into the eighteenth century. Between 1657 and 1732 the grant of about 120 leases is recorded, some tenants taking out several leases for different holdings. About a quarter of these tenants have to pay capons or chickens as well as a money rent, three have to give one harvest day, one has to give two harvest days, four have to give a day's work with plough or wagon. In only one case is an alternative money payment set down by these payments in kind, where 3s. might be paid instead of two capons. The rents in kind and services are by no means restricted to the leases granted during the earlier years of the period. The following is an example of the leases as recorded in the Survey Book:

CORSLEY SURVEY, 1745.

Michael John Dead val 15^{ll}	"Michael Parret holds by Copy from Thos Thynne Esqr the 30th of Sepr 1679 A Tenement with the Lands Meadows pastures & Appurtenances thereto belonging late Meares's for the lives of the s Michael & of John Parret.	1679. ffine 170^{ll} Rent 7^s & a days Carr with a plough & 1^s Court Silver Her^t in kind.

(1727-1760)

GREAT CHANGES WENT forward in Corsley during the reign of George II. At his accession we find a still mainly agricultural community of perhaps seven hundred persons. But in a short space of time industries were extensively developed, and by the end of his reign the population probably numbered twelve or thirteen hundred, including manufacturers and tradesmen, who, with their workmen, were more important and numerous than yeoman farmers and the tillers of the soil.

Much of the wastes and commons had been enclosed either piecemeal or wholesale by agreement, and numbers of new cottages had sprung up. With the rapid increase of population which was taking place, the housing problem must have been a very serious one.

The relation between the number of deaths, marriages, and births, as shown by the parish registers, affords a curious study. Decennial averages between 1715 and 1735 show a rising number of deaths, a very slightly rising number of marriages, but a falling number of baptisms. Possibly there was at this time a considerable overcrowding, and much infant mortality, which is unrecorded in the registers owing to the children dying unbaptized. However this may be, the number of deaths rose enormously, while the number of baptisms decreased. During the two decades from 1706 to 1726 the average number of deaths annually had been 9 and 10 respectively;

during the following ten years (1726-1736) the average number was 15.2 per annum, and from 1736 to 1746, 21.9 per annum, while during the following ten years it fell again to 16.4 per annum.

The great rise in the death rate which occurred between 1726 and 1746 culminated in the five years 1740-45, during which no less than 159 persons died, or an average of 31.8 per annum. 46 died in each of the years 1741-42 and 1743-44.

The cause of this mortality is not clear. Smallpox was a constant visitant from 1730 to 1742, from one to five families being relieved nearly every year by the parish officers in this scourge, but it does not seem to have been heavier in 1742 than in some previous years, and from 1742 to 1748 no cases were relieved. If the deaths in 1743-44 were from smallpox, perhaps the high mortality was the result of neglect on the part of the parish officers, but it seems more probable that the pestilence had for the time being worn itself out, and that the deaths were due to some other and unrecorded cause. Whatever the cause of the mortality, its immediate sequence is striking: from 1743 onwards a great increase in the number of marriages took place, accompanied by a simultaneous, but more gradual, increase in the proportional number of births. One can hardly avoid the conclusion that many young people anxious to be married had been debarred by the difficulty of obtaining a, house, so that the exceptional number of marriages was the direct result of the clearance effected by the high mortality.

To go into the details of these figures: the average number of marriages per annum from 1726 to 1736 was 5, and no increase took place till about 1743-4. During the eighteen years 1743-4 to 1760 the average number is 12, the greatest actual number reached in any one year being 20 in 1755. After 1760 the average falls again, varying between 7 and 11; and it is not until the eighties and nineties, when the total population had greatly increased, that a number of marriages per annum slightly in excess of that of the middle of the century is reached.

In 1743, too, the number of baptisms per annum, which since 1725 had been falling, began to rise. The greatest number of births per annum occurred in the early sixties, if the parish registers, which are incomplete for these years, are rightly interpreted. The annual number of births continued high from 1766 to 1775, and then fell off somewhat.

Though the housing problem would seem to have been urgent about 1730, many new cottages had been erected within the memory of man, as we learn from the leases in the Longleat Survey Book. Between 1730 and 1739 leases were granted of cottages 'formerly built' by John Bartlet, George Greatwood, and William Singer, two of these men, if not all three, being still alive. They had apparently raised these cottages on the waste lands of the manors, and no doubt other people were doing the same thing. George Greatwood also leased the brickkiln, partly in Corsley and partly in Norton parish, now worked by the Open family, which, perhaps, he had himself built in order to supply materials for the growing demand for houses. John Bartlet's cottage was on the lower side of Corsley Heath, and several cottages seem to have been then recently built on this open ground. A newly-erected cottage on the heath was let in 1733.

In 1736 about two acres of newly enclosed waste land at Whitborne Moor were let to George Prowse, dyer, 'with 2 Dyehouses Stove packhouse Stable,' and he was excused the usual fine in consideration of his having laid out £400 in building and enclosing.

About this time it was agreed to divide up and enclose the whole of Corsley Heath. Commissioners were appointed, and a deed of distribution, a copy of which is in the Longleat Estate Office, was drawn up and agreed to in 1741. Land was allotted to twenty-seven persons who had common rights, subject to a reserved rent to Lord Weymouth of, roughly speaking, about 1s. an acre. It was stipulated that three of these allottees, Richard Collins, Thomas Rimell, and Robert Meares, or one of them, should buy the new Warren House, lately built and repaired by Lord Weymouth, paying £20 for a lease of three lives and 2s. annually. The holders of land were to 'inclose their several proportions and plant the same with Quick Set Thorn plants in a husbandlike manner,' and the roads were to be laid out, left, and made according to plan.

We have seen that the population was increasing numerically at a rapid rate; the mode of living of the community and the character of their occupations appear to have undergone quite as rapid a development. The growing prosperity of the cloth manufacture was the primary cause for all these changes, and the Longleat Survey Book shows conclusively how extensive this had become in the thirties.

Leases were granted to about 40 tenants during the ten years 1730-1739: of these 40, 2 were clothiers and 14 or 15 manual workers in some branch of the manufacture, including 3 dyers, 4 cloth-workers, 3 broadweavers, 1 shearman, 1 twister, 1 scribbler, 1 shear-grinder, and also a 'sievier,' who may or may not have had some connection with the industry. Thus of the 40 tenants 16 or 17 were cloth-makers, while only 10 agriculturists took leases, namely, 8 yeomen, a husbandman, and a gardener. This is in striking contrast to the proportions in the earlier decades of the century, when out of 10 or 12 tenants only 1 or 2 would represent the cloth trade, the bulk of the occupations being agricultural.

From 1740 to 1749, again, the proportion of cloth-workers is large, being 5 out of 12. Of these 5, 3 are clothiers, 1 a capitalist dyer, and 1 a twister.

From 1750 to 1759, out of 21 tenants 7 are cloth-workers: these consist of 2 clothiers, 1 cloth-worker, 2 twisters, 1 scribbler, and 1 card-maker.

But though the proportion of agricultural employments falls off during these years, some specialisation seems to have taken place. Between 1740 and 1749 we only have four tenants with agricultural pursuits, but one of these is a 'drowner', who one presumes was employed by different farmers to supervise the proper flooding of their water-meadows. This may indicate the introduction of some improvement of method in farming. The other three are a yeoman, a miller, and a gardener.

Between 1750 and 1759 we find another occupation subsidiary to agriculture not before met with, that of farrier. During these years leases were also granted to two yeomen, two husbandman, two gardeners, and a labourer.

During the thirty years the immigration of well-to-do townsmen observed during the reign of George I continued. Among the newcomers besides the numerous clothiers and Robert Meares, dyer, who probably ranked socially with the yeoman farmer, there was one Thomas Whitaker, of Westbury, gentleman, while the families of Barton, Carey, and others, who had previously come to the parish, continued to renew their leases or take out fresh ones.

Following on the development of the cloth trade we find a set of crafts and trades growing up to provide food, houses, and clothes for this manufacturing population. Between 1730 and 1739 leases were granted to two bakers and a butcher. Bakers may have existed in the parish previously, for negative evidence that no mention of them has been met with is inconclusive, considering the scantiness of the records; but whether or no these were the first in the parish, their appearance indicates a new demand for ready-baked bread. In most of the old cottages remains of baking ovens are found, and it seems probable that about this time many of the people were growing too busy, and, perhaps, too cramped for house-room, to bake for themselves as they had hitherto done.

Besides these caterers for food supply we find in the thirties a brickmaker and a wheelwright, two carpenters and a blacksmith, and also a shoemaker.

In 1749 an inn was set up at Corsley Heath, and lease granted to William Young. William Young had kept a house where the parish officers could meet and drink previously to this,[1] and tradition relates

---

1 MS. Overseers' Accounts, May, 1733.

that the Manor Farm was at one time used as an inn;[1] but this inn on Corsley Heath is the first of which we have authentic record in the parish.

In the decade 1750-1759 leases were granted to a 'victualler' and a tailor, as well as a butcher and a carpenter, so the inhabitants were now able to do practically all their shopping in the parish.

Towards the end of the reign of George II., George Carey, formerly clothier, had developed a malting business, and is specified as 'maltster'.

The Longleat Survey Book affords material for this sketch of the population of Corsley during the reign of George II. But there is one side of parochial life of which we have a fuller and a fairly continuous record. This is the administration of the Poor Law.

The MS. Overseers' Accounts from 1729 till 1755, and again from 1768 onwards, have been preserved in Corsley Parish Chest.

The first book, which commences in 1729, shows a systematic method of administration, which had, no doubt, been handed down from the days of Elizabeth or the early Stuarts.

It would seem that from 1729 to 1740 with the new industrial openings was a prosperous time in the parish; nevertheless, a considerable sum of money was expended annually on poor relief, and persons or families whose number varied through these years from sixteen to thirty-one were relieved regularly. The pensions given in 1729 varied in amount from 1s. to 12s. a month, 2s., 4s., 5s., or 6s. a month being the most common rates.

During the summer half-year in 1729, from May to October, the expenditure on poor relief was £91 18s., so that the annual expenditure can have been little, if at all, short of £200, though it is not probable that the population at this time much exceeded seven hundred.

In the early forties the number of paupers increased, the regular list in July, 1742, containing forty-five names: this was a year

1   Sir R. Colt Hoare, *History of Modern Wilts: Hundred of Warminster*, p. 63.

of exceptionally high mortality, as we find by the parish registers. In the year 1748-49 the total expenditure on the poor was £163 1s. 11½d.

Besides distributing regular doles, the parish officers provided exceptional necessaries required by the regular paupers and others. They clothed them; they housed them, paying their rents, and sometimes repairing the cottages; when sick they provided medical attendance and nursing, and medicines or extra diet when needed, especially after the smallpox, when allowances of bread, malt, or beer were given. They frequently paid funeral expenses, which usually included beer or drink money. Bedding was sometimes provided, and occasionally fuel.

The overseers occasionally assisted adult inhabitants to earn a livelihood: the rent of a loom for this purpose was several times paid by the overseers, and in 1748 they purchased a broadloom for the parish. They also provided a certain John Haines with a pickaxe and spade costing 2s., and from time to time they purchased 'turns' or 'spinning turns' for poor women.

We find the parish officers incurring expenses in taking prisoners to the sessions and to gaol, and much trouble was taken by them in dealing with the parents of illegitimate children in order that the burden on the parish funds might be lightened so far as possible. When it became necessary to provide for destitute children the overseers usually boarded them with some woman until they reached the age of seven years, when they were sometimes apprenticed to a master or mistress for a period of not less than seven years. The reputed father of an illegitimate child was required to pay a weekly sum towards its maintenance during infancy and £4 when the child reached the age of seven years for its apprenticeship.[1]

A poor child, Elisabeth Cragg, was bound apprentice by the parish officers in 1743 to a dairyman of Somersetshire till she

1   MS. papers, A.D. 1737, in the possession of C. N. Phipps, Esq., relating to bastardy cases in Corsley.

was twenty-one or married, to be taught 'the Art or Business of Housewifry'.[1]

Another side of the activities of the parish officers was the jealous guard kept lest strangers should hide themselves in the parish and so gain a settlement; and expenses, usually a few shillings, are paid from time to time to persons, including Francis Mines, a servant of the parish officers, for 'waring' or 'warning' out the 'outcomers'. While thus chasing away any who manifested an inclination to remain without producing a certificate from the place of their legal settlement to hold Corsley 'harmless' should they become chargeable to the rates, the parish duly relieved those who were journeying from one place to another with a 'pass'. Various parties of sailors were relieved in this way in 1742, 1747, and 1748.

Contributions were regularly made to the county rates, and for prisoners in the King's Bench or Marshalsea, this being frequently entered as the 'Jal & Maishel & Vagbun money'.

The parish officers appear to have considered that their labours earned them an annual festivity at the public-house, and the expenses on 'estertusday', varying from £1 to £1 10s., are an annual charge on the parochial funds till 1751. In one case a puritanical critic has added the comment, 'not fit to be allowed'. He appends a similar remark to an entry of 16s. expended at the sessions, so it would appear that the burden of holding the compulsory office of overseer or churchwarden was not without its compensations in Corsley.

In 1757 a lease was granted by Lord Weymouth to the churchwardens and overseers of a cottage, garden, and orchard, about 10 lugs of ground, under Gore Hill.[2] The overseers' accounts for this period are missing, but this was probably the first parochial experiment in setting up a poorhouse.

The system of apprenticeship was by no means confined to the

1   Indenture, A.D. 1743, in Corsley Parish Chest.

2   MS. Corsley Survey, 1745, in the Longleat Estate Office.

children under the care of the parish officers, and any youth would have found it difficult to get a start in his trade or occupation until he had fulfilled his seven years with some master.

An account of the examination of William Chapman in 1739 or 1759, which is found in Corsley parish chest, gives a good illustration of this. He was born thirty-three years before this examination took place, at Rodden. When fourteen years of age his mother bound him apprentice to a chair-maker of Westbury, from whom after four years he ran away and for two years wandered the country. At the end of this period he returned to his master and made an agreement with him to serve out the remainder of his time, which he completed in the service of this master, and afterwards of his master's brother. The account concludes, 'Soon after he married and has five children—he has lived in Corsley ever since'.[1]

William Carpenter, a broadweaver of Corsley, was born in the parish sixty-five years before his examination in 1739 or 1759.[2] He was apprenticed when thirteen to a master at South Brewham, and, after three and a half years, transferred by him, with his assent, to another master at Berkley. Soon after finishing his time with this master he married and had seven children. He declared 'that he has continued ever since working at his hands in ye Parish of Great Corsley Afores'd'. He was then living in a cottage valued at £8, formerly his father's.

These short biographies illustrate the normal life of the handicraftsman of that day, who still, according to the Statute of Elizabeth, served a long apprenticeship, after which he could reasonably aspire to setting up for himself, marrying a wife, and following his trade until incapacitated by old age.[3]

1   MS. account of the examination of William Chapman in 1739 or 1759 (date indistinctly written), in Corsley Parish Chest.

2   MS. account of the examination of William Carpenter, broadweaver, in 1739 or 1759, in Corsley Parish Chest.

3   For extracts from Overseers' Accounts see Appendix, pp. 287-9.

4
Industry and Agriculture

(1760-1837)

CORSLEY WAS NOW entering upon the period of its fullest life and activity. The estimated population in 1760 was about 1,300, or more than half as much again as at the last census in 1901, when the number returned was 824.[1] This population of 1,300, or thereabouts, continued to grow rapidly, though with fluctuations, till about 1830, reaching its highest recorded figure of 1,729 in 1831, when the census was taken but it was probably even greater than this a few years previously, as the tide had already begun to ebb, commencing with a number of emigrations to America, in the years which preceded the taking of the census.

Increased vitality in the various departments of life of the community did not fail to accompany the numerical increase. Something like a religious revival in the Church of England seems to have occurred simultaneously with the introduction and growth of Dissent. The continued development of industries in the parish is shown in the new occupations, or new branches of the old industries, which were followed by the inhabitants. Parochial administration and methods of Poor Relief, the one side of parish life of which full records remain to us, underwent great changes and development, to meet the

1   *Census Report, 1901.*

needs of the growing population. Lastly, one of the most important events in the whole history of the parish, the enclosure and division of the old common fields, occurred in 1783. Probably in no previous century of its existence as a village community did such vast changes take place, both in the outward aspect of Corsley and in the life of its inhabitants, as between the early years of the eighteenth and those of the nineteenth century.

From 1760 onwards cloth-making continued to flourish and increase. It appears that all stages of the manufacture were carried on in Corsley, including preparing, spinning, dyeing, weaving, shearing and finishing. The work was mainly under the control, direct or indirect, of capitalist clothiers, of whom there were several in the parish. The wool would be purchased by them, either raw, or from the spinners, in the form of yarn, and for each subsequent process they would employ a different set of people; at some stages giving out the wool to be dealt with at the workers' homes at piecework rates, at others having it handled in their own factories by wage-earning labourers, and finally disposing of the dyed and finished pieces to merchants at Blackwall Hall, or other purchasers.

Some of the old inhabitants remember how the wool, raw as it came from the sheep's back, and sometimes all matted together, would be fetched from Mr. Taunton's factory at the Mill Farm by the women who performed the unsavoury process of 'woolpicking' in their own homes. Spinning was doubtless also partly, if not altogether, a home industry.

After being spun into yarn, dyed, and prepared at one of the factories, such as that at the Mill Farm, the wool would be fetched thence by the weavers, in large bags which they carried on their shoulders. Some of the weaving was done in weaving factories, where several looms would be kept at work; one of these may be seen half-way up Chapmanslade village street. But the greater part of the yarn was woven by independent workers at their own homes. The loom was fitted up in a long weaving-shed at the back of the house, or else in the dwelling itself. Many of the long, low, weavers' windows are yet to be seen in Corsley and Chapmanslade. Both men and women would work at the loom. It took two persons to fix the threads, and then one could work the shuttle, standing with his back to the light and throwing it to and fro.

When the material was woven it was taken back to the factory to undergo the finishing processes. One of these was the raking with 'teasels', or thistles, to draw all the threads one way and give a surface.

Shearing, again, was often given out to small independent workers whose homes were fitted up with the necessary appliances. One of these shearers, Down by name, resided at Whitbourne Moor, where he had his apparatus, or mill, with a horse to drive it round.

The very important industry of dyeing the yarn was carried on extensively. The dyers were probably a class of capitalists, distinct from the clothiers, by whom the other processes of manufacture were financed.

Besides Sturford, where extensive dyeworks belonging to Mr. H. A. Fussell were in operation during the first half of the nineteenth century, at least two dye-houses existed, one belonging, in 1783, to Thomas Singer,[1] at Dartford or Whitbourne Moor, the other in the fields near Chapmanslade. In Corsley Church is a monument to John Carpenter, 'an eminent dyer of this parish', deceased in 1812. About the year 1770 we learn that dye-stuffs were stolen from Messrs. James and Nicholas Codell (or Cockell?), of Chapmanslade.[2] Soapwort, a plant much used by the dyers, is to be found, growing in a wall near where the lane to Temple branches from the high-road. Mr. Fussell's dyeworks at Sturford included machinery worked by the stream from the pond. In the fields near Temple were white railings or racks, where the yarn was dried under the supervision of 'old Robert Mines'. Towards the middle of the nineteenth century, when the trade was

1   Warminster and Corsley Enclosure Award, with maps, 1783.

2   *Wiltshire Archaeol. Mag.* xvi. p. 325.

declining in Corsley, wool used to be fetched to the dyeworks from Mr. Britten's factory at Colport Road, Frome.

The total output of cloth from Corsley must have been considerable, and probably few houses, from that of the yeoman farmer down to the labourer's cottage, were at this time without a loom; for although the manufacturing handicraftsman was usually a specialised worker who turned with difficulty to farm labour when the cloth trade deserted Wiltshire, yet cloth-making and agriculture were not wholly divorced in Corsley; and not only was the capitalist clothier frequently a farmer, but no doubt weaving was also carried on by the peasants in conjunction with a little farming or gardening. An example of this is found in the will of James Greatwood, dated 1796,[1] whereby he left to his daughter, Elizabeth White, the east part of the dwelling-houses, with the weaving-shop and broad loom, also the upper part of the garden, the cowbarton or yard, and a close of ground of about two acres. To his son Robert he left the west end of the house, the remainder of the garden, and two acres of the close; to his son John the remainder of the close and one and a quarter acres of Corsley Heath Warren. The goods, furniture, and residue of his personal estate were to be divided equally between Elizabeth and Robert, who were to pay the funeral expenses. The sum owed on mortgage was to be discharged by his children, and for every £17 owed, Elizabeth and Robert were each to pay £7 and John £3.

This type of small farmer with a second occupation has continued in the parish to the present day, or possibly may have died out and been revived during the last half of the nineteenth century, in a district where the soil is particularly favourable for the success of the small holding.

During the last twenty years of the eighteenth century the expansion of the clothing industry is shown by the immigration of workers in new branches of weaving; a narrow-weaver, a 'casimere'

1 Loose slip or memorandum in MS. Corsley Survey, 1745, at Longleat Estate Office.

weaver, and a linsey-woolsey weaver took out leases in the parish and settled to work beside the broadweavers, whose predecessors were established there a century earlier.[1]

It seems that even towards the end of the period we are now considering weavers in Corsley could earn a tolerable maintenance by constant work, but, as one of the old inhabitants, Mr. Moses West, remarked, they 'had to be always at it'. Though women as well as men were engaged in this process, children were not able to assist, and child labour was confined to other branches of the clothing industry, such as spinning.

A silk factory was set up at Whitbourne Moor, probably after the clothing industry had begun to decline, and was working until the middle of the nineteenth century, giving employment to about twenty women and girls.[2]

But while weaving and other home industries were carried on simultaneously with work on the land, the workers in factories were a class apart. An old man states that he can remember when little mites of children, aged seven or eight years, worked at the factories, and all the workers, children and adults, would leave the factories together, stinking of the dye to such an extent that their passing by was a nuisance to the other inhabitants of Corsley. The earnings of the men in the factories were higher than those of agricultural workers, and another old inhabitant remembers hearing that at the Lane End Factory workers got 30s., 20s., or 13s. per week, and a certain George Clements earned 14s. per week in Mr. Taunton's factory, sometimes being kept at work till 7 or 8 p.m. This must have been shortly before the trade left Corsley, towards the middle of the nineteenth century, and wages were probably lower than in the prosperous days of the eighteenth century; but they still compare very favourably with

---

1   See MS. Corsley Survey, 1745, at Longleat Estate Office.

2   This is distinctly remembered by many of the older inhabitants of Corsley. Winding silk on to reels appears to have been the particular process carried on.

agricultural wages, which at this time seldom exceeded 8s.

Alongside the manufacturing population the tradesman and dealer increased and throve. There were several tradesmen in the parish, and from the old account-book of Mr. Sparey, who kept a store in 1821,[1] we get a glimpse of the way the inhabitants did their shopping. It was probably those living round Sturford and Whitbourne Springs who dealt chiefly at this little shop, where they could purchase bread, butter, cheese, meat, candles, fat, flour, 'shugar', salt, biscuits, tobacco, tea, bran, worsted, soap, and paint—red, grey, or brown. The bread was sold by the dozen, but the unit, whether it refers to a weight, or, improbably, to a loaf, must have been quite small.

Credit was granted to many of the customers, and debts amounting to £97 7s. 9½d., due from forty-seven persons, appear to have been owing to Sparey at this time. One of the largest debtors, owing £11 1s. 4d., was Isaac Taylor, or, as entered in the account book, 'is taylor,' sexton and bellringer at the parish church, a near neighbour, one of a family whose descendants remark that they were 'Taylors by name and tailors by trade'. Isaac Taylor would sit, cross-legged, stitching, in the large window of his cottage in Sturford Lane, according to tradition, and, doubtless, he found difficulty in getting his accounts settled, so that his neighbour the shopkeeper was obliged to give him long credit till his tailoring bills were paid. Sparey's customers seem to have purchased goods as they wanted them, 7d. or 9d. worth at a time, and to have settled their bills wholly or in part every month or thereabouts. John Moody, who had about five guineas' worth of goods on credit during sixteen months, or an average of 1s. 6d. per week, which goods included bread, butter, cheese, meat, and fat, paid up his account most promptly every month or oftener, with the exception of three months in the summer of 1822, when it ran on, being paid in full on reaching the sum of 19s. 4½d.

Another customer, Phebe Smith, who was receiving 2s. 9d.

1   MS. Account Book, 1821-23, in possession of Mr. Seth Sparey.

per week from the parish as the mother of two illegitimate children, appears, when credit was granted her, to have taken goods to the value of about £1 a month, for which she would then pay a part of the sum owing. She does not appear ever to have settled her account in full, and Mr. Sparey seems to have been naturally reluctant to grant her credit. Martha Singer, a very regular customer, who had goods to the value of £7 13s. on credit during sixteen months, appears likewise to have paid only a portion of what she owed each month. She continued, however, to receive credit.

With regard to his supplies, Sparey probably purchased them mainly from dealers in Warminster or the neighbourhood. In March and April, 1822, he bought ten bags of flour from Mr. Blackmore for £21 19s., which he paid in instalments. He also bought from him tea and sugar, tea being apparently 7s. the pound. In February, 1822, he bought teas to the value of £ 5 15s. from Mr. Gray, at two months' credit.

This tradesman was probably William Sparey, who had migrated from the parish of Boyton, ten miles distant, the grandfather of Mr. Seth Sparey, who at present occupies the small farm and house in Sturford Lane where the shop was kept. His descendants state that William Sparey was a clothier and farmer, and we find from the account-book that he had dealings with London merchants and bankers. On one of the first pages are the addresses of:

Alex. Buckler, Blackwell Hall Factor, 74, Basinghall St.
Boyd's Brock Bank, 28, Bucklersbury.
Vicat Draper, 49, Great Surry (?) St. Blackfrers.

It seems, then, that he followed at once the three separate occupations of farmer, clothier, and retail shopkeeper.

Besides general provision dealers like Sparey there were more specialised tradesmen, such as butchers and bakers, in the parish;[1]

1   See Corsley Survey Book, 1745, &c., in Longleat Estate Office. See also, in various MS. papers relating to the parish, occupations of residents.

and with agriculture and cloth-making, victuallers and tailors, the parish could have produced most necessary articles of consumption.

But at the same time specialisation and division of labour seem to have led to more extensive dealings with the outside world. It is interesting to note that early in the nineteenth century two poor old men were provided by the parish[1] with a donkey, one also with a cart, to enable them to earn a living, an indication that there was plenty of work for carriers, besides that done by the farmers, who drove every week to the neighbouring markets in their wagons.

A new industry probably had its beginning here early in the nineteenth century. In a lease of Whitbourne Farm to 'James Smith of Corsley, Gentleman,' in 1807, besides the usual covenants a special one was made licensing him to keep and use a limekiln on Cley Hill, and to dig stone and burn lime, &c. As far as our information goes, this was the commencement of the operations which now threaten seriously to deface the chief natural feature of our parish.

Another new occupation, which was introduced in the last quarter of the eighteenth century, after the passing of the Turnpike Act, and which henceforth filled a prominent place in the manor rolls, parish accounts, and the private accounts of residents,[2] is the quarrying of stones. It is not quite clear whether 'quarrying' may not sometimes have meant picking or collecting the stones off the fields, or whether in all cases it entailed digging or hewing out. The work was done to a large extent by paupers, sometimes under supervision of the parish officers.

The stones were collected or quarried in a number of fields or localities, and even in the roads of the parish. A presentment of the Court Leet of the Manor of Great Corsley in October, 1786, runs as follows:

1   Corsley MS. Overseers' Accounts, 7th month, 1828, and 7th and 8th months, 1829-30.

2   See Mr. Barton's MS. Farming Accounts, 1801-11 and 1828-36.

Whereas there have frequently been stones quarried by the sides of the Roads and even into the Roads so as to damage the said Roads, we present any person offending in this matter in future (without the leave of the surveyor) to pay five shillings.

It seems also to have been the habit of some of the inhabitants to dig sandpits in the lanes. This was forbidden by the Court Leet in 1791, unless with the leave of the lord and his agents. More presentments on account of sandpits were, however, made in 1795, and in 1796 it was necessary for the same Court to present a sandhole at Dodsgate 'to be dangerous and to be filled up immediately'.

The quarrying of stones would lead us to suppose that an attempt was made to improve the roads, but the method of quarrying in the roads themselves must for the time have rendered them far more dangerous for travellers than before, and throughout the last quarter of the eighteenth century the Manor Courts repeatedly present roads as needing repair. It seems clear that at any rate the lanes and byways of the parish were in a fairly bad state at this time.

We must now consider what was happening in agricultural Corsley.

We saw how in the first half of the eighteenth century the industrial element had begun to preponderate over the agricultural element in the population. An analysis of the people in 1811 shows the extent to which this preponderance had developed by the nineteenth century, and indicates that the number employed in agriculture had remained stationary or had even decreased since the seventeenth century, the surplus of the rapidly increasing population of the parish being entirely absorbed by industries and occupations necessary for the support of the manufacturing community. Of 1,412 persons 698, or about one-half, were employed in trade, manufacture, or handicrafts; 215, or about two-thirteenths, were employed chiefly in agriculture; 499, or more than one-third, were unclassified. The unclassified population presumably included all children too young to work, and the main part should probably be estimated as dependent on manufactures and trades and agriculture in the proportion of, roughly speaking, three-fourths to trades and industries and one-fourth to agriculture. This would make the industrial population 1,072, or rather more than three-fourths of the whole. An indefinite number should be subtracted from the 499 unclassified persons for unoccupied adults, domestic servants, and other occupations which do not come under the given headings, so that the actual numbers dependent on agriculture and industries would be somewhat less than the above estimate. We shall not, however, be far wrong in saying that, broadly speaking, three-fourths of the population were dependent on manufactures and trades and one-fourth on agriculture.[1]

It seems improbable that the total number of persons in the parish in the days when the community was purely agricultural can have been as few as 215, which is the total number employed chiefly in agriculture in 1811. When we add 125, or a quarter of the unclassified persons, we get a total agricultural population of 340, which is not far from the number of the population of Corsley in the earlier part of the seventeenth century, as estimated from the entries in the parish registers preserved in the Diocesan Record Office. It is likely, however, that these registers were incomplete, and the population greater even at that date, when agriculture was presumably the sole occupation and resource of the inhabitants. It appears, then, that the agricultural changes which we must now describe had caused an actual decrease in the number of persons employed, in any capacity, on the land.

In Corsley, as in other parts of the country, the growth of an industrial population had reacted on agriculture, and had led to a step being taken which revolutionised the whole agrarian system, setting a term to the ancient communal method of farming, effecting

1   The above figures are taken from an analysis of the population in [Thomas Davis] *General View of the Agriculture of Wilts*, 2nd ed. 1813, p. 238.

a transformation in the outward appearance of the parish, and deeply affecting the lives of the peasant occupiers of the soil.

The common-field enclosure, while it caused profound and not altogether desirable social changes, and reduced the number of persons who obtained a living by cultivation of the land, gave, however, a new birth to agriculture. Large farms in severalty replaced the old distribution in common fields and commons, and corn was produced in large quantities in response to the growing demand and rising prices.

In 1779 the preliminary measures for enclosing Warminster and Corsley were commenced, and the Act was passed in 1783. Hitherto the land of the parish had been divided into great common fields, closes or enclosures round the homesteads, and commons or wastes. The tenants of the Manor of Huntenhull claimed and enjoyed the right of pasturing their cattle on the commons of Westbury, as well as of Corsley.[1] There had been three common fields, namely, Cley Hill Field, Chedlanger Field, adjoining Norridge Wood, and Bickenham Field, adjoining Scudamore parish. Some enclosures had already been made in these.[2] By the Enclosure Award for Warminster and Corsley the whole parish was in 1783 divided up; strips, patches, and ancient enclosures in the common fields were divided and exchanged among the various persons who had rights; the commons, too, were divided and allotted, and little was left unenclosed of these pastures and wastes, though some portions remained unappropriated within the memory of old inhabitants, to be absorbed by a slow process of encroachment, till only here a wayside strip and there a triangle of grass at the cross-roads remains.

The Enclosure Award map of 1783 shows how the land was allotted among a great number of holders. A large proportion in the centre and other allotments distributed over the parish were assigned

1   See Manor of Huntenhull MS. Minutes of Court Baron, 1785.

2   Warminster and Corsley Enclosure Award, with maps, 1783.

to Lord Weymouth, Lord of the Manor. Cley Hill Farm belonged to John Coope, Esq. Land to the west of Cley Hill, where Corsley House now stands, was in the possession of John Barton, some of whose fields are marked as 'entailed'. A number of detached bits were assigned to Robert Meares, and other owners too numerous to mention had holdings of various sizes in different districts of the parish.

This division and allotment, no doubt, tended to squeeze out the small holder, who lost the advantage of pasturing his cattle on the common, and who could not afford the expenses connected with enclosure and the raising of hedges. It was adjudged by the commissioners that the expense to the Rector of Corsley alone in making fences, barns, &c., which they considered necessary would be £100. Before the enclosure few labourers are to be found among the leaseholders. In 1780 and 1781, the years following the commencement of proceedings, no less than six took out leases, thus leaving evidence that the small holder was being driven to part with his land and become a wage-earning labourer.

The enclosure rendered improved methods of agriculture possible, and the parish became almost wholly arable, so far as farming was concerned. Few cows were kept after the enclosure, though the rich water meadows which border the two small streams of the parish were maintained for pasture and hay crops.[1] In 1828, when a new terrier and rate book was drawn up for the parish, a rough calculation of distribution gives:

Arable land	1,511 acres
Pasture and mead	466
Wood and plantation	194
Water meadows	88
Orchards	49

1 See *General View of the Agriculture of Wilts*, 1794, by T. Davis, where in the map Corsley is coloured chiefly as arable, with two lines of water meadows running through.

the remainder of the parish being occupied by homesteads and a few withy and alder beds.[1]

In 1834 agricultural capital was said to be diminishing owing to the highness of the poor rate,[2] but in 1836, when the Poor Law reform had been carried through, we find that Corsley, unlike some of the neighbouring parishes, was reported as having its people well employed,[3] and though wages were low, no doubt corn-growing afforded amble occupation to the farm labourer.

The Barton family held a large farm in Corsley, partly their own freehold property and partly rented, and their farming accounts between 1801 and 1835 throw light upon the agriculture of Corsley subsequent to the enclosure of the parish.

A valuation of October 18, 1809,[4] and the accounts that follow show clearly that wheat was the main crop, while barley and oats were also cultivated; peas, beans, clover, and vetches were used as rotation crops. The flock of sheep was an important adjunct of the farm, and no doubt the fold was highly valued, as in olden days, for manuring the corn lands, while the wool, sold to yeomen of Corsley, may have been worked up in the local woollen industry. Seven strong horses were kept to draw the plough and drag the heavy corn-wagons into Warminster market. Pigs and poultry, no doubt, grew fat upon the otherwise wasted products. Seven cows were kept, but in 1806 their number was reduced to two and in 1809 to one, and for a time the dairy was probably only sufficient to supply Mr. Barton's household. But in 1828, when the second remaining volume of accounts commences, after an interval of eighteen years, six cows were kept,

1   See MS. Terrier of Corsley, 1828.

2   Report Poor Law Commission, 1834, vol. xiv. Appendix B1, Part III. P. 571c. Evidence of H. A. Fussell.

3   Second Annual Report Poor Law Commission, 1836, vol. 1. P. 300, Warminster Union. Evidence of John Ravenhill.

4   See Appendix, MS. Farming Accounts of Mr. Barton, October 18, 1804, at Corsley House, p. 391.

and some cheese, milk, and butter were being sold.

Women as well as men were employed in agriculture. During the first decade of the century four were working fairly steadily on this farm at a wage of 4s. for a week, or six days' work. In 1828 it appears that the size of the farm had been increased. About twelve men were at this time regularly employed. In January, 1829, their wages were as follows: One 10s., three 9s., one 8s., one 7s., one 5s., one 3s., two 2s. 6d., one 2s. Probably the earners of two or three shillings a week were paupers. Besides these regular workers others were employed on miscellaneous jobs, including 'bird-keeping'. Allen, the mole-catcher, received large sums on account of moles, besides receiving payment for casual labour. From 1830 onwards about six women appear to have been retained at farm work.

We learn incidentally from these accounts that potato-ground was leased in 1805 and later years; the labouring man of Corsley has at least been well provided with allotment land since the enclosure of the parish.

5
The Religious Revival
(1760 – 1837)

FROM THE TIME of the Reformation till 1742 we have scant information as to the religious life of the inhabitants of Corsley. The volume of Churchwardens' Accounts which has been preserved commences in 1742, but the entries for the first forty years or so relate mainly to the usual payments for the destruction of badgers, hedgehogs, polecats, foxes, moles, and sparrows, or to relief granted to travellers, with occasional payments for repairs to the church or bells.[1]

A new element was, however, introduced after the middle of the eighteenth century, when the preaching of the Methodists, followed a little later by a Baptist mission, brought fresh vitality into the spiritual life of the people, and the enthusiasm of these sects appears to have roused the Church of England to greater activity.

In 1769 Corsley was entered in the Wesleyan annals as a 'new place', with thirty-one members.[2] In 1770 it had forty-six members, and in 1777 fifty-one. Wesley himself preached in the parish in September, 1772, visiting Bath, Frome, Bradford, and Keynsham in the same week.[3]

It seems probable that the Wesleyan community was concentrated mainly round Lane End, where the present chapel

1   MS. Corsley Churchwardens' Accounts, 1782-83.

2   Stephen Tuck, 'Wesleyan Methodism in Frome', p. 40.

3   Stephen Tuck, "Wesleyan Methodism in Frome', p. 44. Quotation from Wesley's Journal.

stands, the influence extending from Frome.

The Baptist influence appears to have come a few years later from the direction of Westbury. In 1777 a preacher of this denomination began his ministrations at Chapmanslade, and in 1799 a Baptist chapel was nearly completed in this village.[1] The chapel, if it be the same, or on the same site, as the present Chapmanslade Baptist Chapel, was in the parish of Westbury, but there is no reason to suppose that enthusiasm for the new sect was confined to the northern half of the village, and that the inhabitants on the other side of the road in Corsley parish were not equally affected. On the contrary, we know that the Baptist faith soon spread to the south of Corsley, and in 1811 an offshoot of the Chapmanslade community was established at Whitbourne Temple, where a chapel was erected in 1811.[2]

The Congregational Church at Chapmanslade appears from monuments in the present building to have been established by 1771, the leading members being John Turner and John Barter. No history of this establishment has, however, been preserved.

It is interesting to trace the influence of the new religious fervour on the Church. One of its effects was to stimulate the Rector of Corsley to hold an increased number of Church services on Sunday, as the following entry in the Churchwardens' Account Book indicates:

> *Easter, 1784*
>
> I, Thomas Huntingford, Rector, do hereby declare that I am not bound by any obligation whatever to serve this church twice on a Sunday, but that I am influenc'd thereto purely upon conscientious motives, and that I think myself at liberty to discontinue it at any time whenever there appears to me cause or reason for so doing.

This entry is elucidated by a further memorandum three years

1   W. Doël, *Twenty Golden Candlesticks*, p. 173.

2   Ibid. p. 178.

later, when Thomas Huntingford was succeeded as rector by G. I. Huntingford. It was as follows:

> *Easter, 1787. Memorandum.*
> That it was customary before the time of the late Mr. Thomas Huntingford to have divine service performed in Corsley Church but once on a Sunday, and the present Rector, the Revd G. I. Huntingford is not bound to any further service than what was required by ancient custom. (Signed) John Knight, Nath: Barton, Jno Cockell, George Marven, James Silcox.

In all probability the second service in the church was continued notwithstanding the anxiety which the innovators of this practice displayed to prevent its becoming a precedent, binding on future rectors. And if they cherished a hope that the new heresies would soon be stamped out, leaving the ministers of the Established Church free to follow their old, easy way, this hope was doomed to disappointment.

Dissent had taken a firm root in the parish, which, from its peculiar distribution in a number of scattered hamlets, was specially adapted for the formation of several small religious communities, collected round the nucleus of their chapel or church. And it is interesting to note that each of these Nonconformist settlements gained a footing in the hamlets most distant from the church, with the exception of Chapmanslade, whose nearer end is not more than a mile distant, but which is separated by a hill and valley from the parish church of St. Margaret. At a later time, as we shall see, Church people made efforts to combat Dissent by the erection of Anglican churches in the vicinity of the two Baptist chapels.

But to return to the end of the eighteenth century. It is probable that the successor of Mr. Thomas Huntingford was not less zealous for the religious orthodoxy of his parishioners than his predecessor had been, and in 1788 a Sunday School was established, the Easter

Sacrament money being applied for the purpose to purchase eleven spelling-books, forty-eight catechism books, four horn books, six testaments, and six coats for six of the poor boys.[1] Thus the education of the children of the parish, no less than the ardour of religious life, was stimulated by this rivalry between Church and Nonconformists.

We do not know how far the Church service was a musical one prior to 1817, but the majority of a vestry meeting in this year directed that a clarionet, price £2 2s., purchased for the singers, should be paid for out of the churchwardens' funds.[2] In 1825 Nathaniel Barton's offer of an organ for the use of the parish church was thankfully accepted at a vestry meeting. This barrel-organ was played by the shoemaker, James Cuff, within the memory of inhabitants now living. Tradition relates that it was the custom for the ringers and singers to 'close up in the evening' at Mr. Knight's public-house at Leigh's Green, now the 'Cross Keys'. The inhabitants of Corsley seldom neglected an opportunity for convivial gatherings.

Some evidence of the zeal of Church people at this time was given in 1819, when it was decided at a vestry meeting to build a new wall on the south side of the churchyard, and assumed that a donation of bricks from Lord Bath would be granted, and that the carriage would be rendered free of expense by some of the inhabitants.[3]

In 1830, at a vestry meeting, a momentous decision was come to. It was resolved:

THAT, the parish Church being in a bad state of repair, and its accommodations being insufficient for the Inhabitants of the Parish, it is expedient that the present Church should be taken down and rebuilt on a larger plan.
Proposed by Mr. Ball, seconded by Mr. Meares, &c.

1   MS. Corsley Churchwardens' Accounts, Easter, 1788.
2   Ibid., April 7, 1817.
3   MS. Corsley Churchwardens' Accounts, March 31, 1819.

The old church, pulled down c. 1830

A sketch of the late parish church, which was in the possession of the late Mr. Moses West, shows a picturesque little building; and now that the population has again dwindled, while two additional churches have been erected in or near the parish, one cannot help wishing that some other means had been found to provide accommodation for the worship of the population, whose number reached its maximum about the time this resolution was passed. It was, however, during the following years carried into effect, and the present inartistic building was raised in the place of the pretty old parish church which formerly stood on its site.

While the work of destruction and building were in progress, services appear to have been held in Mr. John Ball's malthouse, which was rented by the churchwardens for the purpose.

A new vestry-room was also erected. The votes at vestry were at this time distributed as follows: John Ball and Mrs. Barton each six votes, the Marquis of Bath five votes, James Knight five, Mrs. Allard five, J. H. Taunton five; other inhabitants had four, three, and two votes, and the majority one vote each.[1]

It is interesting to note that Isaac Taylor was appointed sexton in 1837, the post still being filled by members of his family at the present day (1907).

Appended are a few entries in the Churchwardens' Accounts which have not been noticed in the text, referring to events, historical or otherwise, that affected the parish during these years:

1779-80.	£	s	d.
Mr. Bilbie for Casting the Bell	10	7	4
and for adding 198 new Mettle at 14d.	11	11	0
Expenses Hanging the Bell	0	6	8

1789-90.

	£	s	d.
Four Books for the use of the parish on the Day of Gen. Thanksgiving	0	1	0
Paid the Ringers for Ringing on D°	0	10	6
D° for D° when Lord Weymouth rec'd the Title of Marquess	0	7	6
For a Flag to place on Clay hill when his Majesty Honoured the Marquess of Bath with his Company	0	8	6

March 31, 1807.

it beng agreed on by a Vestry as under:

John Singer to have £1 5s. pr. year for Cleaning the inside of the Church and looking after the Boys Sundays, and furthermor to have;£1 for Cleaning the Churchyard, Cutting the Hedges and Cleaning the Walkes, etc., etc.

July 17, 1815.	£	s.	d.
To the Ringers in ye Parrish Acct. on the news of the Battle of Waterloo	0	10	6

1 MS. Corsley Churchwardens' Accounts, April, 1834.

6

The House Famine and its Results

(1760 – 1837)

WE HAVE SEEN how rapidly the parish was growing and expanding in population, trade, and industry between 1760 and 1837, how the parish was transformed by enclosure, and how new religious elements had quickened the spiritual life of the people. We must now try to discover what was the condition of the population under this somewhat trying process of growth, and especially during those universally terrible years of war and famine which occurred early in the eighteenth [sic, i.e. nineteenth] century.

One result of the rapid immigration and increase in the population was probably a lack of sufficient house-room. In 1813, 1,412 persons, consisting of 388 families, were residing in 278 houses. This gives an average of 1.395 families, or 5 persons, to each house. Nearly a quarter of the houses in Corsley are now small three-roomed cottages,[1] and it is probable that many of the smaller and worse built houses have been pulled down or allowed to fall into decay during the last eighty years, so that it is not likely that housing accommodation was better, or even so good, a hundred years ago as what remains of it at the present day, and overcrowding must have been a serious evil.

An example of the way in which married people continued to

1   See Part 11. p.166.

live with their parents is found in the examination of James Durnford in 1821. This young man, aged about twenty-five, was a native of Upton Scudamore; when about twenty-one he became shepherd to Mr. Gane, of Corsley, at a weekly wage of 9s., still returning to his father's house to sleep for the first two years. He then took to staying the night in Corsley. About a year before his examination he had married a Corsley girl, and they had one child, and since his marriage he had slept at his mother-in-law's house at Corsley. He had not apparently gained a settlement in the parish, the custom of hiring servants by the year having fallen out of use a short time previously to this.[1]

The yearly hiring of servants was still the custom at the end of the eighteenth century. The career of John Moody is a good illustration both of the system and of its abandonment. He was born in Corsley about the year 1780. 'When I was about 11 years old', he relates, 'my father hired me to Farmer Smith at Whitbourne . . . to drive plough and other things'. He remained in this service four years, his father receiving his wages, which, when he left at the age of fifteen, amounted to 2s. a week. His father then hired him to Burgess, at Cley Hill, at '2 shillings and 3d. a week, as he told me. I lived with Mr. Burgess a twelvemonth, and after that twelvemonth my father told me he had hired me for half-a-crown a week for a twelvemonth'. This seems to leave no doubt that the arrangement was an annual hiring. He remained four years with Mr. Burgess, getting a rise of 3d. a week for the first three years, and 6d. a week the last year. He probably left in the year 1799, when he must have been about nineteen years of age. He then hired himself to Mr. John Ball, at Chipps Farm, but was drawn for the militia and was out about eleven months. He then hired himself to Mr. Sainsbury as a weekly servant at Corsley Farm, but did not remain in his service twelve months. 'I then hired myself again to Mr. Ball at Temple Farm in Corsley before which time I was married to my present wife, Hester Warden.'

1   See MS. account of Examination of James Durnford, Feb. 1821, in Corsley Parish Chest.

The cause of this examination, which took place in 1839, then appears: 'George Moody, now chargeable to the parish of Corsley, having a broken leg, is my son. I hired him to Mr. James Burgess of Clay Hill when he was about 12 years old at weekly wages, but nothing was said as to time.'[1] Clearly, therefore, no agreement for an annual hiring had been entered into, though he lived with Mr. Burgess more than a year, lodging the while at his father's house. The abandonment of the custom of annual hirings, which thus occurred early in the nineteenth century, was probably due, as the above examination suggests, to the war, with its constant demands for recruits for the militia.

Although we find no trace of the custom of the farm labourers living in the houses of the farmers in this parish, nor, indeed, in this district of Wiltshire, it seems that tailors or handicraftsmen would board and lodge their journeymen or workmen. Abraham Doël, about the year 1817, agreed with a tailor, Mr. Edward Pearce, at 3s. per week for the year, with bed and board;[2] and a similar agreement was entered into about 1827 between John Wheeler and Mr. James Wilkins, the occupation of these men not being stated.[3] These agreements are incidentally mentioned in disputes as to settlements many years later, and there is no reason to suppose that they are isolated instances; considering the lack of housing accommodation, one may readily suppose that it was usual for the handicraftsman to board and lodge his unmarried workers in his own dwelling.

It is the more remarkable that this practice was not followed by the farmers since there are many roomy farmhouses in Corsley, some of them older than the eighteenth century. But in all the settlement disputes relative to agricultural labourers we find no case in which the labourer was ever boarded in the house of his master; and

1 MS. account of the examination of John Moody, A.D. 1839, in Corsley Parish Chest.

2 MS. paper relating to Abraham Doël, in Corsley Parish Chest.

3 MS. paper relating to John Wheeler, in Corsley Parish Chest.

in the Report to the Poor Law Commission in 1834 Mr. à Court gives evidence that the custom had not prevailed in this part of Wiltshire, at least since the enclosures were made.[1]

The parsonage-house at Corsley was unreasonably small. William Cobbett, in his 'Rural Rides', quotes from the parliamentary returns that it was 'too small for an incumbent with a family'.[2] It must, if still occupying the same site, have been considerably added to or rebuilt since that time, for though not a large house, the present rectory contains a number of rooms.

In the year 1814 Mr. Barton, who owned land in the eastern half of the parish, began to build the new part of what is now known as Corsley House.[3]

It was probably owing to the urgency of the housing problem that the parish officers were led in 1769 to abandon the system of maintaining all the poor in their own houses, and to call a meeting 'for the establishment of a workhouse'.[4] A poor- house seems to have existed near Huntley since 1757,[5] when, no doubt, the population had already begun to outgrow the housing accommodation; but this proposed workhouse was a much larger and more important enterprise. Workhouses were not common in this district; there were never more than forty-one in the whole of Wiltshire, including those in the numerous boroughs and market towns,[6] so that there is ground for believing that exceptional needs led to its establishment in Corsley.

1   *Report Poor Law Commission, 1834, Appendix C*, p. 472.

2   William Cobbett, *Rural Rides*, 1st ed. 1825, p. 437.

3   Mr. Moses West, son of the carpenter who was imported from a neighbouring parish for this job, on which he was employed for many years, had a slab of wood on which a record of the commencement of the work was cut.

4   Corsley MS. Overseers' Accounts, April, 1769.

5   MS. Corsley Survey, 1745, at Longleat Estate Office, lease to Churchwardens and Overseers of premises, cottage, garden, and orchard (about 10 lugs of ground) under Gore Hill.

6   *Abstract Poor Returns, 1815*, p. 504 (Wiltshire).

Little seems to have been done for four years, though the churchwardens and overseers took a lease of a messuage and four closes in the Manor of Whitbourne Temple, and some payments for repairs to the poorhouse were incurred during these years. But in 1773 the matter was again brought forward, and it was agreed at a vestry meeting in April 'that there be a Work-house erected as soon as Possible it can be done for the reception of ye Poor of the said Parish'.[1] A committee was at the same time appointed to carry out the work. Premises were leased at Whitbourne Springs,[2] and a thatched workhouse was erected.[3]

This new workhouse was opened in December, 1773, most of the twenty-five persons who disappear from the list of regular pensioners at this date being in all probability moved into the house. These twenty-five included men, women, and children, widows and spinsters, single men, a married couple, and orphaned or deserted children, admitted without their parents. In April, 1774, there were thirty-six inmates,[4] and in June another batch of regular pensioners appears to have been taken in.[5] About twenty-five, however, remained outside the house, and the usual doles and payments for rent, clothing, and funeral expenses for those in receipt of outdoor relief continue in just the same way as before.

Before proceeding to consider the general conditions of the people and of poor relief during the period, it will be well to follow the history of the workhouse from its establishment in 1773. It was, like all workhouses of that date, as its name implies, a place where

1   Corsley MS. Overseers' Accounts, April 20, 1773.

2   MS. Corsley Survey, 1745, at Longleat Estate Office, lease taken out in 1773.

3   Insurance policy, with Bath Fire Office, in Corsley Parish Chest. The house was insured 'not exceeding £180', and goods and furniture contained in it 'not exceeding £20.'

4   Corsley MS. Workhouse Accounts, April, 1774.

5   Ibid. June, 1774.

work was carried on, and its establishment was an effort to lessen the burden on the ratepayers by making the labour of the paupers profitable. Unlike most of these experiments, the Corsley workhouse seems to have been a financial success, and, on the whole, to have rather reduced expenditure, and this without acting as a deterrent, for the number of persons relieved increased, while expenditure per head diminished. Between 1769 and 1772, before the workhouse was opened, the number of regular paupers varied from thirty-four to forty-two, and the annual expenditure from £244 to £351. The first four years after the workhouse was opened expenses were rather high, about fifty-five persons being relieved in or out of the house, at an annual cost of from £325 to £460. After this expenditure fell, and during the four years 1776-77 to 1779-80 about twenty people outside the house and about thirty inmates were supported for an annual expenditure of from £242 to £278. From 1783 to 1786 the expenditure was higher without any great increase in the number of paupers. From 1786 onwards the number of poor relieved outside the house increased, but expenditure only once exceeded £350, though the number of persons regularly relieved varied probably from sixty to eighty, or even exceeded that number.[1] It cannot, therefore; be said of the Corsley workhouse, as of many of these institutions, that its maintenance led to an extravagant waste of the ratepayers' money.

We must now see what treatment the inmates received. We have already noticed that persons of both sexes and all ages were sent here. The house received the sick as well as the able-bodied, and at any rate by 1796 it was also an asylum for the insane or feeble-minded. There were several rooms in the building, sometimes as many as four chimneys being swept in the spring, so some classification was possible if desired. The whole was ruled over by a salaried master, whose chief business it was to supervise the work of the inmates. The

1   See Corsley MS. Overseers' Accounts for these years for total annual expenditure on poor relief, and see ibid. and Corsley MS. Workhouse Accounts for total number of persons in receipt of regular relief.

workhouse never seems to have been left without a master from 1774 till 1802, except possibly for a year, in 1794-95. The master's salary was usually £20 per annum, but during part of the period he was paid a smaller sum, receiving in addition a twelfth part of the profits of the work of the paupers. The number of inmates ranged, roughly speaking, between twenty and forty, though there were sometimes more or less than this.

The work to which they were set was very varied. Linsey was manufactured, being sometimes given out for the processes of weaving, milling, and dyeing, and finally sold for the benefit of the parish. Weaving was, however, carried on in the workhouse itself at least during part of these years. Some of the other occupations were spinning and scribbling of wool, knitting, netting, and shoemaking. A garden was kept, and pigs and potatoes were sometimes sold. No doubt the workhouse inmates made their own clothing and grew their own vegetables, pork, and bacon, as well as producing these commodities for sale. The paupers were also employed to quarry stones, and pickaxes, spades, and shovels were sometimes purchased. From 1786 onwards some of the inmates appear to have been hired out regularly to various employers. The age of these workers does not appear, nor the nature of the work performed by them, but the payments to the workhouse account for their labour were small, 1s. 6d. per week being the most common, and it seems probable that they were either children or feeble old men; 4s. 6d. was received in 1796 for 'Yeudles maid 4½ weeks Bird Keeping at 1/P', and 4s. 1½d. was received in 1789 of Mr. Dredge, a regular employer of the paupers, for 'Aple Picking.'

Each month a few pounds would be received from various sources for sales of the materials manufactured, or for the work of paupers. This amount was deducted from the expenses incurred for maintenance of the workhouse before the account was presented to the parish officers.

The inmates of the workhouse appear to have lived well – wheat, beef, cheese, milk, and malt and hops being purchased in considerable quantities, and no doubt the house brewed its own beer and tobacco was sometimes provided. During the year from April, 1776, to March, 1777, the purchases included:

> 9 cwt. of cheese.
> About 42 sacks of wheat (or its equivalent in flour).
> 12 sacks of malt and 18 lbs. of hops.
> 11 lbs. of tea.
> About 150/- worth of meat, chiefly beef.
> About 4/- worth of milk per month, or 48/- for the year.
> 1 lb. of tobacco.

There was probably an average of at least thirty inmates during this year, besides the master. Other articles of which small quantities were purchased were salt, butter, oatmeal, currants, figs, sugar, treacle, broad beans, cabbage, peas, and barley; the latter may possibly have been for the pigs, and not for human food. Together with the produce of the workhouse garden and pigstyes, this gives a fair range of variety.

In 1795-96 the provisions for thirty persons are analysed as follows:

	cwt.	qr.	lb.	£	s.	d.
Cheese	12	3	1¾	23	3	11
Meat (including						
2 pigs killed)	19	2	24½	33	18	11¾
Bags flour, 28½				75	17	6
Sacks wheat, 22				42	8	0
Grinding and baking				5	0	0
Coals, 50 qrs. and 2 bushels				13	16	0
Soap, 103¼ lbs.						

It is stated this year that when earnings were deducted the maintenance cost about 2s. 4d. per head per week, or, with inclusion of the master's salary, about 2s. 7d. per head. In the following year over five pounds' worth of malt and hops were purchased.

The bills for clothing indicate that the paupers were well dressed as well as well fed. Seven pairs of gloves were purchased for them in 1774.[1]

At the beginning of the nineteenth century, when the labouring classes were half starved and corn at a fabulous price, the expense of maintaining the workhouse became very high. Consequently, in 1802 the master was dismissed, and all attempts to set the people to work in the house apparently abandoned; and it would seem that the workhouse from this time forward became merely a poorhouse, where the destitute could lodge, rent free. The yearly expenses incurred by the parish on account of the workhouse during the next few years amount only to from £10 to £16,[2] and cannot have included food or clothing. Presumably each inmate received a monthly pension from the overseers and catered for him or herself.[3]

In 1812 a woman was paid 8s. for looking after the old people in the workhouse,[4] and with this exception the inmates were left to their own devices to look after themselves or each other.

It cannot be supposed that the withdrawal of all authority over this community of thirty persons or so, of every age, sex, and condition, who were thus left to live as they could or pleased, would conduce to good order. In 1819 a committee was appointed to make regulations for the governance of the workhouse and its inmates, and one of the parish officers or the assistant overseer were desired to

1 For all particulars of workhouse receipts and expenditure, number of inmates, &c., see MS. Workhouse Accounts.

2 See Corsley MS. Overseers' Accounts.

3 This is borne out by the recollections of an old inhabitant who remembers the years previous to the Poor Law Reform. Another old inhabitant states that the workhouse 'seemed to be everybody's house, for any one to go in and out as they liked'. So far as he remembers there was no supervision.

4 Corsley MS. Overseers' Accounts, September, 1812.

attend once a week to see that the orders were duly observed.[1] This seems rather insufficient, especially as we find that the insane were still housed here, expenses being incurred in bringing a lunatic hither in 1822.[2] Nothing further, however, appears to have been done.

In 1830-31 the workhouse or poorhouse was paved[3] and newly thatched,[4] and it lingered on as an institution until the erection of the Warminster Union workhouse, after the Poor Law Reform, in 1836.

1   Corsley MS. Overseers' Accounts, Lady-day, 1819.

2   Ibid. February, 1822.

3   Ibid. 12th month, 1830-31.

4   Ibid. 13th month, 1830-31.

7

Corsley under the Old Poor Law

(1760-1837)

THE GENERAL ADMINISTRATION of poor relief outside the workhouse continued from 1768 on the same lines as during the first half of the century,[1] with gradual changes which naturally followed on the increase of poverty on the one hand, and on the other the growth of knowledge and of new ideas, whether true or false. House rents and repairs were paid by the parish, and relief in money or kind was distributed, the poor, when not too infirm, attending at the vestry to receive their portions. Medical relief was freely given, three or more different doctors often receiving an annual settlement of their accounts. Sometimes a contract was entered into with some doctor to attend all the poor for a fixed sum per annum, but further expenses were always added before the year was out. In 1772 the parish began to subscribe to the Salisbury Infirmary, and occasionally to send its sick thither. In 1779 it became usual to send poor people to Bath Hospital, and from 1782 onwards subscriptions were paid regularly to the hospitals at these cities, both more than twenty miles distant.

The small-pox was still a frequent visitant, and in 1773 the practice of inoculation was begun, the patients being brought to the church porch for treatment, as tradition relates. Whole families would

1 See Corsley MS. Overseers ' Accounts for the administration of poor relief prior to 1836. The accounts are missing for the years 1742-57 and 1756-68.

be inoculated with small-pox by order of the parish. In 1779 a number of families, comprising thirty-six persons, were inoculated wholly or partly at the parish expense. In 1798 again, £13 13s. was paid to a doctor for inoculation alone. Probably this inoculation often caused serious illness, and necessitated relief to the sick. We sometimes find it noted early in the nineteenth century that a case relieved was 'natural small-pox,' which still seems to have found victims throughout these years in spite of the wholesale inoculations.

After 1753 the parish incurred law expenses from time to time in disputes relating to settlements. The most serious of these was settled in 1776, the lawyer's bill amounting to £207 3s. 2½d., of which, however, Warminster parish paid £74.[1]

The moderate sum of £1 was charged to the parish account for the Easter dinner in the seventies, but in the nineteenth century the custom was kept up with unnecessary expense, the bill for this social gathering in 1824 amounting to nearly £5. The parish, too, bore the expense of the 'possessioning,' presumably beating the bounds, which took place at intervals of eighteen to twenty years. These expenses included a bountiful supply of beer and stronger drinks, besides some meat and cheese. But the official expenses at sessions, and for 'signing the book,' which, no doubt, included refreshments, during the first half of the eighteenth century, became much smaller, and also less frequent, during this period.

The parish officers continued to show a readiness in helping poor parishioners to earn a living, and besides from time to time providing tools or stock-in-trade of some description, they would now and then assist a needy family to repair their loom or twisting mill. But the great standby from 1774 onwards, after the passing of the Turnpike Act, was the quarrying of stones. Any unemployed who applied for relief could be set to this occupation, and the parish paid for the work accomplished, apparently on a piecework system.

1 See Corsley MS. Overseers ' Accounts for the administration of poor relief, April, 1776.

It is noticeable that between 1774 and 1791 no expense for premiums was incurred for the poor children apprenticed, their labour being, perhaps, of sufficient value in the clothing industry to induce employers to take them free. Between 1792 and 1799, however, premiums were paid with most of the seven children apprenticed by the parish. After 1830 it became usual to send the children out to service instead of apprenticing them, the only expense to the parish in this case being a clothing outfit.

From 1778 to 1784, and again between 1793 and 1815, the parish had to provide for all the various expenses connected with finding recruits for the militia, and providing for the families of the absent men. A large part of this outlay was, however, received back from the county treasurer.

We have in the Overseers' Accounts in 1787 a curious memorandum, which indicates that destitution was not the test for granting relief. A woman in receipt of relief, Jane Lumberd, received special indulgence and commendation on account of her honesty in giving up her house for the benefit of the parish, it being sold for £28. It was evidently considered that she was fully entitled to relief without sacrificing her property had she desired it. After the new Poor Law of 1834 the one grievance of the poor people of Warminster Union, we are told, was the demand of the guardians that an applicant for relief who possessed a cottage should sell or mortgage the latter. It was not usual under the old system to make such demands, though the parish officers were ready to make a bargain with a cottage owner when occasion offered. In 1796 the house of Uriah Gritt was repaired, in return for which it was to become the property of the parish. Another cottage was 'signed to the parish' in 1804 when expenses on account of this cottage were met by the parish officers. It was thus only when relief was granted on account of the house itself that it was the custom to appropriate it under the old system.

Some light on parish customs and manners is thrown by the following undated slip found in one of the parish books. Gane was overseer in the year 1808, so it may have been drawn up at this date:

> In consequence of a report of there being Mad-dogs in the Parish of Corsley, the paymasters are determined to lessen the number kept, and the following resolutions ordered, and entered into, this day at a Vestry Meeting.
>
> 'Resolved whoever keeps a Dog after this time shall have no relief of the Parish, whatever. They shall not be permitted to live in any House, belonging to the Parish. To have no part of the Gift at Christmas, or be entitled to either of the Half-Crowns given by the will of the late Mr. Adlam.
>
> (Signed) W. GANE, Overseer.
EB'R COOMBS.
JOHN BALL.
JOS JONES'.

It would seem that, besides participation in the charitable bequests with which Corsley is rather richly endowed, to live rent free and receive poor relief were advantages widely enjoyed at this time. One or two curious entries having some relation to this may be quoted. In February, 1775, the parish paid 6d. for 'catching rats at Widow Hainses'. In 1790, 3s. was given to Thomas Pewsy 'to begin housekeeping'. A generous conception of the province of poor relief was thus in existence prior to the commencement of wholesale pauperisation in the early years of the nineteenth century.

As a rule, relief was ordered to the poor by the Vestry Meeting, but now and then, when refused help here, the applicant would refer to the magistrates, and relief was given, as the entries record, 'by order of ye Justices'.

Towards the end of the eighteenth century, probably marked by the year 1795 in Corsley, began a period the darkest since the time of the Black Death in the fourteenth century for the English labourer. War abroad and famine at home rendered the means of a decent livelihood practically unattainable for the labouring classes. An old inhabitant of Chapmanslade would relate with horror the tales which his father had told him of the terrible years about 1801, when he resided on the border of Wilts and Somerset. Men would go about with a piece of sacking tied round their necks, with holes for their arms and legs, as sole clothing. The people would feed on acorns, or anything they could obtain. So high was the price of corn that a man could carry a guinea's worth of bread on his head.

Another old inhabitant tells how his aunts could remember the 'barley times', and when 'their supper was lack of food'. Clothing, too, was very expensive; his father, born in 1790, had to pay £5 for his first Sunday coat, and though the winters were very severe, people could not afford to buy warm clothes.

A third relates that his father, who was born about 1790 , never ate meat as a young man; the poor could not buy bread, but ate barley bannocks; and flour was in those days £7 7s. the bag.

The Poor Law accounts bear out the tales as to the hardness of the times. In June, 1801, no less than 236 cases were relieved in Corsley in a population 1,412, and, as a large proportion of these doubtless represented a family, the total number dependent on relief must have been far greater. This number, too, does not probably include any of the inmates of the workhouse.

In 1802, as we have seen, the main part of the workhouse organisation was abandoned, supervision of the work in the house being no longer kept up, and the inmates being no longer catered for. About the same time a paid assistant overseer was appointed to perform the work of paying the poor of the parish.

The custom of hiring out the inmates of the workhouse to employers in the parish continued, and a new practice first made its appearance, payments being made to an employer on account of a certain labourer, Shadrach Singer. This has every appearance of being the first definite rate in aid of wages made in Corsley. The practice was continued, though it never seems to have become a very prominent evil in the parish. At the time of the Poor Law Commission in 1834 it was reported by Mr. Fussell that there were four or five able-bodied labourers in the employment of private individuals in receipt of relief to make up their earnings to the scale allowed by the Warminster magistrates.[1]

In 1802, £1,640 3s. 5¼d. was expended on poor relief by the parish of Corsley. But things soon began to improve here, if expenditure may be taken as a test, this not again exceeding £1,000 till seventeen years later.

The rise of the rates in 1827 marks the beginning of a time when the prospect was again looking black for the labourer of this district, owing principally to a decline in the cloth trade, which threw numbers of unemployed weavers upon the hands of the farmers, who took on inefficient workers rather than leave them entirely a burden on the rates. This was detrimental to the farmers and disastrous to the genuine agricultural labourers, these being often crowded out by inferior workers, whose competition also lowered the standard of wages.

Hard as were the times, it is probable that Corsley suffered rather less than many of the neighbouring parishes. Industry was still in a fairly thriving state here, and we do not learn that any Corsley men joined in the agricultural riots of the district in 1830.

Some of the women and children, as well as the men, worked for wages in those days, but the united earnings of the whole family were very small. From the report to the Poor Law Commission[2] we learn that there was employment for the women in hay-harvest and in the silk factory which was being worked at this time at Whitbourne Moor. Many of the boys were employed in agriculture, probably be-

1 *Report Poor Law Commission*, A.D. 1834, vol. xiii. Appendix (131) II. p. 571b. Evidence of Mr. H. A. Fussell.

2 *Report Poor Law Commission*, A.D. 1834, vol. xii. Appendix (B1), I, p. 571a. Evidence of Mr. H. A. Fussell.

ginning work at seven or eight years of age.[1] The girls were employed in woollen and silk manufacture. Mr. Fussell, in his report, states that women and children under sixteen could probably earn £10 per annum, 'when the domestic duties of the woman will permit her to do anything, which, I think, must seldom be the case'.[2] It does not appear, therefore, to have been a universal custom in Corsley for the women to go out to work. The wages of men, in the district were 7s. or 8s. per week.[3] Mr. Fussell reported that it was possible for families to subsist on these earnings, but only on a diet composed almost wholly of vegetables, with bread occasionally.[4]

Corsley may have been slightly better off than its neighbours, owing to the extensive emigrations to Canada which took place from the parish in 1828 and the following years.

In 1830 the parish shipped off at its own cost sixty-six of the least desirable of its inhabitants, about half being adults and half children, or 'under age'. This was only following the example set by natives of Corsley who had previously emigrated on their own account.[5] Emigration became the fashion, and this means of drafting off the surplus population must have helped to mitigate the misery which followed on the decay of the clothing industry in the neighbourhood, with the consequent pressure on agriculture, which thus became the sole occupation of many formerly busy cloth-making parishes.

1   An old inhabitant, Mr. Alfred Down, born about 1820, states that he and his brother went out to work at the age of seven. Probably the employment of children of this age continued in the parish till the passing of the Education Act, in 1871.

2   *Report Poor Law Commission*, A.D. 1834, vol. xii. Appendix (B1), i. p 571a. Evidence of Mr. H. A. Fussell.

3   *Second Annual Report Poor Law Commission*, 1836, vol. i.,p. 300, Warminster Union. Evidence of John Ravenhill.

4   *Report Poor Law Commission*, 1834, vol. xiii. Appendix (B1), ii, p.571b.

5   1831. About two hundred persons are stated to have emigrated within the last three years: *Accounts and Papers*, 1852-3, vol. lxxxv. Population of England and Wales – Corsley. Numbers of the inhabitants 1801-51.

To raise money for shipping off these sixty-six persons, some houses belonging to the parish were sold, and a considerable sum was raised by subscriptions. Clothing as well as money was contributed. These emigrants consisted of 'several families of the very class one would wish to remove – men of suspected bad habits, and bringing up their children to wickedness'! There were several poachers among them, and other reputed bad characters. The captain of the ship came up to arrange as to taking them on board his vessel at Bristol for Newport, whence the ship of Quebec would sail. Finally it was arranged that the whole party were to leave Corsley on a certain day in wagons, accompanied by the assistant overseer and some of the ratepayers, who, avoiding the towns on their route, were to deliver the party safely to the vessel in the river below Bristol.[1]

This was probably the largest party which left Corsley in a body, but other families were helped to emigrate by the parish in subsequent years,[2] and doubtless some of the people who owned a little property sold it and sailed for America at their own cost. Thus the congestion of unoccupied population caused by decaying industries was relieved, and we learn, after the Poor Law Reform of 1834 had been carried out, and conditions possibly improved thereby, that the people in the Corsley district were 'well employed,'[3] although there was still much able-bodied pauperism in neighbouring districts, and fifty labourers out of work in other parts of the Warminster Union. Other parishes in the vicinity soon followed the example set by Corsley,[4] in emigrating some of their surplus population.

We must not leave the history of the people of Corsley under

1 See paper re Corsley emigration at the Longleat Estate Office, and Corsley MS. Overseers ' Accounts for this year.

2 Corsley MS. Overseers ' Accounts.

3 Second Annual Report, Poor Law Commission, 1836, vol. p.300, Warminster Union. Evidence of John Ravenhill.

4 See pamphlets by Paulet Scrope, relating to emigrations in Wiltshire, in the Devizes Museum.

the old Poor Law without alluding to the Corsley Walking Club, which was founded about 1798 or perhaps earlier.[1] This club, which had a large roll of members during part of the nineteenth century, has recently come to an end, being practically superseded by larger societies, such as the Shepherds, Wiltshire Conservative Benefit, and Hearts of Oak.

1   In an article in the *Warminster and Westbury Journal*, June 17, 1905, is stated that the club was founded years before this date. Allusions to a club are found the Corsley MS. Overseers' Accounts in 1789 and 1794. Whether or no this was the Corsley Walking Club does not appear.

8

Corsley in the Nineteenth Century

A T THE ACCESSION of Queen Victoria an era of steady decline and depopulation had already set in for Corsley; and its story during her reign is one of the constant mutual adjustment, on the one hand of population to the changes and decreasing requirements of industry and agriculture, and on the other of agricultural methods to the variations in the supply of labour. At the census of 1841 the population numbered 1,621 persons, in 1901 it was reduced to 824.[1] The parish was therefore about twice as populous at the Queen's accession as it was when she died. The decrease was most rapid between 1841 and 1861, the term when Corsley was finally deserted by the cloth trade and other manufactures. Since then the population has declined at an average rate of about one hundred every ten years, the movement being greatest during the seventies, when agricultural changes were going forward.

By 1837 the new Poor Law, and a more stringent system of relief, was established. The old workhouse premises were sold in 1838,[2] and indoor relief was thenceforth administered in the newly-erected Warminster Union, other cottages belonging to the parish being disposed of in subsequent years.[3] Some confusion and difficulty was met with at first by the Corsley people in administering the new

1   For census returns of Corsley, 1801 to 1901, see Appendix I. p. 290.

2   MS. Corsley Vestry Minutes, August, 1838.

3   MS. Corsley Vestry Minutes, November, 1839, and February 6, 1840.

law. At Lady Day, 1843, it appears to have been formally discussed at a Vestry Meeting whether or no the old custom of the parish should be maintained in preference to adopting the new modes of procedure, and the decision come to is entered in the minutes, 'that at this and all future Meetings the Law should be the Guide'.[1]

The year 1844 was a hard time in Corsley. This was very probably owing to the closing of a large cloth factory, which we learn from the Census Report[2] occurred between 1841 and 1851. Though several families migrated elsewhere in search of employment, many persons became a burden upon the rates. A resolution passed at a Vestry Meeting in January that rates levied upon cottages and gardens should be paid by the tenants, allowance being made to them by the proprietors in the rents,[3] was presumably an attempt to make the bulk of the population realise the incidence of the burden of pauperism. Later in the year the Vestry decided that the unemployed paupers should be divided among the ' paymasters ' according to the number of acres in their occupation. A committee was appointed to investigate the matter. From their report we learn incidentally that 7s. a week was considered the minimum wage in Corsley for an able-bodied man, and in computing the number already employed, two women were to count as one man.[4] How the scheme worked, or whether, indeed, it was ever carried into effect, is not recorded.

In 1854 a salaried assistant overseer was appointed for Corsley.[5]

In December, 1856, the Vestry, anticipating lack of employment during the winter months, agreed that persons seeking work were to be referred to the Waywardens, who were promised

1   Ibid., March 5, 1843

2   See Appendix I. p. 290.

3   MS. Corsley Vestry minutes, January 15, 1844.

4   Papers in Corsley Parish Chest. Minute of Vestry Meeting, October, 1844, &c.

5   MS. Corsley Vestry Minutes, September 4, 1854.

Cottage with weaver's window, inhabited by John Mines, the last weaver in Corsley

an additional way rate, when necessary, to defray the expense of providing employment.[1]

In 1889, and again in 1893, the Corsley Vestry pressed for greater publicity of the proceedings of the Warminster Board of Guardians, and demanded that copies of the financial statement should be distributed among all the larger ratepayers.[2]

Having briefly surveyed the action of the Corsley Vestry in regard to pauperism, under the new law, we must turn our attention to the chief cause which aggravated poverty, namely the decline in the cloth trade. Within the memory of the older inhabitants now living there were three manufacturers who employed a considerable number of workpeople. These were Mr. Fussell, the dyer, at Sturford; Mr. Taunton, clothier, miller, and farmer, at the Mill Farm; and Mr.

1   Ibid. December 2, 1856.
2   Ibid. March 5, 1889, and March 5, 1893.

Coombs, who had a silk factory at Whitbourne Moor. The factories were situated on the small streams of water which flow through Corsley. By the middle of the century, or shortly after, all these works were closed.

The last factory which is remembered was just without the parish at Lane End. This was burnt down and never rebuilt, but was made into a logwood mill, in connection with the dyeing factories. The loss of this factory was keenly felt. After its destruction many Corsley people went to work in the factories at Rodden, or Frome, from which also spinning and other home work was fetched by Corsley women. We have already seen that some of the men thrown out of work were billeted upon agriculture, while the majority probably migrated to other parts of England or to the colonies.

The agriculture of Corsley was in a prosperous state in the earlier part of the reign. Since the enclosure, nearly the whole parish had been converted to arable, and wheat was the principal crop. The land was mainly in the hands of large farmers, and the big farmhouses were the scene of busy life and activity, especially Cley Hill Farm, with the neighbouring hamlet of Chipps, then belonging to Mr. Barton, which the people say seemed like a little town. Very few cows were kept, and milk was not easily obtainable by the poor, but the farmers would always allow the labourer to rent potato ground at 1s.[1] a pole.

But the prosperous days for the English producer of corn were drawing to a close. The agriculture of the New World was developing, means of transport were improved, and the competition of American wheat brought down prices in the English market to such an extent that its cultivation became unprofitable in most districts of England, and after much loss, and even ruin to some farmers and landlords, the country has for the most part been turned down to grass, acre by acre, and converted into dairy, and cattle-rearing farms or broken up into market gardens.

1   This rent is given on the authority of one old lady's recollection. Probably the price varied as in the allotments at present.

Between 1871 and 1881 a marked increase in the movement of depopulation occurred in Corsley, and this corresponds with the crisis of the change in agriculture, which in less than thirty years converted Corsley from a wheat-growing to a dairy-farming parish. The conversion of arable to pasture was mainly effected between about 1870 and 1885,[1] though it continued on into the twentieth century.

The difficulty of letting large farms at this time led to some of them, such as that at Whitbourne Temple, being broken up, and leased in small holdings. This reversion to something more nearly resembling the old system of distribution in Corsley was ultimately a great boon to those of the inhabitants who remained. The rich sandy soil is peculiarly favourable for the success of the small holding, and there are probably at least thirty families in Corsley at the present day with less than twenty acres, who as market gardeners or dairy farmers make their living mainly from the land. Dairy farming is also a reliable and satisfactory form of agriculture for the larger farmer, though the small amount of labour it demands, and the consequent lack of encouragement which it gives to the labouring lad to remain on the land, is to be deplored.

When the land was laid down to grass, women, too, ceased to be employed in agriculture. Forty years ago women worked in the fields of Corsley gathering stones off the plough-lands, planting beans, tying corn, hoeing roots and corn, and cleaning up the fields at a wage of 10d. per day, and four women were employed by Mrs. Barton in her garden.[2] But with the conversion of arable to pasture, and a further reduction in the demand for agricultural labour caused by the use of machinery, women ceased altogether to be employed as agricultural wage-earners, though at the present day the wives of small holders, and many cottagers, work on their own land or gardens.

1   When questioned in 1905, most of the inhabitants stated that the change occurred mainly twenty to thirty-five years previously.

2   These details are related by an old inhabitant of the parish.

The demand for women's work in industry having failed, and the demand for women's work in agriculture having failed, the young women naturally took to migrating elsewhere, and for the most part entered domestic service in the towns. The migration of the female population of Corsley is at the present day greater than that of the male. It has been suggested that this departure of the young women has contributed to make the young men unwilling to remain on the land, and undoubtedly the parish is far duller for the few young people who stay here than it was a couple of generations ago, before most of the youth had departed.

Owing to the gradual adjustment between population and the demand for labour, together with the revival of the small holding, the reign of Victoria, which began with painful and violent cataclysms, sudden loss of employment, the breaking up of homes, and departures from Corsley, drew to a peaceful conclusion in this village.

The only industries now carried on in the parish besides a few to supply local needs, such as shoemaking, tailoring, dressmaking, baking, and the like, and the domestic industry of gloving, are building and cart-building. Mr. Eyers at Chapmanslade carried on a considerable business, and in the winter of 1905-6 employed about twenty hands in building and plumbing. Mr. John Pearce employs some twenty-five carpenters, wheelwrights, painters, &c. at Corsley Heath, besides about twenty masons and others elsewhere. The largest shop remaining in the parish is that of Mr. Henry White, at Lane End, who supplies bread, groceries, and general provisions. Several smaller bakeries and shops are yet to be found scattered over the parish.

Notwithstanding the steady decline in the population since 1830, considerable additions have been made to the accommodation for religious services in Corsley. In 1849 the Wesleyan Methodist chapel at Lane End was rebuilt, at a cost of £244 12s. 4½d.[1]

---

1   Corsley Wesleyan Methodist Chapel MS. Baptismal Register, note on flyleaf.

In 1867, on the far side of the road at Chapmanslade, just outside the parish of Corsley, an Episcopal church was built,[1] and a few years after the period we are considering, in 1903, the new Episcopal church at Temple was completed, according to the will of the late Mrs. Barton. Nonconformist chapels already existed at Chapmanslade and near Temple, which are, however, a mile or so distant from the parish church, and a missionary zeal for religious orthodoxy was probably the motive which led to the establishment of churches in these districts.

Among the events which have most profoundly influenced the life of Corsley in the Victorian era we must count the establishment of the National School in 1848, and the law which enforced compulsory school attendance in 1871. Previous to 1848 there were private schools in the parish, such as the 'Ranters' shop', belonging to the Primitive Methodists at Whitbourne Moor, kept by Thomas Ansford, and the school kept by Miss Mines at Longhedge, who is remembered as a very old woman, with a long stick with which she could reach all the children from where she sat. At Leighs Green, Mrs. Haines, a 'turrble strict woman', had a small school where she taught five to eight children to read and write. Another school is said to have been kept by the Gutch family at Temple.[2] There is no reason to suppose that this is an exhaustive list. Any man or woman who could read was in those days considered qualified to keep school, and probably many such small institutions were distributed over the parish.

In 1846 a collection was set on foot for the establishment of a National School, and £678 16s. 6d. was raised. By 1848 the work of building appears to have been complete.[3]

In 1861 Lord Bath made a gift to the parish of the site of the National School House. It was stated at this time that 535 children had

1   W. Doel, *Twenty Golden Candlesticks*, p. 172.

2   These schools are remembered by old inhabitants.

3   MS. Papers relating to Corsley National School.

passed through the school since its establishment, and the number on the books in this year was 105.[1]

In 1870 statistics in the matter of education in Corsley were collected,[2] which show that of 175 children between the ages of five and twelve years, 94 were being educated in the National School and 70 in 'adventure schools', leaving only 11 who were receiving no education. As, however, a large proportion of the population at the present day, of forty years old and upwards, are unable to write, and read only with difficulty, there is reason to doubt whether in all cases the education was very efficient. A proposal was made at this time for the erection of a 'Chapel' school at Temple, the National School premises being inadequate, but the scheme seems to have been dropped.

In 1873 the Rector stated that the attendance at the National School had increased, funds being needed to provide a more adequate teaching staff.

Some of the 'adventure schools' continued. George Stevens, a one-legged man, kept a school, attended chiefly by the sons of farmers

1   Ibid.

2   Ibid. Population 1,235

	Present Supply.	
National School, on the books		83
National School, provided for in Dilton's Marsh		
of Chapslade		11
		94
	Adventure Schools.	
	[Not recognized by the Government]	
Ann Morgan		17
Ann Hyatt, Lane End		6
Jane Watts, Long Edge		16
George Stevens, Dartford		26
Miss White, Temple		5
		70
	Total	**164**
Census of children from one year to twelve years:		
	Result	290
	Those under five years	115
		175

and tradesmen, whom he taught reading, writing, arithmetic, and book-keeping, until in 1891 free education gave the death-blow to his institution. One or two of the small schools for infants yet remain in the parish.

The last great influence, which has perhaps done more to change the habits and mode of living of country people than any other single factor, was the introduction of railways. In 1850 the Great Western Railway opened the line to Frome, and this line has since undergone improvements and extensions. In 1856 the G.W.R. line from Warminster to Salisbury was opened.

The railway development further encouraged the movement of population to the towns. It also brought about a strong reaction of town life on country life. The youth or maiden who left his or her native village could easily return, and within living memory urban habits and fashions in dress and amusements have come down and overset the ancient customs of nearly every village in England. We shall conclude this chapter with a description of the early Victorian personnel of Corsley, with their distinctive characteristics, habits, and amusements, as remembered by the older people of the parish, before this last disturbing influence was brought to bear.

The principal family in the parish were the Bartons, of Corsley House, who lived in a homely way, farming their own land and taking part in the incidents of rural life, whilst occasionally entertaining the neighbouring gentlemen at a large dinner or banquet, commencing at an early hour. Residing continually in the parish, they lived in close relations with their humbler neighbours, especially their own employees, and many tales are told of the chaff, repartee, and practical jokes which passed between them. Harvest was the great festival of the year, when, the work being concluded, all partook of a generous feast, neither meat nor beer being stinted.

Mr. H. A. Fussell, the dyer, was residing in the house he had built at Sturford Mead, with his family of twelve sons and daughters. They likewise lived quietly, going in very little for show, and walking to church, instead of driving as was the habit of well-to-do people in those days. Mr. Fussell made it a rule that all the men employed in his dye-works should attend a place of worship on Sundays, but they were free to choose among the church and chapels of the parish.

Mr. Taunton, the clothier, of the Mill Farm, is always spoken of as a great benefactor to the parish. He employed probably forty hands, and if any man went to him wanting work he would find him a job if possible. He also ground corn, killed pigs, made cheese and bars of soap, and he would let his poorer workmen have bacon, flour, cheese, and soap at cheap rates, this system of 'truck' being much appreciated by the receivers. But this Mr. Taunton, who was a kind and a businesslike man, had children who turned out wild. One was accused of the murder of a Corsley man, and he fled to America, though the crime was never brought home to him.

Mr. Coombs, the silk manufacturer, had daughters, who, when the factory was broken up, went to live with their uncle, Mr. James Sainsbury, at Sturford Cottage. This Mr. Sainsbury is said to have been a self-made man. He began by buying a sack of corn and dealing with it. He then took to riding to Salisbury market every week, and eventually accumulated a considerable fortune, which he left to his nieces. He was a very reserved man, holding conversation with no one if he could avoid it. He 'kept no company', except that once every month he gave a dinner to all the people in the parish who had only one leg, one arm, or one eye.

Near by, at Whitbourne Springs, in the house now occupied by Mr. Harry Ball, and formerly in all probability the residence of the Carey family, Mr. Dredge, a very stout man, carried on his malting business.

Somewhere in the neighbourhood of Leighs Green lived Mrs. Eyers, who kept an old-fashioned gig, in which she was driven every Sunday to the Whitbourne Baptist Chapel, taking the preacher back to dinner with her. This lady bequeathed to the chapel £500.

Among the larger farmers were Mr. Bailey, of Pool Farm, and Mr. Ball, of Church Farm.

Big farmers in those days, say some of the old people, did not live as well as working people do now. These two farmers would drive or ride to Warminster market every week, always attired in a smock frock. When driving they would have wagons with four horses and bells. Warminster market must have presented a very different appearance to the markets of to-day, when every small farmer, and many market gardeners and others, drive in small carts, dressed in the conventional ready-made great coat and bowler hat.

At Corsley Heath there lived a blacksmith, who with his wife saved £1,000 in twenty years. These people would fatten a pig from time to time, and eat salt bacon. They never ate fresh meat more than once a week, though they had no children to save for. One old lady relates that it was the custom for working men to take out with them half a small loaf and a large onion for their dinner, never meat or cheese. Breakfast and supper generally consisted of home-grown potatoes, with a little of something to flavour it. Very little meat was eaten. The period of famine appears to have taught a hard lesson in thrift, which was not forgotten for more than a generation, either by the labourer whose wage was still not more than 8s, a week, or by the more well-to-do country people.

Among the notable characters we must not omit to mention John Moody, a labourer, who early in the nineteenth century brought up a family of six sons and one daughter, who is still living, without receiving any assistance from the parish. He was afterwards presented with a sum of money in recognition of this remarkable independence, together with a book for 'religious and moral conduct'. One of his sons, John, worked as a labourer for Farmer Ball's family for over forty years. Another son, Robert, became butler to the Bartons, and on his death left the Moody Charity, including the church clock, to the parish. Some of the descendants of the first John Moody, yet living in Corsley, display the same extremely independent spirit manifested by their ancestor.

There were plenty of people with horses and carts and a great deal of trade going on in Corsley in early Victorian times. An elderly couple were able in a few minutes to recollect about ten men besides the farmers who kept traps in their young days, and they say that there were many more, though whether as many as there are to-day it is not possible to guess.

There were many gipsies about, who camped on the remaining bits of waste land. These men would fight among themselves or with the inhabitants for money, and murder was sometimes done. A certain old Jack Youdall, who is said to have killed a man, was a 'vagabond upon the earth'. He was allowed to dig up a bit of the waste land at the lower side of Corsley Heath and plant potatoes. He used to make up people's 'banks' for them, and when his daughter, a housekeeper, married her master, she was said in a local newspaper to be a 'banker's' daughter.

At Norton Common lived an old lady mysteriously clever in curing wounds, bruises, and sores, who was visited by patients from far and near.

The inhabitants of Corsley had several amusements early in the century which are now obsolete. A skittle-ground used to exist at Longhedge, the gipsy fights have already been noticed, and the great events of the year were the Corsley Fairs. There had been one at Whitsuntide, and one on July 27th from ancient times. This latter used to be held fairly recently at Corsley Heath on 'Cock Heap', a large artificial mound which has now disappeared. Cheese was pitched here, and teams of horses were brought to be sold. There were stalls where gingerbread and fancy things could be bought. There were ponies for telling fortunes, cheap jacks, and other shows and amusements. The Corsley fairs have now been entirely dropped.

One old amusement, which probably dates from time immemorial, yet remains. This is a game played up Cley Hill with a ball and sticks on Palm Sunday.

But though we still find many old people, with the old ideas and old tales of the past, though many ancient superstitions yet linger on half-concealed among the population, though many of the young people who remain are true children of their parents, conservative in ideas and habits, yet the youth of Corsley as it grows up tends more and more to assimilate to the modes of thought and habit of the dweller in towns, and the more energetic, unless withheld by the prospect of becoming the master of a small farm or gardening business, continue to migrate to districts where their urbanised tastes may be gratified.

What, however, Corsley has lost in picturesqueness it has undoubtedly gained in solid comfort; and with an extension of educational methods better adapted to foster a taste for rural life, with fuller prospects in the future for those who remain on the land, and with ever increasing facilities for bringing the more varied, more exciting, or more intellectual life of the towns into the country districts, a reaction against emigration to the towns, or a counter current of emigration into the country, some indications of which are already discernible, may set in, and an increasing number of people may find that this parish, with its healthy climate and its singularly beautiful scenery, is, after all, a good place to live in.

PART TWO

CORSLEY IN THE PRESENT

An Old Inhabitant

9

Introduction
Method of Inquiry

THE FOLLOWING DESCRIPTION of life in Corsley is based on the results of systematic inquiries, addressed to the inhabitants, and others who were able to furnish the desired information. Before giving the conclusions, it will be well to describe the nature and method of the investigation. The bulk of the information was collected by a house-to-house inquiry in November and December, 1905, and the first weeks of January, 1906. During these visits the following form was filled up, so far as possible, for nearly every household, from information given by the householder, his wife, or one of his children.

1. Name.
2. Age.
3. Place of birth.
4. Occupation.
5. Name of employer (or state if on own account).
6. Wife's name.
7. Wife's place of birth.
8. Father's name.
9. Father's occupation.
10. Father's place of birth.
11. Paternal grandfather's name.
12. Paternal grandfather's occupation.

13.   Paternal grandfather's place of birth.
14.   Maternal grandfather's name.
15.   Maternal grandfather's occupation.
16.   Maternal grandfather's place of birth.
17.   Names and sex of all children born, and date of birth; marking those which are still living; and trade or occupation of those who have left school.
18.   Have any of your children left the parish ? and if so, state where they went to, and what occupation they are following.
19.   How many rooms are there in the house that you occupy ?
20.   Does any one else, and if so, who, dwell in the house ?
21.   If occupying land state the number of acres.
22.   If employer, state occupation and number of persons employed, men, women, and young people.

Towards the end of 1905 a second inquiry was made as to the characteristics of the various households. Several reports were obtained for most of the families, care being taken in each case to question persons likely to be well acquainted with the characters of the persons concerned, and to have no personal interest in concealing or exaggerating the facts. The inquiry as to earnings was somewhat difficult, and this investigation was spread over a whole year, from the winter of 1905-6 to the winter of 1906-7. Information was obtained in three ways. In the first instance, employers were usually approached. When willing to give information at all, some of these stated fully the wages and all extras which they gave; others stated only a sum, without explanation as to whether this was money wage, or the real wage including all extras, and, in the latter case, what estimation they made for a cottage, beer, or other extras given; some, again, refused definite information, but stated that they paid 'about' so much. Further inquiry revealed a strong tendency amongst some of the employers to estimate the extras given at a rather liberal rate. When, therefore, an employer stated that a man was paid 'about' so much, it has been assumed that this was not the exact wage given, but that, taking into consideration the observed tendency, it was probable that the man received a little less.

Secondly, in a large number of cases, earnings have been ascertained from labourers or their wives. These were not, as a rule, directly questioned, but in many cases the information was volunteered, and persons keeping a diary of their food were paid a small sum, in return for which they were usually quite willing to answer any inquiries. Two tendencies were noticed among wage-earners in regard to giving information as to their incomes. Firstly, some of the more independent were unwilling to reveal their income at all. Secondly, those people, especially the women and housekeepers, who were anxious to participate in public or private charities, were sometimes inclined to understate it, either by omitting some of the extras given by employers, or by mis-stating the money wage. It is quite possible that in the latter case the women were sometimes ignorant of the exact weekly sum received by their husbands, though the amount retained as pocket-money by married men in Corsley is not usually large, and is generally kept with the approval of the wife.

Thirdly, in addition to these two sources, valuable help was given by a person who knew the parish intimately, and could give information as to the wages, in money and kind, of the large majority of wage-earners in Corsley.

All these sources of information were liable to more or less error, and at first sight the results appeared to be in disagreement. A closer scrutiny, however, showed that this was not the case. The apparent discrepancies were usually fully accounted for by the omission or over-estimation of the extras given. These have been generally ascertained, and allowed for at the rate as given in the section on Labourers, in Chapter 10, so that, with a few exceptions, it has been possible to estimate the real wage and money wage of nearly all the workers with a considerable degree of accuracy, the margin of doubt in most cases being nil or very small. In a very few cases hopelessly contradictory information has been received, owing mainly to confusion of names in a parish where most of the people are related to one another, and possibly in one or two instances in consequence of a wish to mislead. But the earnings of these men have been assumed to be the same as other workers of the same class and about the same ability in the parish. These doubtful instances are in any case too few to appreciably affect statistical results, though if wrongly estimated the family may not have been placed in the right economic class in the chapters on Poverty.

The family budgets were collected at various dates during 1906 and 1907, and notes as to diet were also taken while the other inquiries were being carried on. The diaries of food were kept in prepared copy-books by some member of the family, usually one of the children, or the mother. The person keeping the diary was requested to write down after each meal what had been put on the table, and a small sum was paid for the trouble. Frequent calls were usually paid to the houses to see that particulars were being carefully entered at the time. In most cases the mother also gave an account of her receipts and expenditure for each week.

Inquiries were made in the winter of 1905-6 as to religion, friendly societies, insurance, amusements, and many other things. In the autumn of 1907 supplementary information was sought on various points, including women's earnings, medical attendance, and rents.

Though the investigation has been spread over a period of two years, the result may be considered a picture of Corsley in 1905-6, when the bulk of the information was obtained. It is not probable that any appreciable change has taken place in the particular departments on which information was obtained later, for such changes, had they recently occurred, would undoubtedly have been remarked on. To obviate confusion, when necessarily omitting all names, each household in the parish was allotted a number. Care was taken to avoid any sort of order in numbering which could assist in establishing the identification of any particular household. In the section on Character, in the diaries of food, and other parts where separate households are referred to, this index number is given, each household being always identified by the same number.

In order to avoid identification and to obtain statistical results the households have been divided into groups under the heading of their occupations. Some arbitrary classification was, however, necessary, to include people such as the lime-burner and the road-mender. Where, as in the case of these men, there were only one or two of a class they have been included in a group earning similar wages, and it is stated that they are so included.

The whole inquiry was greatly facilitated by the willingness which most of the inhabitants displayed to give the desired information, as soon as it was made clear to them that the names of present inhabitants would be treated confidentially and that the inquiry was only being undertaken with the object of describing their parish as an example of rural life.

10

Who the Corsley People are and How they get a Living

THE GEOGRAPHICAL POSITION of Corsley has been described in the opening chapter of Part I, and we have seen that the population is scattered over the area of 3,056 acres in a number of hamlets and scattered homesteads, being most thickly congregated in the westerly and southerly districts. We must now consider the people who inhabit these lonely houses or more sociable hamlets. When the last census was taken in 1901 there were 824 persons in Corsley. In the winter of 1905-6 the population was distributed in 220 households. The occupations of the heads of these households may be roughly classified as follows:

				Per cent.
Agriculture	...	...	...	57·7
Trades...	...	...	...	4·5
Artisans	...	...	...	11·3
Miscellaneous ...	...	...	...	15·7
Women living without a male relation		...		10·8
Total	...	...	...	100·0

Any accurate analysis is rendered wellnigh impossible by the fact that in Corsley it is the exception rather than the rule for each man to depend on one source of income alone. To take an example, one inhabitant holds three public offices under the central government and local governing bodies, besides following the occupations of farmer and also of timber-haulier and coal-merchant. The public-house keepers are all either farmers or artisans. Artisans are sometimes also small farmers. Lastly, gardening is a source of income in Corsley which is difficult to estimate for individual cases. Most labourers add to their earnings by selling garden produce, and the market gardeners range between people having no other source of income and the labourer working regularly at full time for another employer, with such imperceptible gradations that it is often impossible to guess whether the living is made principally from the garden or from the wage. The following is an attempt at classification, including each man under what appears to be his most important occupation. All working as artisans are included as such. All farmers, not artisans, are grouped under this heading. In this classification, therefore, the publicans, of whom there are five, are not mentioned, but are included as artisans or farmers. There are in reality a few more farmers included among the unoccupied or the artisans, a few coal-hauliers and traders classed as farmers, and many more market gardeners who have some other source of income, regular or occasional.

With these qualifications the occupations of the householders are as follows: The rector (Church of England), 1 Congregational minister; 3 private gentlemen (migrated to parish since 1890); 1 retired estate agent; 1 schoolmaster; 32 farmers, including all grades; 10 market gardeners, marketers or gardeners, with no other occupation; 7 head gardeners, coachmen, and grooms; 1 thatcher; 1 woodman with high earnings; 2 dairymen earning over £1; 72 labourers (including carters, agricultural or other, cowmen and dairymen earning less than £1, a shepherd, woodman, under-gamekeepers, a roadman, a mason's labourer, under-gardeners, a worker at the limekiln, and men who work at malting in winter and do casual labour in summer); 1 warrener; 3 shopkeepers; 1 coal and timber merchant, having no other occupation; 2 shoemakers; 1 'naturalist'; 1 builder and wheelwright, large employer of labour; 1 plumber and builder, large employer of labour; 9 wheelwrights or carpenters; 1 sawyer; 2 plumbers; 4 masons; 1 plasterer and tiler; 2 painters or glaziers; 3 blacksmiths; 3 brickmakers; 1 commercial traveller; 1 assistant clerk of works; 1 police-constable; 1 platelayer, Great Western Railway; 1 worker in Westbury Iron-works; 1 worker in cloth factory, Frome; 12 persons retired with means (including a house decorator, a 'bus-driver, an engineer and publican, a shopkeeper, 2 farmers, a head gardener, a shoemaker and factory hand, a shoemaker, a policeman, and a signalman; these, with the exception of 1 farmer and 1 shoemaker, spent their working lives elsewhere); 5 labourers retired; 1 labourer ill; 1 retired schoolmaster; 1 retired mole-catcher; 2 retired market-gardeners; 1 plasterer out of work; 24 women householders who have no male wage-earner living with them. There are in all 38 households whose head is a woman; but 14 of these women having a son or other male wage-earning relative residing with them, their households have been included under the heading of the male relations' occupation in the above classification.

The occupations of the 24 women without male relations living with them are as follows: Seven living on private means, 1 farmer and coal-haulier, 3 laundresses, 2 who keep a shop and also take in sewing or other work of some description, 2 charing and washing, 2 widows kept by children, 7 occasional jobs and miscellaneous, including 4 who have poor relief.

Farmers

THE MAIN PART of the land of Corsley is now laid down to grass, and the majority of farms are chiefly, or entirely dairy farms.

In 1904 out of 3,056 acres only 512 were returned to the Inland Revenue Office as arable, viz.:

Under crops and bare fallow	361 acres

| Under clover and rotation grasses | 151 acres |
| Total arable land | 512 acres |

But as returns are made in each case under the parish where the farmer resides, though his land may lie partly in an adjoining parish, and as no returns are made by holders of less than one acre, the actual area of arable may be estimated at anywhere between 500 and 550 acres.[1]

This is, roughly speaking, one-sixth of the total area. An indefinite area is covered by homesteads, 280 acres or upwards by woods, and the remainder is pasture or grass.

A considerable amount of milk is sent from the dairy farms to London all the year round. Some is sold to the United Dairies Factory in Frome. Milk is also sold in small quantities and is easily obtainable in the parish, but it is said that good butter is now hard to get locally. On some of the farms cheeses are made in summer and butter in winter.

There is some cattle-rearing. Pigs and poultry are frequently kept.

The size of farms varies from 454 acres down to 3 acres, the smaller farmers merging sometimes into market gardeners. The market gardeners often have a second occupation, and most of the cottagers do a little market gardening; it is therefore impossible to draw distinct lines between the different sections of people who rent or own land for productive purposes, though under the heading of farmers and market gardeners we have to include people at opposite ends of the social scale, some being among the most important of the parishioners and employers and others being actually in receipt of poor relief.

Again, some of the farmers, both large and small, have a second occupation; among them are publicans, coal-hauliers, artisans, a

---

1   I am indebted for this information to Mr. Lewis P. Bunn, Inland Revenue officer.

carrier, a postmaster, a postman, a man who undertakes miscellaneous jobs such as pig-killing, a sexton, a small baker, and a pensioner.

It is thought that thirty-four who call themselves farmers may fairly be classified under this heading,[1] at least twelve of these have a second occupation or, source of income.

> Five of these have over 100 acres of land.
> Four between 50 and 100 acres.
> Seven between 25 and 50 acres, twelve between 10 and 25 acres.
> Four under 10 acres.
> Of three particulars have not been ascertained.

Some particulars of each of these farms will give the best idea of the agriculture of Corsley. No farmer not residing in Corsley has been included, and gentlemen who do a little farming are also omitted (see tables, pp.145-6).

Coal Hauliers and Timber Merchants

FOUR OF THE farmers are also coal hauliers and timber merchants. There are besides these at least two other coal and timber merchants in Corsley. These people are the successors of the wagoners who in the olden times carried the corn from the renowned Warminster market to Bath and Bristol, and returned, via Radstock, where they loaded up with coal.

They now carry timber from the Longleat estate to the collieries and return with coal.

One of these people hauls the Longleat coal supply, another carries coal to Warminster, a third supplies Corsley House, a fourth supplies the villagers, going round with small quantities, a fifth resides

---

1   On p. 106 only 32 have been classified as farmers, but in this list we include 2 who are there classed as artisans.

No.	No. Acres.	Nature of Farm.	No. Men and Boys employed, including Sons or other Relatives.
102	454	Arable and grass. Wheat, oats, beans, sold Frome and Warminster markets. Calves reared. Sheep. Butter-making. Sometimes milk sold	10 regular.
74[1]	327	Dairy	—
93	255	25 acres arable, the rest grass. Dairy. Milk sold in London. Grow enough wheat to supply own straw, and roots for own supply.	7
75	224	80 acres arable, the rest grass. Dairy. Cheese-making, summer, Milk sold in London in winter. Wheat, barley, peas, and beans sold Warminster and Frome Markets	7
87	195	70 acres arable, the rest grass. Cows, horses, pigs, poultry. Milk sold to United Dairies Factory, Frome, and in the parish. Wheat, barley, oats, swedes, &c., sold Frome and Warminster markets ...	5
86	90	5 acres arable, rest pasture. Dairy. Cheese-making summer. Butter-making winter. Both sold at Frome. Pigs and chickens.	1
85	83	... ...	2
101	80	Dairy, &c.	3
89	48	Dairy. Cheese-making summer. Sometimes make butter. Sometimes sell milk. Poultry, especially turkeys	2
82	47	Chiefly arable, but also dairy	—
76	45	Dairy. Cheese-making summer. Butter-making winter. Poultry and pigs ...	1
79[1]	77		3
103	39	Dairy. Cheese-making — cheeses sold to dealers	1
78	28	Dairy	None.
98[2]	26	Dairy. Butter-making. Milk sold in parish	2
90	19+?[3]	Dairy. Milk sold to Frome factory. Pigs and poultry. Some arable, where corn and roots for the cattle are grown ...	1 regularly.
95[4]	18		None.

[1] Also publican.   [2] Also postmaster, coal and timber merchant, &c.
[3] Unknown amount in another parish.   [4] Also carrier, &c.

No.	No. Acres.	Nature of Farm.	No. Men and Boys employed, including Sons or other Relatives.
84	17	Dairy. About 12 cows kept in summer and 10 in winter. Poultry and turkeys. Rear upwards of 200 chickens and 50 turkeys, besides ducks and geese. Butter and eggs sent to London. Dealer in calves and pigs	
77[1]	17	Dairy	1 Man 2 hours daily.
92[2]	—	Dairy, &c.	2 regularly.
97	13+?[3]	Dairy	2
169[4]	14	... ...	None.
96[5]	13	Dairy	None.
81[6]	13	Arable. Corn and vegetables, sold to market gardeners locally, who carry it to Frome. Pigs and poultry	1
112	13	Dairy. Poultry. Butter merchant (buys butter in the market and sells in Corsley) ...	None.
83	13	Dairy	1
88	11	Dairy. Poultry and market garden ...	None regularly.
91	11	Market garden. Two or three cows. Poultry	None regularly.
80	9¾	A few cows. Butter-making. Poultry. Butter fetched by Frome purchaser. Eggs sold to local marketer ...	None.
99	8	... ...	None.
195[7]	7½	Two or three cows. ½ acre arable	None.
150[8]	3	Cows. Poultry	None.
94[9]	—	Dairy (50 cows). Cheese-making — cheeses sold to dealer at Yeovil. Winter, milk sold in London	1
184[10]	47	Dairy	2 (no male in family.)

[1] Also does odd jobs, such as pig-killing.
[2] Also coal haulier and timber merchant.
[3] Unknown quantity in another parish.
[4] Also artisan.   [5] Pensioner.   [6] Sub-postman and sexton.
[7] Also baker.   [8] Also brickmaker and labourer.
[9] Dairyman, rents the cows.   [10] Also coal and timber hauliers.

in Chapmanslade, and probably supplies the inhabitants of that part of the parish.

Market Gardeners and Marketers

MANY OF THE cottagers do some market gardening to supplement their wage-earnings, but besides these and two or three who have been counted among the farmers there are ten or more men, not always heads of households, who make a living mainly by market gardening or marketing.

These include men with a few acres and some capital and people who have fallen back on this occupation owing to the failure of other sources of income. If a man loses an arm, becomes rheumatic, or in any way is so disabled as to have difficulty in finding an employer as an agricultural labourer, he cultivates his garden, perhaps manages to obtain a horse and cart, builds himself a rough stable of corrugated iron and some pigstyes, and, working with his wife, manages to make a hard living, probably being reduced to dependence in his old age.

On the other hand, a small capitalist, often a labourer who has saved money, invests it in a market garden or small farm, and makes a good thing of it, thereby raising himself in the social scale.

The most important of these people, and such as have no other source of income, are included in the following table, which, however, is not exhaustive. Some of the lesser people, not sole earners in the family, are picked at random as examples.

The business of marketing is frequently carried on with that of market gardening, but there are also people, mostly women, who follow this business solely. The marketers range from capitalists with a horse and cart, or wagon, to old women who walk to Frome with a basket and hawk the produce from door to door. The marketers collect butter and eggs, fruit and vegetables from farmers and others, paying a little less than market price, and carry these goods to customers or the markets in Frome or Warminster.

No.	Size of Holding.	Remarks.	Men Employed.
113	6 acres.	Vegetables. Pigs and poultry. Business has been in family fifty years. Horse and cart to take produce to market.	1
118	Big garden and allotment.	Has horse and cart and goes to market Saturdays. Occasional labourer for other people. Wife takes in washing	None.
114	—	Horse and cart. Does some carrier's work as well as market gardening.	None.
117	Two gardens.	Wife nurse.	None. Son sometimes.
116	Garden and ½ acre.	Market garden. Pigs. Poultry. Horse and cart, does some carrier's work, but no marketing for others.	None.
115	6 acres (?)	Horse and cart. Market gardener and carrier.	None.
111	Large garden.	Market gardeners and marketers for other people. Walk in with basket. Poor relief.	None.
72	About 1 acre.	Market gardening. Pony and cart. Living with father, who is pensioner.	None.
24	About 50 poles.	Market gardening. Mainly marketers—collect eggs, butter, &c., from farmers, &c., and sell in Frome. Horse and cart. Head of household a wage-earning labourer.	[Continued on next page.]

In Warminster these people are allowed to hawk without a licence. In Frome they pay, with baskets, 2s.6d., with a donkey 5s., and with a horse and cart 7s. 6d. per annum for the right to hawk from door to door.

Marketers, besides taking Corsley produce to market, bring in supplies for Corsley people. One marketer, included in the list of farmers, buys butter at the market and sells it in this parish, for though a considerable amount of butter is made in Corsley, it is difficult to

No.	Size of Holding.	Remarks.	Men Employed.
190	Allotment and garden.	Old woman. Grows fruit. Son a labourer.	None.
207	10 acres (?).	Market gardener. Horse and cart.	Occasionally a man.
109	3½ acres.	Horse and cart. Also blacksmith.	Occasionally a man.

obtain locally.

It may be noted here that besides well-to-do people who keep a carriage or pony-cart, and about thirty farmers with holdings of three acres upwards, who keep a horse or pony, there are at least twenty men with a pony or horse and cart. These include a few tradesmen, such as builders, coal hauliers, and shop-keepers, but are mainly cottagers. Probably fifty-five is an under-estimate of the number of persons keeping a horse or pony and cart, and there can be no doubt that at least one-quarter of the Corsley households have a 'trap' of some description to drive about the country.

Labourers

THE MAJORITY OF labourers are employed in agriculture, and include carters, cowmen, woodmen, a shepherd, and under-gardeners, as well as general labourers; and for convenience a few others, such as under-keepers, road labourers, a lime-burner, and a mason's labourer, have been included in the group.

The money wages of the majority of wage-earners in the parish, whether householders or subsidiary earners, have been carefully ascertained, every effort being made to check inaccuracies, either accidental or intentional, in information given, by supplementary evidence.

The extra payments given to agricultural labourers in money or kind have also been inquired into. These consist mainly of house and garden rent free, harvest money, and beer or ale daily; also in a few cases milk or meals are given.

These have been estimated at fixed rates as follows:

House and Garden	1s. 6d. per week
Beer	1s. 0d. per week
Harvest money, where amount given is not stated, £2 12s. 0d, or	1s. 0d. per week

Some of the cottages and gardens are, no doubt, worth more than 1s. 6d., but a special assessment in each case was not found practicable.

In certain cases farmers give 1s. a week extra above the usual wage instead of beer; this seems, therefore, to be the commonly accepted value, and 1s. has been taken for beer in all cases where it is given, though in fact the amount given by different employers varies.

In many cases the amount of harvest money given has been ascertained. Where this has not been done £ 2 12s., or 1s. per week, has been taken, this being a mean between sums given in ascertained cases.

In the case of milk the market value of the amount given, or 3d. per quart, is allowed.

Carters

THERE ARE EIGHTEEN carters, sixteen of whom may be considered to be earning full men's wages.

The normal carter's wage is 15s.

Omitting the two who earn 10s., which is not the wage of a full-grown, able-bodied man, the average money wage for the sixteen men is 15s.; the average real wage for the sixteen men is 16s. 9d.

No. of Men.	Money Wage.		No. of Men.	Real Wage.	
	s.	d.		s.	d.
2	18	0	1	20	6
1	16	0	1	19	0
7	15	0	1	17	6
4	14	0	4	17	0
2	13	0	2	16	6
2	10	0	5	16	0
			1	15	6
			1	15	0
			1	10	6
			1	10	0

Dairymen

TWO DAIRYMEN WHO receive more than £1 a week real wages are not counted among labourers.

A third included below receives rather more than the average cowman.

Cowmen

There are 10 cowmen. Their normal money wage is 13s. or 14s., 6 out of 10 receiving this amount.

No. of Men.	Money Wage.		No. of Men.	Real Wage.	
	s.	d.		s.	d.
1	16	0	1	18	0
2	15	0	1	17	6
3	14	0	2	17	0
3	13	0	1	16	0
1	12	0	1	15	0
			1	14	6
			2	14	0
			1	13	0

The average money wage is nearly 13s. 11d., the average real wage 15s. 7d.

Agricultural Labourers

(1 road labourer, 1 worker at the limekiln, and 1 keeper's labourer are included.)

The parish contains 37 agricultural labourers regularly employed, 1 road labourer, 1 keeper's labourer, 1 labourer at the limekiln, and 6 boys or lads employed in agriculture.

The normal labourer's wage is 14s.. or 15s.

Out of 27 labourers whose earnings have been ascertained, two-thirds receive one of these sums – i.e., 11 get 15s. and 7 get 14s.. More than half the labourers in receipt of 15s. are given beer as well; in the other cases the wage is nominally 14s. and 1s. extra in lieu of beer.

No. of Men.	Money Wage. s. d.	No. of Men.	Real Wage. s. d.
11	15 0	2	17 0
7	14 0	6	16 6
5	13 0	6	16 0
3	12s. to 13s. according to season	2	15 6
		2	15 0
1	10 0	1	14 6
13	unknown	3	14 0
		1	13 6
		1	13 0
		3	12 6
		13	unknown

The average money wage of the 27 men is nearly 13s. 11d.; the average real wage is 15s. 3½d.

If we divide the 27 into 2 groups, the first including the 18 men with a wage of 14s. or 15s., the second the 9 men with lower wages, we get the following results:

	s. d.
GROUP I.—Average money wage	14 7
Average real wage	16 1·2

These 18 men are working for farmers or employers resident in the parish.

			s.	d.
GROUP 2.—Average money wage	...	...	12	6
Average real wage ...	...	...	13	4½

The striking fact of this group is that though the money wage is exceptionally low they receive very little addition in kind. This appears still more forcibly if we omit the ninth, an old man working for a farmer at 10s. a week, who receives considerable additions, such as a roomy house which shelters a large adult wage-earning family. The rule has been followed of reckoning this at 1s. 6d., though it is worth more, but even so this man brings down the average of the money wage, and raises that of real earnings in the group.

The other eight men receive 13s. in the summer, but three of them probably have their wage reduced to 12s. in winter.

This group includes the road-mender and other workers for employers not resident in the parish, who, so far as can be ascertained, receive no extras whatsoever.

About half are in an employment which offers some advantages over that of small farmers, such as less supervision and easiness of work. In certain cases, too, a pension may be gained after twenty-five years' continuous service.

This group remains, however, the lowest paid in the parish.

Taking the whole 27 labourers together, it is not probable that if particulars had been obtained respecting the remaining 13 the result would be materially affected. Their omission is due to accidental causes, which do not seem likely to give any particular bias; 3 are working for employers likely to give the highest customary wage, 3 for very small employers, who labour on their own land. In 1 of these cases the wage is likely to be very low. Four are omitted owing to confusion of names which prevents proper identification, and one or two of them are working for farmers in other parishes. One was out of work at the time the investigation was made.

The following is a table of the earnings of boys and lads employed in agriculture in Corsley.

Boys and Lads.

No.	Money Wage.		No.	Real Wage.	
	s.	d.		s.	d.
1 (aged 18)	12	0	1	12	0
3	9	0	1	10	6
1	7	0	1	10	0
1	6	6	1	9	0
			1	8	0
			1	7	6

Under-gardeners

TEN MEN HAVE been classified as under-gardeners; normal wage 14s.

No. of Men.	Money Wage.		No. of Men.	Real Wage.	
	s.	d.		s.	d.
1	16	0	1	16	0
1	15	0	1	15	6
4	14	0	1	15	0
2	13	0	3	14	0
2	unknown		2	13	0
			2	unknown	

The average money wage of the 8 men is 14s. 1½d.; the average real wage, 14s. 3¾d.

Under-gardeners might be counted with agricultural labourers without materially affecting the average money wage, which is 13s. 11d. for agricultural labourers. Their real wages, however, are greatly less than those of farm labourers, since they seldom receive a cottage, harvest money, or beer.

Possibly perquisites of some description are given in certain cases, but these have not been discovered or estimated.

Day Labourers and Woodmen

THERE ARE EIGHTEEN men in the parish who do not work regularly for any employer at a fixed wage, but work by the day, or at piecework, as farm labourers, woodmen, drainers, hedgers and ditchers, mowers, etc. There is also a woodman working regularly for a low wage who can probably supplement his earnings considerably by doing piecework jobs.

The normal rate for an able-bodied man with no special skill such as that possessed by woodmen is 2s. 6d. per day.

No. of Men.	Rate per Day. Summer.	Winter.	Average Weekly Wage.	Weekly Wage when in full Employment.
1 (wood-cutter) —		—	25 0	—
1	—		18 0	—
1	3 0	3 0	—	18 0
4	3 0	2 6	—	15s. to 18s.
1	—		15 0	—
9	2 6	2 6	—	15 0
1	2 0	2 0	—	12 0

The general idea in the parish is that the day-labourer can earn more than the regular labourer.

His money earnings when in work are, no doubt, higher than the average, but besides the uncertainty of employment he probably receives less payment in kind, such as house and garden rent free, than the regular farm labourer, and his real earnings are probably considerably lower.

Gardeners

THERE ARE TWO head gardeners and one foreman gardener in the parish, all in receipt of good wages and earnings.

Groom-gardeners

THERE ARE THREE groom-gardeners, whose earnings are probably equal to or higher than those of labourers.

Thatcher

THERE IS ONE thatcher in Corsley, who works with the assistance of a lad who lives in his house. He probably gets constant employment either in Corsley or in neighbouring parishes. He is paid on a piecework system.

The Building Trades and Artisans

WITH A DECLINING population there is no great scope for the speculative builder in Corsley. There are, however, two builders resident here, who are the chief employers of labour in the parish.

Mr. Pearce, wheelwright and builder, living at Corsley Heath, employs over twenty inhabitants, besides about twenty workmen who are not resident in Corsley.

Mr. Eyers, builder and plumber, at Chapmanslade, employs fifteen to twenty men resident in the parish.

The work carried out by Mr. Pearce at his Corsley workshop is mainly that of cart-building; he also undertakes house carpentering, painting, etc.

There are some good cottages in the parish built by Mr. Eyers, though his business consists more in executing repairs than in the construction of new buildings.

The greater number of artisans living in Corsley find employment at the workshops of one of these tradesmen, while the remainder, or most of them, work for employers residing in other parishes.

In considering the earnings of artisans it will be convenient to include under this heading wheelwrights, carpenters, masons, plumbers, plasterers and tilers, blacksmiths, some brickmakers, and a sawyer.

Corsley Heath Wagon Works

Artisans' Earnings

THE EARNINGS IN this group usually run from 20s. to 25s. per week. A few get less than this and a few get more; none, however, receive more than 30s. per week.

Information given as to the earnings of plumbers, carpenters, and masons is somewhat conflicting.

One informant states that the best men in these trades can earn 5d. to 6d. an hour; but though this is true for wheelwrights and carpenters, no case has been found where plumbers or masons resident in the parish receive more than 4½d. per hour. Individual earnings have not, however, been ascertained in every case.

Masons

THERE ARE SIX masons, two mason's labourers, and one plasterer and tiler (out of work) in the parish. Masons' wages are 4d. to 4½d. per hour. For a week of 56 hours this amounts to 18s. 8d. or 21s.

Plumbers

THERE ARE 4 plumbers and 1 lad learning the trade. Earnings appear to be similar to those of masons.

Painters

THERE ARE 5 painters (1 out of work), also 2 lads and 1 apprentice in the trade.

Wages have not been satisfactorily ascertained but the average is probably 21s. per week.

Carpenters and Wheelwrights

THERE ARE 5 wheelwrights and carpenters and 6 carpenters in Corsley. Wheelwrights, working full time, can earn 24s. to 25s. per week. One worker is said to be able to earn 27s.. per week. The rates are 5d. and 5½d. per hour, for a week of 59 hours. But some workers do not work full time.

Carpenters usually receive 20s. per week. One is said to receive not much short of 30s.

Brickmakers

ONE OR TWO Corsley men work at the Rodden Brickyard, where it is said men can earn £2 to £2 10s. a week in the summer.

The brickyard at Dartford, on the borders of the parish, is worked by the tenant, with the help of his own sons.

Blacksmiths, Sawyer

THERE ARE ONE or two wage-earning blacksmiths and one sawyer in the parish.

WOMEN'S WORK

IT REMAINS TO consider the work and the earnings of women in Corsley. The chief occupations followed by women are laundry-work, charing, gloving, nursing and midwifery, dressmaking, sewing, marketing, shopkeeping, and baking.

Laundry-work

SEVERAL WOMEN IN Corsley take in sufficient washing to oblige them to employ other women to help them, and many more take in a small amount regularly, or occasionally, earning from a few pence to a shilling or two weekly. There are four laundresses living at Longhedge, one at Temple, and one at Corsley Heath. These do the washing of the larger houses in the parish, and also take in some from Warminster. The prices charged for washing are not uniform, but most charge at a low rate, leaving a very small margin of profit. A laundress whose gross earnings are 12s. weekly has to pay a woman for two days' work and provide her food. She must provide materials such as soap, and extra firing, which amounts to something considerable in damp weather. If 3s. be allowed for the extra labour and 1s. 6d. for firing and materials, her nett earnings are 7s. 6d. For this she has to work hard. Whatever the weather may be, the washing has to be finished by a certain time. Should wet weather set in on drying day, she must often remain up all night drying the linen before the fire. There are few washerwomen in Corsley who have attained middle-age without being seriously affected by the trying conditions of their occupation, rheumatism in many forms being prevalent among them. It is absolutely necessary that they should feed well, and with the strictest economy most of them can save little towards a provision for old age, notwithstanding the fact that to end their days without coming upon the parish often appears to be the chief anxiety of their hardworking lives.

One or two Corsley laundresses charge rather higher prices than their neighbours, and, no doubt, make larger profits; one takes in a large amount of washing and by hard work probably makes a fairly good income; in two other cases the laundress is not the only supporter of the family. The fact remains, however, that the remuneration for laundry-work is in most cases unreasonably low.

The women employed by the laundresses receive 1s. per day and their food. They expect good food; probably meat is provided every day. This may be estimated in money as a total of 1s. 6d. per day. Many women go out for the day washing, but they cannot as a rule get employment for more than two days a week at this work. They are sometimes able, however, to get charing work on other days.

Charing

MANY WOMEN SAY that they do occasional charing, and some have regular employment at this occupation. The customary wage appears to be the same as for laundry-work – 1s. per day and food. Some, however, are able to obtain 2s. per day without food or 1s. 6d. with food, and it is to be hoped that this rate may become more general.

Gloving

ALARGE PROPORTION OF the married women and girls in Chapmanslade, and a few in other parts of Corsley, take in 'gloving' from the two glove factories at Westbury and Westbury Leigh. They have to fetch the work from the factories, three or four miles distant. They bring home the leather ready cut into shape, stitch the seams by hand, and return the gloves to be finished in the factories.

The work is poorly paid. The women have to provide their own needles and thread and they receive 4½d. or 5d. per pair according to the quality of the glove. Each pair takes four hours' steady work, so that three pairs are considered a good day's work. This at six full days a week only yields eighteen pairs at 7s.6d. for the better class of glove, and means toiling at high pressure for an excessive number of hours, the work being very trying to the eyesight; and even by the most skilled workers this output is only accomplished now and then as a record, although occasionally a small pair of ladies' gloves may be done in less than the four hours. Married women with a household to look after probably seldom earn more than 2s. 6d. or 2s. per week at gloving, and girls living at home with their relations, and working regularly, but not at high pressure, probably earn about 4s. per week. No case has been found where a single woman or widow is able to support herself by this work, though several women in receipt of poor relief add a little to their incomes by gloving. It must, therefore, be considered entirely a parasitic industry.

Sewing

A FEW WOMEN TRY to support themselves by taking in sewing. This, like gloving, is usually badly paid. One single woman said that she could make 4s. to 5s. per week at sewing, sitting at it all the time.

Nursing and Midwifery

WE NOW COME to an occupation where women have been able to raise their standard of earnings somewhat. Three of the five nurses or midwives residing in Corsley parish were questioned, with the following results:

No. 206 serves the very poor. In the case of confinements in the near neighbourhood she charges 5s., not staying in the house of her patient but making occasional visits for one week. If the patient is more than a mile or so distant, she charges 7s.6d. She is not, she says, able at this price to provide herself with all that is required by the inspector.

No. 1 seldom nurses the very poor. When she does so she says that she charges 5s. or 6s. for a confinement, her usual rate being 7s. 6d. for the, week. A labourer's wife recently attended by her paid 10s. per week, no doctor being called in, and this is probably her customary charge.

No. 180 seldom nursed the inhabitants of Corsley. She usually attended farmers' wives, etc. in other parishes. Her charge was 10s. per week.

The fourth midwife residing in Corsley does not practise in the parish.

The fifth woman, who goes out nursing occasionally, is said to be a very capable attendant. Her scale of charges was not ascertained.

Since the winter of 1905-6 a Benefit Nursing Association has been established, which enables the cottagers, by subscribing, to obtain attendance in sickness or confinements at a much cheaper rate.

Dressmakers

THERE WERE IN the winter of 1905-6 at least three dressmakers in Corsley. The rates of payment are low, being about 3s. 6d. for making a skirt or a blouse, and probably less is charged in some cases.

Nevertheless, a clever dressmaker, working alone, is able to make as much as £1 a week, or, allowing for slack seasons, holidays, and illness, over £40 per annum. Those who have to assist in housework, who are slower workers, or who do not get fairly regular employment, cannot, of course, make so much. Probably the actual takings of the dressmakers vary from 7s. to £1 per week.

Girls going out to work for the day as dressmakers, having received a training, get 1s. per day and food, like laundresses and charwomen. Apprentices taken by village dressmakers receive no remuneration or food during the first year. During the second year they are paid 1s. a week.

Marketing

THIS BUSINESS, WHICH is largely followed by women, has already been dealt with in the section on market gardeners and marketers. It is not possible to discover the nett earnings of such people, these being made up of a number of small and miscellaneous items.

Shopkeeping

AT LEAST THREE women keep shop, in addition to other occupations, or to supplement the earnings of their menkind. One of these does a good business, but little is done by the others, the people of Corsley now buying their provisions mainly from the towns, or from people who hawk round from door to door.

Baking

AT LEAST TWO women earn a little by baking. They usually bake twice a week, and send a child round to their customers with the bread. It has not been ascertained what profits they are able to make in this way.

This exhausts the principal remunerative occupations followed by women in Corsley, as far as can be ascertained.

Speaking broadly, the wage of a woman, be she laundry-worker, charwoman, or dressmaker's assistant, is 1s. per day and food. Few women, however, can get more than four days' employment in a week, unless in regular service. This, calculating food as 6d. per day, gives a maximum of 6s. per week, which may be sufficient for a single woman, but cannot allow her to provide for children or other dependants, nor to save much towards a provision for her old age. When, however, a woman is supported by her husband or son, and works only for pocket money, she is able to make a good thing of it. One woman, the wife of a labourer, was able to save £70 out of her earnings working at farmhouses, and has set up with her capital as market gardener and marketer.

Women's work is to a large extent parasitic, those women who are able-bodied and without dependants or family naturally preferring to enter domestic service or migrate to districts where remuneration is higher. It is to be feared, therefore, that women's wages will not easily be raised, those who are solely dependent on their own earnings being too few and too isolated to fight effectively against a rate of payment which usually forces them in the end to seek relief from the Board of Guardians. It is, as might be expected, from the more well-to-do, those who have substantial savings or are being kept by their male relatives, that the only efforts to raise the rates of pay have come. These can refuse the work as not worth their while to undertake should the reward be too small, and in a few cases such women have succeeded in obtaining a higher scale of payment than their less fortunate sisters.

11

Houses and Gardens in Corsley

THE PARISH OF Corsley boasts of no great house, the lord of its manor for the past three hundred and fifty years having been the owner of Longleat, in the neighbouring parish of Horningsham. It is, however, well provided with houses of a moderate size. There are, firstly, Corsley House and Sturford Mead, and the small house of Sandhayes, occupied by the households of the three gentlemen mentioned in the last chapter. These houses were built, or received considerable additions and alterations, during the nineteenth century. Next we find two old houses, now used as farmhouses, the one the Manor Farm, an Elizabethan house built by Sir John Thynne, and the other Cley Hill Farm, probably in part of more ancient date, and the dwelling of the Kington family prior to the Reformation.

Another picturesque old farmhouse at Whitbourne Springs was in all probability the home of the Carey family in the seventeenth century.

In addition to these there are a number of comfortable-looking houses studded all over the parish, most of them not much more than a century old and some of quite recent erection. These are chiefly occupied as farmhouses.

There are about 165 inhabited cottages in Corsley, in addition to the farmhouses and other substantial dwellings. It is not, however, possible to draw any very firm line of division between houses and cottages.

The cottages appear on the whole to be neither specially good nor specially bad. It is a grievance that few have a parlour as well as a kitchen, and this is asserted to be a reason why young married people often refuse to set up house in the parish, but the influence of this demand for a newly-coveted mark of social distinction is probably much exaggerated.

There is a fair proportion of really good cottages, mainly owned by residents in the parish.

Cottage property in Corsley is owned by a number of different persons, including builders and tradesmen, private gentlemen and farmers, besides cottagers who own their own dwelling, but the majority of the houses belong to the principal landlord, Lord Bath.

Peasant owners of one or two cottages are fairly numerous, and are sometimes the successors of squatters on the once extensive commons of Corsley.

Some of the cottages are still let on a lease of lives, but ordinary yearly or weekly tenancies have during the last forty years been gradually substituted for this old system as the lives fall in.

The population of the parish is declining, being now less than half what it was in 1831, and numbers of cottages have been pulled down or allowed to fall into disrepair since that date.

At the present day if a cottage stands empty, it is usually allowed to fall into ruin, while its garden can generally be let at a good rent.

The 165 cottages contain 689 rooms and are inhabited by 624 persons.

The size of the cottages is as follows:

No. of Cottages.							
8	...	...	...	...	with	2	rooms.
51	...	...	...	...	,,	3	,,
45	...	...	...	...	,,	4	,,
33	...	...	...	...	,,	5	,,
18	...	...	...	...	,,	6	,,
4	...	...	...	...	,,	7	,,
5	...	...	...	...	,,	8	,,
1	...	...	...	...	,,	9	,,
165							

It will be seen from this table that nearly one-third of the whole are three-roomed cottages, though four or five roomed dwellings are also numerous. The larger dwellings of six rooms and upwards are frequently two small cottages rented by one tenant.

As there are 689 rooms, or thereabouts, in these cottages, and only 624 persons, including children, there is more than one room per head for the cottage population.

An examination of the distribution of population among these cottages shows only three cases of overcrowding according to the Registrar-General's definition, of more than two persons to a room.[1] Forty-two cottages have more than one person, but not more than two to a room. The remaining 120 have one or more rooms for each inmate.

Occupations of Householders.	Total No. of Cottages.	No. Rooms.	No. Inhabitants.	No Cottages with		
				1 or more rooms per head.	Less than 1, not less than 2 rooms per head.	Less than 2 rooms per head
Small farmers and market gardeners	14	69	58	13	41	
Brickmakers, shoemakers, &c.	5	20	17	4	1	
Carters	13	51	66	5	7	1
Cowmen	7	30	31	5	2	
Labourers	33	136	148	20	13	
Miscellaneous agricultural ...	14	56	60	9	3	2
Miscellaneous gardeners, retired labourers, and others, and persons working outside parish	25	89	75	20	5	
Artisans	20	104	85	14	6	
Women householders ...	34[1]	134	84	30	4	
	165	689	624	120	42	3

This number 34 includes all women householders living in cottages, some having sons or other male relatives living with them.

1   See *Poverty: a Study of Town Life*, by B. Seebohm Rowntree, p. 145

Rents for cottages in Corsley run from about £3 to £6 a year. Probably the two-roomed houses are less, and a few of the best cottages are more.

Practically every cottage in Corsley has a garden, which is included in this rent.

The rent for an ordinary cottage with three rooms and a pantry, and a good garden of 20 to 40 poles, is £4 a year. A cottage of better type with about four rooms and a garden is £5. If the garden be very large, or the cottage larger or better built than the average, rents are naturally higher, amounting to as much as £8 in one case for a good house of eight rooms and garden. Whilst some of the inhabitants, including those who own their cottages, and also many of the tenant occupiers, have resided in the same house for a number of years, a constant movement is going on among another section of the population. In the autumn of 1906 it was found that besides a few families who had left the parish, and a few who had newly settled there, many had changed from one cottage to another in Corsley or Chapmanslade since the preceding winter. There are families who have moved their house three or more times within the last ten years. The reason for change is not always apparent, though it is sometimes accounted for by the growing up of the children, the need for more accommodation, and an increased income which makes it possible to rent a larger house.

One or two of the smaller farmers, a few of the widows or single women, and some of the tenants of the large and well-built cottages take lodgers. Orphans from the Union workhouse are occasionally boarded out with women in Corsley.

Besides the regular lodgers, who are usually working lads or men employed in the parish, 'visitors' from the towns find accommodation here in the summer, when many strange faces may be seen about the parish. These visitors are sometimes put up in the smaller cottages, and the crowding must be great.

Allotments

THERE IS A considerable amount of land available for allotments in Corsley, viz., about 30 acres in Corsley and 15 acres at Broadpath, Chapmanslade.

Rents are reasonable, being from 3d. to 6d. per lug or pole, or £2 to £4 the acre. It is let in 20-pole holdings, one man often getting three or four into his hands, though, nominally, this is forbidden; the holders, too, will sometimes sublet to other villagers. The actual amount held by any individual is, therefore, not easy to ascertain.

The rents for grass land are high, and cause grumbling, nevertheless, when any grass land is to be let, people 'tumble over each other' to get it. There are a number of people in the parish renting small plots of land which they use either as gardens or dairy farms. The soil is particularly favourable for the success of small holdings and these people usually thrive.

Some of the cottagers also keep pigs or poultry, and the majority add to their income by selling garden produce, even when not holding an allotment.

The garden is, of course, usually cultivated as an additional source of income, but there are, or have recently been, several persons in the parish who, cut off from other means of earning a livelihood, contrive to make one from the garden alone, either with or without a small preliminary capital invested in a horse and cart.

These people probably work very hard, and have a struggle at first, but they seldom come upon the parish until extreme old age.

This proves what a valuable asset the labourer's plot of land is to him, under favourable conditions, and the following account from the wife of No. 131 is an example of what can be done with an ordinary cottage garden in Corsley.

I have a patch of the garden to myself; in this I have a strawberry bed, raspberry bed, gooseberry-trees, currant-trees (black and red), apple-trees and a fowl pen. I have to look after this myself and keep it clean; the fowls enjoy all the weeds which I hoe off and throw into the pen.

Below is what I sold:

	£	s.	d.
Gooseberries	0	11	4
Strawberries	1	11	5
Raspberries	1	14	8
Black and red currants	0	9	2
Apples	0	19	5
Poultry	1	5	0
From other parts of the garden :			
Young potatoes...	0	8	6
French beans and peas	0	6	5
Flowers	1	2	6
Total during year	8	8	5

When I am selling my fruit in the summer, I sell the finest fruit, and boil down into jam all the small fruit, which makes quite as good jam, but does not command so good a price at the market. The jam I find very useful in the winter when butter is dear.

The man in this case had no time to work in the garden, so that a woman, working alone, and having her household duties and cooking to attend to, was able to supply all the fruit and vegetables and some eggs and poultry for home consumption, and in addition to make a profit of over £8 from garden produce and poultry out of a garden of 50 poles, rented, with a five-roomed cottage, for £5 5s. per annum.

12

Poverty

OF THE 220 households comprising the population of Corsley, how many are living in a condition of poverty? In order to ascertain this we have firstly to discover the income of each working-class family, and secondly to define what we mean by poverty.

Every effort has been made to get accurate information as to the incomes of most cottage households. It is as a rule possible to ascertain the receipts of male wage-earners with a fair degree of precision. Real wages, including value of cottages and beer given free, are taken, though wages given as beer are not, as a matter of fact, available to contribute to the efficient nourishment of the family.

It has been less easy to discover whether the wife supplemented her husband's earnings and if so to what extent. When no definite information could be obtained it has been generally assumed that a woman working nearly full time at charing or laundry-work could earn 6s. a week.[1] In the case of married women living at or near Chapmanslade it is assumed, if there is no special pressure to induce them to work very hard, that they earn 2s. 6d. a week gloving, except when they have very young children, or another occupation, or it has been definitely ascertained that they do not undertake this work. In the case of a girl living at home it is assumed, unless definite information has been obtained, that the girl earns 4s., and that the mother does not work. Married women living in other parts of the

1   This is an estimation of the real wage made up by four days' work at 4s. with four days' food value 2s. – total, 6s.

parish are not assumed to earn anything, unless it is known that they do so. Under Family Income, the supposed earnings of all members of the family are included, although sons and daughters living at home do not as a rule contribute the whole of their earnings to the family purse.

In households where the male worker is not a wage-earner, it has usually been impossible to estimate the income with any accuracy. Appearance of houses and inmates, and opinion of neighbours have in these cases been taken into account and an estimate formed; but this is very liable to error. Even if it be ascertained that a family does not have sufficient food, there is the possibility, in the case of the small gardener or farmer, that this may be due to a miserly habit acquired in the effort to save capital and gain independence.

It is believed, however, that the incomes of the great majority of the cottagers have been ascertained or estimated with sufficient accuracy to leave very slight doubt as to whether they are or are not in poverty, primary or secondary.

Primary Poverty

IN ORDER TO define primary poverty, we have followed the precedents set by Mr. Rowntree and Mr. H. H. Mann. An estimate has been made of the minimum cost at which food, fuel, dress, household sundries, and house-room, sufficient for efficiency, can be obtained in the parish, and it has then been seen how many families were below this standard, or in primary poverty.

Mr. Rowntree, in his *Poverty: A Study of Town Life* (pp. 88-106), enters into a scientific inquiry as to the nutritive value of various dietaries, and adopts a certain standard, less generous than that of the Local Government Board dietaries for workhouses, since it omits meat, as the cheapest upon which efficiency is obtainable. He then calculates on a scientific basis the amount required for men and women, and for children of different ages, and from this deduces an average of 3s. for a man or woman and 2s. 3d. for a child as the minimum necessary cost of food, though ignorance and prejudice would prevent the poor from actually selecting any such scientifically economical diet.

To estimate the necessary cost of food per head in Corsley, comparison has been made between the prices paid here and those given for York by Mr. Rowntree.[1] From this we find that provisions as bought by the poor are dearer in Corsley than in York. On the other hand, the inhabitants of Corsley obtain potatoes, vegetables, and fruit from their gardens cheaper than could be obtained by the inhabitants of York. Mr. Rowntree's minimum, based on the cheapest diet sufficient for efficiency, has therefore been adopted, viz. 3s. for an adult; 2s. 3d. for a child.

This standard has likewise been taken by Mr. Mann in his study of the village, of Ridgemont, in Bedfordshire, published in *Sociological Papers,* Vol. 1.

Rent is omitted, since practically every cottage in Corsley has a good garden, and the value of garden produce in some cases more than equals the rent. Probably, in an average case, rent and value of produce (including that consumed by the family) about balance. An old person unable to work his garden would, no doubt, have to pay more in rent than he could get back by the lease of his garden, and in such cases the minimum will therefore be placed a little too low, while in the instances where a man is able to earn more than the total rent from his garden produce it will be placed a little too high.

Mr. Mann estimates that, allowing for wood, etc., picked up, 1s. per week per household would probably be sufficient for fuel, irrespective of the number of persons. He allows 2d. per week per head for household sundries. For dress he has followed Mr. Rowntree's standard of 6d. per week for a man or woman and 5d. for boy or girl under sixteen.

1   See *Poverty: a Study of Town Life,* by Seebohm Rowntree, p.104.

As there seems no reason to suppose that conditions are materially different in Corsley, I take these figures as the minimum necessary. The table then stands as follows, these figures being estimated as the very lowest on which, with the most judicious and economical expenditure, efficiency is possible.

Food, 3s. per adult.

Food, 2s. 3d. per child.

Rent, none, as garden produce equals rent.

Firing, 1s. per household.

Sundries, 2d. per head.

Dress, adult, 6d. per week.

Dress, child, 5d. per week.

The following table gives the minimum necessary income for families of various sizes.

				Food.		Dress, Fuel, and Household Sundries.		Total.	
				s.	d.	s.	d.	s.	d.
1 adult		...	...	3	0	1	8	4	8
2 adults		...	...	6	0	2	4	8	4
3 ,,		...	...	9	0	3	0	12	0
4 ,,		...	...	12	0	3	8	15	8
5 ,,		...	...	15	0	4	4	19	4
2 ,,	1 child	...		8	3	2	11	11	2
2 ,,	2 children	...		10	6	3	6	14	0
2 ,,	3 ,,	...		12	9	4	1	16	10
2 ,,	4 ,,	...		15	0	4	8	19	8
2 ,,	5 ,,	...		17	3	5	3	22	6
2 ,,	6 ,,	...		19	6	5	10	25	4
2 ,,	7 ,,	...		21	9	6	5	28	2

For every child 2s. 10d. is added.

For every adult 3s. 8d. is added.

This corresponds with the table given by Mr. Mann, except that rent is here omitted.

Having thus discovered the minimum upon which efficiency is possible, we find that 28 families, comprising 144 persons (57 adults,

87 children under sixteen), are living in primary poverty in Corsley.

These may be divided into three groups:

(a) Where there is at least one A.B. male wage-earner, but where, through largeness of family or smallness of wage, earnings are insufficient.

(b) Where the wage-earner is incapacitated through old age or illness.

(c) Households without a male wage-earner.

(a) The first of these groups is largest. It contains 17 families, 40 adults and 82 children. If one family of 9, whose earnings are unknown, be omitted, this gives 113 persons with a total weekly income of 297s. and a weekly deficit on what is required for efficiency of 70s.

(b) The second group contains 7 families, 12 adults, and 3 children. Some of these families are in receipt of poor relief and some are not.

Five are persons or families of good character who, through some misfortune, such as illness or accident, were unable to earn good wages in their younger days, and hence have been unable to provide for old age and sickness, or else they have been defrauded of the fruits of their thrift, by the recent breaking up of the old Corsley Walking Club.

The other two are of more doubtful character, and may owe their poverty to wasteful expenditure, or drink.

(c) The third group consists of 4 households containing 5 adults and 2 children, being women with or without children or other dependants, who, through old age or illness, are unable to earn and do not obtain from any other source sufficient for efficiency for themselves, or for themselves and dependants, as the case may be.

The occupations of the heads of the 28 households in primary poverty are as follows:

A.B. labourers ...	...	...	...	16
Retired market gardeners		...	...	2
Labourers retired from old age or sickness ...				5
Warrener ...	...	...	...	1
Women householders ...		...	...	4

The following tables show the economic position of each family:

(A) HOUSEHOLDERS IN PRIMARY POVERTY OWING TO LARGENESS
OF FAMILY AND LOWNESS OF WAGE.

Index No.	Adults.	Children.	Income. s. d.	Deficit. s. d.
5	2	3	13 0	3 10
11	3	5	25 0	1 2
12	2	4	16 6	3 2
28	2	7	17 3	10 11
29	2	3	16 0	0 10
32	2	6	17 0	8 4
36	4	4	23 6	3 6
37	2	6	24 0	1 4
42	2	6	20 6	4 10
44	2	5	15 0	7 6
45	2	4	17 3	2 5
49	3	5	15 0	11 2
51	2	4	16 0	3 8
54	2	3	15 6	1 4
58	3	5	25 6	0 8
62	2	6	20 0	5 4
63	3	6	unknown	unknown deficit.
	40	82	297 0	70 0

(B) HOUSEHOLDS IN PRIMARY POVERTY OWING TO OLD AGE OR
ILLNESS OF WAGE-EARNER.

Index No.	Adults.	Children.	Income. s. d.	Deficit. s. d.
65	1	0	4 0	0 8
66	3	0	unknown	prob. deficit.
67	2	3	12 0	4 10
68	1	0	3 6	1 2
70	1	0	4 6	0 2
73	2	0	unknown.	deficit.
111	2	0	unknown.	deficit.
	13	3		

(C) Households without Male Wage-Earner in Primary Poverty.

Index No.	Adults.	Children.	Income.	Deficit.
183	2	0	unknown	prob. deficit.
179	1	0	unknown	certainly deficit.
205	1	1	6 0	1 6
212	1	1	unknown	prob. deficit.
	5	2		

Total number of persons in primary poverty: 57 adults, 87 children.

Secondary Poverty

IT WILL HAVE been noticed that in estimating the minimum income necessary, nothing is allowed for clubs, insurance, and provision against old age and sickness generally, though it is the practice even of the poorest labourers of Corsley to make such provision. Nor is anything allowed for waste owing to ignorance of the most nourishing and economical foods, or accident of any kind.

It does not appear, therefore, that a family has a secure position above the line of primary poverty, unless it has a surplus of at least 1s. per head per week.

It is usual in an analysis of this kind to take a section who are described as in secondary poverty.

Under this heading we shall include all households whose income does not give this margin of 1s. per head above primary poverty, as well as those households where the income should be sufficient, but where it is squandered and the members are obviously living in want. Probably a few families who might be included for this reason are omitted, since an appearance of dirt and untidiness has not been taken by itself as a proof that a sufficient diet was not provided, though this is likely to be the case.

There are 37 households which, for one or other of the causes mentioned, come under this definition of secondary poverty. These contain 80 adults and 48 children. Thirteen are labourers, 3 being included on account of drink or other wasteful expenditure, or bad management, though the incomes should be sufficient. The other 10, including a carter, cowman, underkeeper, and road labourer, have not the margin of 1s. per head.

A small farmer, a small shopkeeper, and four market-gardeners are included. It is not possible to do more than make a guess at the income of these people, but they appear to have a struggle to keep going, and their incomes do not probably exceed the limit to secondary poverty.

Four are families where the head of the household is aged and the margin of the income over the primary poverty line is small. Nine are women householders.

Five are carpenters, masons, or blacksmiths, with five or six in family, but no supplementary earners. In one case grown-up daughters are kept at home idle. Another case, owing to want of work, drink, and extravagance, is probably in primary poverty, in spite of substantial help from relations and others.

The total number of households in the parish is 220; of these, therefore, 155 are above the margin of secondary poverty, though it must be remembered that even artisans and others, well above this line, are liable to be plunged into extreme poverty, by misfortune, such as serious sickness in the family.

About five-sevenths of the households are above poverty, rather less than one-sixth in secondary poverty, about one-eighth in primary poverty.

But as poverty is mainly due to the presence of non-productive members, we find that numerically the group of primary poverty with 144 persons is greater than that of secondary poverty with 128 persons. Similarly these two groups, which form about two-sevenths of the households, in all probability contain more than two-sevenths of the population. If the decline of the population has continued since the last census, this is certainly the case, although the higher group contains many well-to-do households swelled by the presence of domestic servants and grown-up children.

	Adults.	Children.	Total Population.	No. Families.
Primary poverty ...	57	87	144	28
Secondary poverty ...	80	48	128	37
Over line of secondary poverty	—	—	—	155

Having defined poverty, it will be interesting to investigate its incidence in the households of labourers and artisans.

Out of 70 households[1] whose head is a labourer only 16 are in primary and 13 in secondary poverty; the remaining 41 are, therefore, above this line.

Of these 41, only 13 have a child or children in the household.

We will take first the group of 28 households having no children below fourteen years old.

(A) These contain 78 adult persons.

Nearly all the male wage-earners are labourers (as defined above); but among the subsidiary earners are found one coal merchant, one mason, one labourer in iron-works, and one employee in gas-works. An electrician is also included in this group as a lodger.

(B) The second group of 13 is similar to the above, except that each household contains one or more child. These families are composed of 47 adults and 20 children. The number of adults and of wage-earners is, therefore, preponderant over that of children, many of the women in this group being wage-earners.

Like the first group, the male earners are labourers with the exception of a market gardener, a blacksmith, a worker in Frome foundry, and an engine-driver.

1   On p. 141 (Chapter 10.) the number of labourers is given as 72, but two sons of widows, who are usually away malting in winter, which were included there, are here omitted.

The households in Groups A and B are all well above the line of primary poverty, having a margin of at least 1s. per head.

(C) Group C consists of 13 families in secondary poverty, containing 29 adults and 25 children.

Ten of these are households where there are not more than two children, or where a second male member of the family has just reached an age to contribute to the family income, and has thus enabled the family to rise above primary poverty.
The other three are families where, owing to laziness or drink, the household appears to be sunk in poverty, but where earnings should be sufficient if work was regularly undertaken and the money properly expended.

There are few subsidiary earners in this group. All are labourers. No household in this group has more than 1s. per head over the minimum required for efficiency.

(D) Group D has 16 families in primary poverty, containing 37 adults and 76 children. There are about 6 subsidiary earners in this group, 2 being wives with large young families. In all cases but one the poverty is entirely due to the wage of the man being insufficient to provide efficiently for his family. The one exception is where poverty is due to illness of adult members of the family, and in this case, probably help is received from private charity.

The most striking fact that emerges from this analysis is that, though only 16 out of 70 households in which the head of the family is a labourer are in primary poverty, yet 76 out of 121 of their children are being brought up in this condition, which precludes a sufficient supply of nourishing food or good clothing; and of the other 45 children the great majority have either passed their infancy, or will pass their later childhood should more children be born to their parents, in a condition of primary poverty.

It would appear that only in households where adults outnumber the children can these be brought up under conditions which give scope to full development of their faculties.

Turning to the artisans, we find 25 families whose head has been classified in this group. These 25 householders contain altogether 69 adults and 41 children.

Among the supplementary earners, besides artisans and brickmakers, are several labourers.

The wage-earner in this group very frequently has a second occupation, and among the 25 artisans and brickmakers are 3 publicans, 2 small farmers, and a small shopkeeper. The public-houses and the shop are carried on partly or mainly by the wife. This, of course, raises the income of these households above what it would be were the craft the sole source of earnings.

But among those who have no second occupation we find four families who have not a margin of 1s. per head above primary poverty. Two of these have each 4 children, one 3, and in one adults are kept at home idle. Twelve of the 41 children in the whole group belong to these four families.

There are no artisans in primary poverty, none having more than four children under fourteen. A fifth child would frequently reduce a family in this group, having no additional source of income, to primary poverty. But none of the younger married people have had more than four children, and the majority have only one or two, in this contrasting with market gardeners, and other independent workers, who, when they have any children at all, usually have a long family. There are two large families, however, among the older artisans, some of their children being already grown up and themselves wage-earners.

13

Character and its Relation to Poverty

Relation of Poverty to Character and Ability

FULL REPORTS HAVE been obtained from various sources as to the characters of parents and children in the majority of families in the parish. The households omitted are those of most of the larger farmers and publicans, and most of the gardeners, coachmen, and grooms in private service, except in cases where the man is practically a labourer, and has been born and bred in the parish. Tradesmen and dealers are omitted with the exception of one or two cottage shopkeepers. The inhabitants of the larger houses, professional people, and clerks or agents are omitted, and also about ten respectable poorer households, mostly of men retired from work. Many of the respectable women householders have been omitted, these being both comfortably off and of good character.

But where any of these households have children attending the parish schools, reports of the children have been obtained. Full reports have been obtained of 162 households, and school reports of 7 more. These are printed, together with particulars of the circumstances of the families, on pp. 187-201. The authorities at Corsley and Chapmanslade schools have reported on the children belonging to 66 families, resident in Corsley parish and attending one of these schools. The circumstances of each family were ascertained from other sources, and a comparison made of the results.

Primary and secondary poverty are taken in the senses defined in the chapter on Poverty. In each division all the families have been marked with an asterisk where one or more children show characteristics which might be the result of poverty and insufficient feeding. These marks of *deficiency* are dulness, nervousness, laziness, 'strangeness' or 'peculiarity' of disposition, dirtiness of disposition. Signs of neglect on the part of the parents, resulting in untidiness or dirtiness of the person, for which the child itself is not responsible, are omitted. The inclusion of these would emphasise the facts which are brought out by the former, as an examination of the reports will show.

1. We have, first, seven respectable families, who, owing to the uniqueness of their position in the parish, cannot be reported on separately. These include three farmers, a policeman, a head gardener, and a groom, and a cook in a private house. There are no deficient children in this group.

2. There are children of school age in ten families of artisans, three being in secondary poverty. Only two of these families have children who can be included under our definition of deficiency, the first being a 'neglected, strange' family of naughty children, in secondary poverty, and the second a large family where the eldest child, still of school age, is rather dull. It is noteworthy that during the earlier childhood of this boy the family was probably in primary or secondary poverty, though the united earnings of the family are probably now quite sufficient.

3. There are 16 households other than artisans' above secondary poverty, whose full characters are given in the tables on pp. 193-201. The children of five out of these sixteen have characteristics which might, were their home conditions unknown, be put down to malnutrition. Of these five, one is the family of a respectable and prosperous carter, one is a batch of boarded-out workhouse children, one is the family of a labourer, who was probably in primary poverty till recently, when his elder children became wage-earners, one is an illegitimate child living with its grandparents, and the fifth a farmer's

child who is characterised as 'lazy'.

4. Fifteen families with school children are in secondary poverty, either from the small margin of the income over primary poverty, or from the bad character of the parents.

Six or seven of these fifteen families have deficient children; in regard to one of the seven the teachers remark that the children would be all right but for the bad home, so this should, perhaps, be excepted.

5. There are 18 families with children of school age in primary poverty. No less than 10 of these have deficient children. In only 4 of these 10 cases is any fault found with the parents and homes, as an examination of the tables will show, and of these four, one is a case where poverty appears to have had a lethargic effect on parents as well as children.

These facts show emphatically that the dulness and deficiency of the children, even in a rural district where every advantage of good air and healthy surroundings is obtained, is mainly due to malnutrition; for though a certain proportion of dulness is found in all or most classes, whether well fed or otherwise, the greatly larger percentage among the children of the very poor, even where the parents are in every respect satisfactory, can hardly be due to any other cause.

Circumstances of Family.	No. of Families.	No. where there are Deficient Children.
Well-to-do	30	6
Secondary poverty	18	7 or 8
Primary poverty	18	10

Full particulars have been obtained from various persons likely to be well informed as to the characters of 162 households, including all the poorer and practically all the less respectable families. In about eighteen of these we find that there is one or more member who drinks either more than he or she can afford or sufficient to make him drunk. The following table gives the proportion in each economic group:

Circumstances of Family.			No. of Families.	No. where one or more Members drink too much.
Well-to-do ...	...	...	101	8
Secondary poverty	...	...	33	6
Primary poverty	...	...	28	5

The larger proportion who drink too much, among those in primary poverty, is due to the inclusion under our definition of those who drink more than they can afford; the proportion of drunkards is greater among the people in secondary poverty.

Honesty, Promptness in paying Debts, and Thrift

NEARLY EVERY WORKING man in Corsley belongs to a friendly society; these will be dealt with in a later section.

Some of the cottagers insure their children or themselves. There are two kinds of insurance, death insurance and life insurance; in the latter case payment is made by the Company if the persons insured live to a certain age. No statistics have been obtained as to insurance, but the custom is not general, and the sum insured for, as death insurance, is not usually more than 30s. or 40s., 1d. per week being collected from the person insuring. There are indications that the insurance of children has been lessened since the opening of the Corsley School savings bank. About twenty-three children pay money into this, and in some cases at least this plan has been substituted by the parents for insurance.

Besides the very universal thriftiness and foresight displayed by the working classes in joining friendly societies, to which they make regular and prompt payments for fear of sacrificing the benefits which they hope to derive, a very large amount of honesty and careful management is displayed in the regular and prompt payment of debts to tradesmen. The characteristics of the various households in this respect have been ascertained from people with whom they have dealings, and the results are given in the tables on pages 187-201. A summary of the results, classified according to the circumstances of the families, is as follows:

Circumstances of Family.	No. of Families.	No. where one or more Members are bad at Paying or Thriftless.
Well-to-do	101	6
Secondary poverty ...	33	5 (also 1 where sons have spent parents' savings)
Primary poverty ...	28	6

Of the six families in primary poverty who are 'bad at paying', five have each five or more young children; the sixth is an extravagant aged couple.

[The following tables are printed as reduced facsimiles of those originally published in the 1909 edition. Each table was rotated to occupy a double page (152-84) in that edition.]

REPORTS ON CORSLEY HOUSEHOLDS.

PRIMARY POVERTY.[1]

Households are marked, if having a member who drinks † ; who is unthrifty * ; a deficient child ‡.

No.	Family.	Probable Income in Money or Kind.	Amount above + or below − Primary Poverty.	General Character.	Promptness in Paying Debts and Thrift Generally.	School Report.
5.	Labourer, wife, 3 children (eldest 8).	13s.	− 3s. 10d.	Quite respectable.		Very nice child.
11.	Labourer, wife, son (15), 5 younger children.	25s. (irregular).	− 1s. 2d.	†Rather rough family. Convicted once or twice for drunkenness.	*Shocking one to pay. Has owed one tradesman money for four or five years. Earns plenty of money in summer, and spends it on drink.	Three children fair ; nothing special about them. One boy mischievous.
29.	Labourer, wife, 3 children.	16s.	− 10d.	Very respectable. Wife respectable since marriage. "Quiet, steady young fellow."	Nothing against them.	Nice children. One boy bright.
28.	Labourer, wife, 6 children.	17s. 3d.	− 8s. 1d.	Respectable man.	Nothing against them.	Nice children. Very clean.
12.	Labourer, wife, 4 children.	16s. 6d.	− 3s. 2d.	†Man best of the two. Wife very free with the drink, like her mother.	Pays very well. Nothing against them.	‡Not particularly tidy or bright. Not satisfied with eldest (aged 11). School-attendance poor.
32.	Cowman, wife, 6 children (eldest 8).	17s.	− 8s. 4d.	Never seen out, so does not go to public-house. Gives no trouble.		‡Very tidy. Inclined to be dull.
36.	Cowman, wife, 1 daughter (invalid), 1 son (agricultural wage-earner), 4 children (youngest of family of 10).	23s. 6d.	− 3s. 6d.	Respectable man and family.	Always pay their way. Has always been a lot of sickness in the family.	‡ Extraordinary family. Very untidy. Can't afford to keep the children very well. Parents very ignorant.
37.	Labourer, wife, son (agricultural wage-earner), 4 children.	24s. (estimate).	− 1s. 4d.	"Bad party ; no good to anybody." Poacher by trade, but can't be caught, as he has leave to catch his employer's rabbits, &c.	Not long in parish.	Good character, but rough. Very untidy. Have not much clothes, but mother tries to keep them clean.
42.	Carter, wife, 6 children (eldest 9).	20s. 6d.	− 4s. 10d.	Can't say much for them, but man does not get into trouble. Neither of parents have any energy.	*Shocking at paying debts. Cannot get anything out of them. Can't say much for them.	‡Several very bad children. Worst family in the school. "Haven't a good word for them in any way. They swear, &c. Are neglected at home, untidy, dirty."
65.	Retired stone-breaker, afterwards marketer (has lost one leg), over 80 years old.	4s.	− 8d.	Respectable.	"Has always been a straightforward, hardworking man, so long as I can remember." He has not been on the parish long.	

1 In these tables "labourer" has been substituted for lime-burner and warrener, to prevent identification of these families.

No.	Family.	Probable Income in Money or Kind.	Amount above + or below − Primary Poverty.	General Character.	Promptness in Paying Debts and Thrift Generally.	School Report.
66.	Retired labourer and market gardener, wife, daughter.	Unknown and irregular.	Probably inadequate.	Very respectable old man.		
67.	Retired labourer (aged 80), wife, 3 children.	Say 12s.	− 4s. 10d.	(1) Nothing to say about him. Present wife used to bear a bad character, but appears clean and hard-working. (2) First wife was "a brute of a woman and tried to make him the same. Don't know anything against his present wife —very hard-working."		Children rather clever, but very much neglected. Inclined to be untidy. Mother not at all a nice woman.
68.	Retired labourer.	3s. 6d.	− 1s. 2d.	"Poor old man— respectable old chap."	Nothing against him. Was farm labourer as long as he was able. Belonged to local club, which has come to an end, therefore destitute.	
70.	Retired labourer (aged 87).	Say 4s. 6d.	− 2d.	Very old man. Know nothing about him.	Has always been a very good man to pay. Is over 80, and has only just come on the parish owing to break-up of local club.	
73.	Labourer (retired on account of ill-health), wife.	Unknown.	Probably inadequate.	"Nothing for nor against."	All right. Always paid very well. Not doing much work now.	
212.	Widow, child (grandson, illegitimate child of daughter).	3s. 6d. poor relief and something from daughter.	Probably inadequate.	Respectable.	Not long in the parish.	‡Peculiar boy. Dirty little rascal. Sharp at lessons.
183.	Widow (aged), daughter. Baking, &c.	Unknown.	Probably inadequate.	"Very nice old lady."	Always paid up. Daughter very hard-working.	
44.	Carter, wife, 5 children (eldest 11).	15s.	− 7s. 6d.	(1) Respectable. (2) *Employer:* "Has rather a hard family."	*Got a "little hard family, and bad manager in his wife. A bad one to pay."	‡Eldest boy not very satisfactory. Bad attendance. Only fairly clean and tidy.
45.	Carter, wife, 4 children (eldest 11).	17s. 3d.	− 2s. 5d.	(1) Respectable. (2) *Employer :* Very nice man ; wife dirty and untidy.	Nothing against him.	‡Dull children. Tidy.
49.	Carter, wife, 5 children, son.	15s.	− 11s. 2d.	†Man gives no trouble. Wife inclined to drink ; respectable otherwise. Son out of work ; was bad at getting up in the morning some time back.	*"None of the briskest to pay. Does not earn high wages and has a large family."	‡"Don't think much of parents." Eldest child slow, second dull, fourth *very* sharp.

No.	Family.	Probable Income in Money or Kind.	Amount above + or below − Primary Poverty.	General Character.	Promptness in Paying Debts and Thrift Generally.	School Report.
54.	Odd jobs (labourer), wife, 3 children (eldest 7).	15s. 6d.	− 1s. 4d.	(1) Quite respectable. (2) *Employer* : " Very satisfactory."	Satisfactory to deal with.	
58.	Agricultural engineer, wife, 1 daughter, 5 children.	25s. 6d.	− 3s. 6d.	(1) Man best of two. Wife often in debt. Children all right. (2) Wife not up to much. Nice man, quiet and steady.	*Don't know much about him. *School*: " Spend all they get as they get it ; live very extravagantly."	‡Extraordinary tribe. Children inclined to be tidy, but mother very thriftless, &c. Fairly sharp.
62.	Labourer, wife, 5 children (youngest of family of 9). One son apprenticed to trade.	20s.	− 5s. 4d.	Very respectable. Wife one of most contented women in the parish.	" Never heard anything against him."	Very good attendance. Inclined to be sharp. Clean. Nice little children.
51.	Carter, wife, 4 children (eldest 8).	16s.	− 3s. 8d.	A steady, industrious fellow.	They always pay cash.	‡Two children, rather strange children. Nervous disposition. One has chorea.
63.	Casual labourer, wife, daughter (afflicted), 6 children (youngest of family of 9).	Earnings unknown.	Inadequate.	†" Likes a drop of drink sometimes," but not seen drunk. " Wife poor, helpless creature."	Not long in the parish.	
179.	Widow. Does a little washing—not strong enough to do much.		Certainly deficit.	Respectable old lady.	" Don't know how she gets a living ; she goes out to work. She has a son in London who is very good to her." She will not apply for poor relief. Can earn very little. Son can only help a little. She sometimes has a meal from a neighbour.	
205.	Widow (charwoman), niece (aged 12).	? 6s.	− 1s. 6d.	Very decent woman—hard-working.	Very honest woman.	"Nice little maiden." Clean, fairly intelligent.
111.	Market gardener, wife.	Probably 2s. 6d. + earnings marketing and garden.	Deficient.	†Market people. Seem fairly broken down now.	*First labourer. Has been market gardener, but has given it up now. Both on parish. Had always worked hard. Drank a good deal of their profits. Wife got so drunk she could hardly sit in the cart. Seen one day in public at Frome having glass of port — more than such people could afford.	

No.	Family.	Probable Income in Money or Kind.	Amount above + or below – Primary Poverty.	General Character.	Promptness in Paying Debts and Thrift Generally.	School Report.
116.	Market gardener and carrier, wife, daughter (dressmaking), 2 children.	Say 16s. 10d.	+ o (on − margin of primary poverty).	"I think he and his family are all right."	"Maimed and got no compensation. Just manages to make a living. Could not do much else (*i.e.*, other kind of work). Know nothing against him."	‡Very nice children. Very clean. One very dull.
118.	Market gardener and labourer, wife (takes in washing).			(1) "Don't know how he lives—hard to say. Has pony and trap and does a bit of greengrocery. Drives to market on Saturdays. Wife does some washing. Quarrelsome man ; drinks a lot of beer at home and at Frome Market. Not often seen in public-houses, except to fetch some in jar. Never knew anything against wife." (2) *Employer :* "Fairly satisfactory."		
135.	Labourer (in brick-yard), wife, 4 children.	Say 30s. (earnings unknown).	+ 10s. 4d. (secondary poverty owing to character).	†Can't say much for them. Wife hard-working woman, but bad manager.	*"Not much of it. A poor lot. Drink too much and don't pay. Dirty lot. Inspector has been down on them once or twice—woman keeps house so dirty."	‡Dirty children. Noted family. Have been on point of reporting parents to Officer of Society for Prevention of Cruelty to Children. Yet children wouldn't be so bad with careful training. Attendance bad ; they take turns to come.
109.	Market - gardener, wife, 4 children.		Probably sufficient.	Very respectable.		Cantankerous parents. Chapel people. *Very* sharp children. Very clean and tidy.
191.	Widow (char-woman), nephew (out of work), niece (12).	6s. and probably income from some undis-covered source.	Probably not below poverty line.	Very respectable woman and nephew.	Very nice woman ; very hard-working and industrious.	Nice child ; good-tempered, very clean, &c.
200.	Widow. Kept by children.		Probably sufficient.		"Never heard anything against her. She pays all right."	

No.	Family.	Probable Income in Money or Kind.	Amount above + or below − Primary Poverty.	General Character.	Promptness in Paying Debts and Thrift Generally.	School Report.
203.	Two spinsters.		Probably sufficient.		In reduced circumstances.	
204.	Widow (charing and washing), lodger (male), 2 children. Poor relief.	Say 19s.	+ 5s.	†(1) Drinks. Accused of being a prostitute. (2) House bare, dirty, and neglected. Appear to feed well.	• " Better not put her down at the top of the tree."	‡Clean and tidy as far as she can keep them. Very poor. Lazy, difficult to manage, sulky. One of poorest houses.
209.	Spinster. Takes in a little washing and has poor relief.	Say 4s. 8d.	Say ± o.		Appears to pay up all right.	
195.	Widow (baker and farmer), son (labourer, &c.), daughter.		Have struggle to keep going.	Respectable. Son rather rough (bad language). As much as they can do to make both ends meet.	Very good, straightforward, hard-working people, "so far as I know."	
127.	Retired schoolmaster.	Poor relief and help from neighbours.	Probably sufficient.	Respectable.		
148.	Shopkeeper and wife.	Owns cottages and small shop.	Probably sufficient.	Very respectable man and wife.	Belonged to a building society, so got his cottages.	
69.	Retired labourer, daughter (washerwoman).		Probably just sufficient.	Very respectable, all of them.	" They keep themselves —are not beholden to any one."	
71.	Retired agricultural worker, wife, son (agricultural earner).	Say 12s.	± o.	Respectable man and wife; latter a gossip. Son would be all right if he left the drink alone.	" Has always been a straightforward sort of man. I know nothing good about the son. He could do any sort of skilled work, such as grafting trees, if he liked, but does not work more than about two days a week."	
208.	Widow, 2 sons (agricultural wage-earners), 3 children.	21s. 6d.	+ 1s. 8d.	†Don't know much about her; used not to bear good character. " Eldest son lazy, drunken, little beggar." Those young men generally in any mischief going.		‡Clean and lazy children. Bigger boy slow and plodding. Mother clean and hard-working; very poor. Husband was very lazy; she always had to keep the children.

No.	Family.	Probable Income in Money or Kind.	Amount above + or below − Primary Poverty.	General Character.	Promptness in Paying Debts and Thrift Generally.	School Report.
176.	Widow (laundress), daughter.		Probably sufficient.	Quite respectable.	" Ought to have been pensioned years ago— is 85 years of age. Husband spent a good deal. She had nearly to keep the house going when he was alive."	
185.	Widow, son (artisan learning trade).	10s.	+ 1s. 8d.	(1) " Not a woman of best character at one time. Know nothing about her now." (2) " Has had 1 or 2 illegitimate children."		‡Child (now left school) was lazy and slow ; not very intelligent. Clean and tidy.
187.	Widow (laundress), daughter, grandson.		Probably sufficient.	Very h a r d-w o r k i n g woman.	Always made her living by washing. " I never knew anything against her. Always found her all right to deal with."	Nice boy ; rather smart. Clean and tidy.
6.	Labourer, w i f e, boy (16), 2 younger children.	20s. 6d.	+ 2s. 4d.	Very respectable people. Wife very hard-working woman. He occasionally goes to the public-house.		Very nice children. Learn very quickly. Are clever with t h e i r h a n d s. " Want to be kept in their places."
7.	Labourer, wife, 1 child at home and pay 1s. per week for a child away.	14s.	+ 1s. 10d.	Very steady man. Have had much trouble with delicate children.	Pays all right.	
10.	Labourer, wife, 2 young children.	17s. 9d.	+ 3s. 9d.	Respectable man.	Satisfactory.	
13.	Labourer, wife, 2 young children.	16s.	+ 2s.	†Hard - working people, Man " not one of the best of them, rather free with the drink and foul-tounged s o m e - times." Wife respectable.		Eldest child (aged 4) attends school 1 mile distant in summer.
21.	Labourer, wife, 2 young children.	17s.	+ 3s.	" Don't think you could say very much for them."	"Nothing against them."	Eldest (5). V e r y nice and tidy.
25.	Labourer and wife.	Could earn 12s.	+ 3s. 8d. (secondary poverty owing to character).	" No good. Was compositor and t a i l o r. Would not work at either. Has deserted his wife time after time. Used to go on the tramp. Has stopped at work now nearly six years."	*" Too lazy to do anything. Spends all he earns. Does not pay up."	
30.	Labourer, wife, 2 young children.	16s.	+ 2s.	(1) " Very decent young fellow—not often at the public-house." (2) " Steady man."		Very nice children.

No.	Family.	Probable Income in Money or Kind.	Amount above + or below − Primary Poverty.	General Character.	Promptness in Paying Debts and Thrift Generally.	School Report.
33.	Labourer, wife, niece (mentally deficient).	19s.	+ 7s.	†(1) "He is a man who works all the time, but you always see him in the public-house. Gives no trouble. Quiet man, and never saw him the worse for drink. (2) "Don't know much as he might have been better."	Wife hard-working woman.	
53.	Labourer, wife, child.	13s.	+ 1s. 10d.	Very decent man now. Some years ago was one of worst drunkards in village, now a teetotaler. "In my opinion an under-minded man—won't stick to his opinions."	Straightforward man.	‡Nervous child, not very sharp; fragile. Nice and clean.
64.	Underkeeper, wife, son (agricultural wage-earner), 4 children (youngest of family of 10).	25s. 6d.	+ 2s. 2d.	Nothing known of him in parish.		‡Two elder boys very sharp, one a strange boy. Third child dull. Youngest "can't make anything of." Clean and tidy.
100.	Retired farmer, &c., wife.			"All right; used to be tidy old nut (swore) in his time. Got over it now."	Had a little money together. Sons have spent it.	
78.	Farmer, wife.		? Sufficient.		Doesn't allow himself enough to eat, and takes very small amount of coal. Always letting dealers get the upper hand of him. He had a few hundred pounds to start with, but probably has nothing left but his stock.	

ABOVE LINE OF SECONDARY POVERTY.

No.	Family.	Probable Income in Money or Kind.	Amount above + or below − Primary Poverty.	General Character.	Promptness in Paying Debts and Thrift Generally.	School Report.
48.	Carter, wife, 2 children, 3 sons wage-earners (labourers or artisans).	58s.	+ 33s.	Respectable. Sons good at athletic games.	Very good, straightforward people. Pay their way. "I don't know a man who works harder in Corsley—he is working day and night; always willing, never tired."	‡Extraordinary children. One girl with all the ideas of a lady. The other very dull. Fairly clean; not very tidy.

No	Family.	Probable Income in Money or Kind.	Amount above + or below − Primary Poverty.	General Character.	Promptness in Paying Debts and Thrift Generally.	School Report.
52.	Carter, wife, 1 young child.	16s.	+ 4s. 10d.	Fairly respectable. Wife rather loose character at one time.	Appears to pay all right. "Know nothing against him."	
72.	Labourer (retired), married daughter with children, son (market-gardener).	Pension 6s. and earnings of others.	Probably quite sufficient.	Man respectable. Daughter "has not been any too respectable."	Son satisfactory to deal with.	
206.	Widow (midwife), 1 child, 2 sons (agricultural wage-earners).	37s. (Poor relief for child).	+ 12s. 2d.	Passable. Lads fairly respectable, but room for improvement.	"Always paid up very well, so far as I know."	"Very nice, most sensible boy." Plenty of common sense.
181.	Widow, 2 sons (mainly agricultural wage-earners), widowed daughter, 1 child.	32s.	+ 13s. 6d.	†Husband killed in drunken brawl. Children have not been very respectable.		
199.	Widow (aged), granddaughter (14).	Private means.	Probably ample.			
174.	Widow, 2 sons (artisan and agricultural wage-earner).	Say 22s.	+ 7s. 10d.	Owns her own house. She bought it.	Nice sort of woman and son.	
2.	Labourer, wife, 2 daughters, 4 sons (agricultural wage-earners), 1 child.	72s. 6d.	+ 39s. 4d.	"Agricultural people. Can't say anything against them, nor very much for them. Rather rough family."	Nothing to say against them. Have always been straightforward and pay very well.	
3.	Labourer, wife, 1 child, wife's brother.	30s. (half irregular).	+ 15s. 2d.			
15.	Labourer, wife, 2 sons (agricultural wage-earners), 5 children.	41s. (irregular).	+ 11s. 2d.	Very hard-working man. Man and family "respectable so far as I know." Have had a "long family."	Pays very well "for aught I know of."	Four children. A year or two since very untidy. Now most clean and tidy, also reformation as to attendance.
20.	Labourer, wife, 3 children (boarded-out orphans).	17s. 6d.	+ 6s. 4d.	Hardly ever goes to a public-house. Seldom seen about.	Hard-working man.	*Very nervous children (from Warminster Union). "Want some one with strong will to look after them."
22.	Labourer, wife (invalid), daughter, son (agricultural wage-earner), 1 grandchild.	30s.	+ 11s. 6d.	Respectable man.	Nothing against him.	*Tidy, rather dull.

No.	Family.	Probable Income in Money or Kind.	Amount above + or below − Primary Poverty.	General Character.	Promptness in Paying Debts and Thrift Generally.	School Report.
24.	Labourer, wife, and son (market-gardening), 1 grandchild.	15s. + market garden earnings.	+ earnings of garden, &c.	†Respectable man, except when he goes on the drink for a week or fortnight. Son respectable young fellow. Wife hard-working woman.	Very good to pay. Wife earns a lot of money, and has saved money.	
31.	Labourer (crippled), son (18), daughter, 2 children.	22s.	+ 6s. 4d.	Fair.	Know nothing against him.	Very nice. Very clean. Not very sharp.
35.	Cowman, wife, aged mother, lodger, 1 child.	25s. 3d.	+ 6s. 7d.	Respectable.	They pay up all right.	Very nice little child.
40.	Dairyman, wife, 1 young child.	23s.	+ 11s. 10d.	Very steady man.		
60.	Woodman, wife, child.	25s.	+ 13s. 10d.	(1) Satisfactory. (2) Husband and wife said to quarrel.		Cleverest boy in school.
34.	Cowman, wife, 1 young child.	17s.	+ 5s. 10d.	Respectable.	Very industrious young man.	
46.	Carter, wife, aged mother-in-law, son (blacksmith), 2 children.	36s.	+ 14s. 8d.	All right.	Always pay their way very well. Thrifty parents. Saved up money to provide children with costumes for school concert.	Very nice. Very clean and tidy.
96.	Farmer, wife.		Ample.			
81.	Farmer and other occupations, wife, son (helping father), daughter (gloving).	15s. 6d. and profits of small farm.	Probably ample.	†" Very respectable man and wife, but she is not particular about running into debt. He visits public-house pretty well. Has plenty, but have never seen him the worse. Very quiet man and son."		
92.	Farmer and coal-haulier, wife, 2 sons, daughter.			All right, sons and father.	Very fair man ; hard-working.	‡When at school was nice boy, but lazy.
77.	Farmer, wife.			Respectable man.	" Don't know much about him. He never would push on and go away from home."	
84.	Farmer, wife.			He is all right.	Was farmer's son. Earned a bit of money, and so got on. Has always paid his way so far as I know.	

No.	Family.	Probable Income in Money or Kind.	Amount above + or below – Primary Poverty.	General Character.	Promptness in Paying Debts and Thrift Generally.	School Report.
90.	Farmer, wife, aged mother.			Very respectable. Used to attend public-house years ago, but now not more than once or twice a week, perhaps. Used to be bad drinker years gone by. Reformed.		
95.	Farmer, carrier, &c., wife, son (agricultural wage-earner), 1 child.			Hard-working man.	Pays all right. Has saved a bit of money. Was only a working man. Very industrious.	Very nice child.
114.	Market gardener, wife, 3 sons (agricultural wage-earners or mechanics), grand-daughter (a child).	64s.	Very ample.	Respectable.	Has always been a very good man at paying.	Always very clean and tidy.
83.	Farmer, wife, son.		Ample.	Very respectable family.	Pension. Quite straight.	
113.	Market gardener, wife, 4 children.			Very respectable people.	Hard-working. Always at work.	
112.	Farmer and poulterer, two daughters.			(1) Respectable. (2) Daughters are very kind when people are ill in neighbourhood.	Dealings very satisfactory and straight.	
88.	Farmer, wife.			No trouble with him. Always been a respectable man.	Used to work at brick-making, and saved money.	
117.	Market gardener, wife (midwife), two sons (artisans out of work), daughter (gloving).	19s. 6d.	Ample.	(1) Man that visits public-house very little. Very respectable family. Three sons have been in army. (2) "Satisfactory family."		When at school very nice and clean.
91.	Farmer, wife, 2 daughters (teaching and dressmaking).			Respectable man.		
80.	Small farmer, wife.				Always very industrious man ; tree-feller. Had money left him by his mother. Saved up a bit of money and went into farm. Kept both jobs up for some time. Old employer wanted to keep him.	

No.	Family.	Probable Income in Money or Kind.	Amount above + or below − Primary Poverty.	General Character.	Promptness in Paying Debts and Thrift Generally.	School Report.
99.	Farmer.			Respectable young fellow.		
97.	Farmer, wife, son, and daughter.			Very respectable people.	Hard-working.	Girl of 16 still at school. Sharp at music, not sharp at lessons.
110.	Retired labourer, wife, 2 sons (agricultural wage-earners).	29s. +indefinite amount.	Ample.	(1) All very respectable, steady, quiet young fellows. (2) *Employer :* "Very respectable family."	Must have saved money when young. Has not done anything for nearly 20 years. Quite straight with money.	
108.	Brickmaker, wife, 2 daughters, 2 sons (helping father), 2 children.		Ample.	Respectable people.	They pay very well.	
150.	Farmer and brickmaker (wage-earning), wife, daughter (servant), son (labourer), 1 child.	Say 58s.	+ 37s. 6d.	Hard-working people. Boys respectable.	Has saved up. He goes out to work, and wife has worked nearly all her life.	Very clean and tidy. Smart-looking. Average at work.
105.	Shoemaker, daughter, 2 sons (artisan and agricultural wage-earner).	Say 30s. (Difficult to ascertain earnings.)	+ 14s. 4d.	Respectable man and family.	Pay up very well.	
106.	Labourer, nephew (artisan).	30s. (probably)	+ 21s. 8d.	†Addicted to drink, but doesn't get drunk. Not very energetic man.	‡Can't say much for him. Wife helped with business when she was alive. He drinks more than he can afford, but does not get drunk. Has not paid rent for about 12 months. Formerly had little farm as well as business. Now labourer.	
134.	Worker in factory (Frome), wife.	19s.	+ 10s. 8d.	Very respectable man.		
133.	Labourer in iron-works, wife.	15s.	+ 6s. 8d.	"Husband and wife quarrel. Has been summoned several times for filthy language. She governs him a bit now."	Recently married. Hard-working, steady man. Honest, I should say.	
132.	Gardener, wife, 2 sons (agricultural wage-earners).	37s.	+ 21s. 4d.	(1) Very respectable. Boys remarkably steady, quiet lads. (2) *Employer :* "Very respectable."	(1) Always very good people ; steady and industrious. (2) A very honest woman.	

No.	Family.	Probable Income in Money or Kind.	Amount above + or below − Primary Poverty.	General Character.	Promptness in Paying Debts and Thrift Generally.	School Report.
189.	Widow.	Private means.	Probably ample.	" Should think she is a very respectable woman. Should think she has a little income."	Some arrangement by which she lives rent free. " I think her two children are good to her."	
182.	Widow.		Probably ample.	Very straight woman.	All right.	
177.	Spinster (takes in sewing and keeps small shop), lodger (female).		Probably sufficient.	Very respectable.	Owns house where she lives. Pays up all right.	
188.	Deserted wife (laundress).		Probably ample.	Fairly respectable, but " gift of the tongue."	Always very good at paying.	
193.	Widow (aged; kept by children).		Sufficient.	Very respectable woman.		
210.	Spinster (washer-woman).	Say 6s.	+ 1s. 4d.	Very respectable.		
180.	Widow (midwife), son (artisan), daughter.	Say 23s.	+ 11s.	Nothing against woman. Son up to all the mischief he can get into. A sly one—ringleader. Don't know that there is any harm in him.	Deserted by husband. Son satisfactory.	Children before they left school very, very clean. Rather nice children. Not *very* much intelligence.
142.	Retired railway-man, wife.	Savings.	Sufficient.	Very respectable.	Has saved enough money to keep him the rest of his days.	
136.	Retired tradesman (London), wife, daughter.		Probably ample.	Quite respectable.	‡Often had bailiffs in house when he was in business in London. " He does not trouble."	
143.	Retired weaver in factory, wife.	Savings and garden.	Sufficient.	Very respectable; rumoured that years ago he used to be a poacher.	Know nothing against him. A man who has always kept himself, though he has done no work for some time.	
41.	Carter, wife, 1 daughter.	20s. 6d.	+ 8s. 6d.	(1) Very decent man. Wife a bad woman; would do any one harm if she got the chance. (2) Very nice, hardworking man; wife not so good as he is (tongue).		
38.	Cowman, daughter (laundress), son-in-law (labourer).	35s. or more.	+ 21s.	(1) All very respectable. (2) *Employer:* "A very good servant."	Steady old man.	
190.	Widow (grows fruit), son (agricultural wage-earner).	Unknown.	Probably quite sufficient.	†Always full of complaints; " comic old customer as a neighbour." Son inclined to drink, but gives no trouble.	(1) "Very honest woman. Always pays up for what she has." (2) Son not up to much. Likes to go rabbiting or do odd jobs; will not stick to a constant job.	

No.	Family.	Probable Income in Money or Kind.	Amount above + or below − Primary Poverty.	General Character.	Promptness in Paying Debts and Thrift Generally.	School Report.
194.	Widow, 2 daughters (one "afflicted," mother and other do needlework and charing), son (agricultural wage-earner).	24s. 6d.	+ 8s. 10d.	Respectable.	Has maintained herself since death of husband. Has poor relief for daughter.	
211.	Widow (infirm), son (agricultural wage-earner or malting).	Poor relief 2s. 6d. + help from son.	Probably ample.	"Son a little rowdy."		
196.	Widow, daughter (laundress), son (market gardener, marketer and odd jobs).		Probably quite sufficient.	Very respectable.	Very old. Has been doing washing till quite recently. Son was tailor by trade, but didn't much care for it. Now does odd jobs.	
207.	Widow (midwife), 2 sons (market gardener and agricultural wage-earner), daughter.		Ample.	Very respectable woman. Very quiet young men.		
1.	Labourer, wife (midwife).	19s.	+ 10s. 8d.	Quite respectable. Man constitutionally delicate. Wife supposed to drink formerly.	*Both hard-working, but though both earning money, and no family, very difficult to get money from if allowed credit.	
8.	Labourer, wife, 3 sons (2 agricultural wage-earners, 1 artisan).	63s. 6d.	+ 44s. 2d.	"Fairly respectable. Don't get drunk, but like their drink." One son sent to reformatory as a boy for stealing flowers.	Always paid very well.	
9.	Labourer (old soldier), wife, son (agricultural wage-earner), daughter (gloving).	36s.	+ 20s. 4d.	Very respectable people.	Very straightforward.	
14.	Labourer, wife.	14s. 6d.	+ 6s. 2d.	Not long in parish.		
16.	Labourer, wife, daughter (dressmaker).	25s.	+ 13s.	(1) Very respectable people. Informant had once seen him with "a little beer" and then very quarrelsome. A man scarcely ever seen at public-house. (2) "Hard-working, steady man."		

No.	Family.	Probable Income in Money or Kind.	Amount above + or below − Primary Poverty.	General Character.	Promptness in Paying Debts and Thrift Generally.	School Report.
18.	Labourer, wife.	15s.	+ 6s. 8d.	(1) "Goes on better than formerly." Used to be very fond of drink. His family rather rough. (2) Doesn't care for constant employment. Works in woods on piecework jobs.		
19.	Labourer, wife, son (agricultural wage-earner).	40s.	+ 28s.	†Fairly respectable. Son a "drunken sot," not his own fault—father always in the habit of going to public-house, but does not get drunk.	*" None too extra well to pay." All wage-earners; man and wife get a lot of money, but they "tipple" and live above their income and only just "keep the wheels going." He always stands out for foreman's work with high pay, but is no better off on Saturday night than other people.	
23.	Labourer, son (miner, iron-works).	30s.	+ 21s. 8d.	Respectable father and son.	Very good to pay up.	
26.	Labourer, daughter, 3 sons (agricultural wage-earners).	37s. 6d.	+ 18s. 2d.	†Man better than his wife (now dead). She was very fond of drink. Can't say much for the children — nearly all inclined to drink.	Nothing against him. Belonged to local club which recently came to an end.	
27.	Labourer, wife.	16s. 6d.	+ 8s. 2d.	All right. Very steady man.	Nothing against him. Belonged to Shepherds' Friendly Society.	
4.	Labourer, wife, daughter.	18s.	+ 6s.	(1) All right. Has stayed at same place long time. (2) *Employer*: "Very satisfactory."	Always a good man to pay.	
61.	Woodman, daughter, son (coal merchant).	13s. + son's earnings.	Ample.	Respectable. Has been offered pension but will not give up work.	All right with money. Very steady man. Has probably saved.	
59.	Tree-feller.	13s. to 15s.	+ 9s. 4d.	Respectable.	All right.	
57.	Shepherd, wife.	15s.	+ 6s. 8d.	Respectable. Not long in parish.		
56.	Agricultural worker, wife, daughter (dressmaker), lad (assistant to householder).	Say 30s. to 40s.	+ 20s. 4d.	Very respectable man.	All right.	
55.	Labourer, wife.	14s. 6d.	+ 6s. 2d.	†Respectable man. Wife rather fond of drink.	Used not to pay up formerly. Do not know at present.	

No.	Family.	Probable Income in Money or Kind.	Amount above + or below – Primary Poverty.	General Character.	Promptness in Paying Debts and Thrift Generally.	School Report.
50.	Carter, wife.	17s.	+ 8s. 8d.	Respectable man.	Nothing against him. Have always paid their way very well.	
47.	Labourer, wife, 2 sons (agricultural wage-earners).	43s.	+ 27s. 4d.	Respectable.	Nothing against him. Wife was a bad one to pay in years gone by. [probably while 7 children were not above school age].	
43.	Carter, wife.	15s.	+ 6s. 8d.	Very respectable man.	Very steady man. Belongs to benefit society of a village where they formerly resided.	
17.	Piecework labourer, wife, daughter, grandchild (illegitimate).	Savings and odd jobs.	Probably sufficient.	Respectable, hard-working people. Have allotment and keep pigs. Wife does "marketing."	Very good man to pay. Only goes out to work occasionally; has saved a bit of money. Wife goes marketing—carries basket.	Mischievous. Clean and tidy.
115.	Market gardener and carrier, wife.		Sufficient.	Respectable. Newly married.	¦Is not much of a one to pay, before he was married, at any rate. Don't know how he and his mother managed to live. They were supposed to do market gardening, but didn't do much.	

Artisans

THE ARTISANS, 22 in number, are so uniformly reported as respectable and prompt in payment that they have been omitted from the foregoing tables and only the few exceptions need be noted.

No. 159. A very respectable man, but has a bad wife, who drinks, squanders all money, including any capital which comes into her hands, and spends her time writing begging letters. The home is in a squalid condition.

No. 156. Very decent people—too grand to visit public-house much, but extravagant and frequently in debt.

No. 168. With a large family, is reported as fairly respectable, but "none too bright to pay."

No. 166. Thoroughly respectable in every way, is having a struggle owing to much serious illness in the household.

All except possibly No. 159 are above primary poverty and have good homes, but when there are children the margin is frequently small.

School reports on all who have children of school age are given below.

SCHOOL REPORTS ON ARTISANS' CHILDREN.

No.	Family.	Circumstances.	School Report.
154	Man, wife, 4 children	Secondary poverty	Very nice children. Very clean and tidy. Fairly sharp. Seem to have very good home from appearance in school.
155	Man, wife, 4 (or more) children.		" Exceedingly nice children, nice manners. Brain power all right, but not clever with hands."

No.	Family.	Circumstances.	School Report.
163	Man, wife, 2 children, son (agricultural wage-earner).		Very clean and tidy. Not very bright.
162	Man, wife, daughter, 2 children.	Secondary poverty	Good family
158	Man, wife, 4 children, maid-servant.		All right.
157	Man, wife, 1 child.		Nice little child and quick at learning.
171	Man, wife, 4 children	Secondary poverty.	Neglected. Strange family. One girl most innocent-looking child, very naughty. Bad little boy, not truthful.
170	Man, wife, 4 children		Very nice children. Two of boys very clever. Always very clean and tidy.

| 168 | Man, wife, 4 children, 3 sons (agricultural wage-earners, 2 out of work). | Clean and tidy, but eldest rather dull. Little ones fairly sharp. |
| 166 | Man, wife, 2 children | One a nice child. These two boys would be better if parents at home more. Rather neglected. One rather wilful. |

SCHOOL REPORTS ON CHILDREN OF FARMERS, GARDENER, GROOM, COOK, AND POLICEMAN.

No.				School Report.
128	...	...	...	Very nice children indeed. Some of best in school and very clean and tidy.
No. 121	...	...	...	Very good family.
76	...	...	...	Children all right. Fair—tidy. Not specially bright.
93	...	...	...	Boy—very regular. Very good family, sharp, plenty of common-sense.
75	...	...	...	Very clean and tidy. Spoilt children.
216	...	...	...	Sharp—common-sense. Spoilt. Very nice boy in school.
214	...	...	...	Sharp—very clever little girl. Sweet little child. Has good home.

State of Education

BEFORE LEAVING THE subject of character it may be remarked that a large proportion of the adults in the parish are unable to write and some are unable to read. This fact was discovered partly from statements of the people themselves, and also from secretaries to friendly societies, who assert that men of forty years of age and upwards are often unable to sign their names.

Pauperism in Corsley

THE PAUPERS HAVE already been included in the preceding lists, but it will be convenient to give a table of these separately .

In addition to the fifteen families or persons in receipt of relief during the year 1904-5 who were still residing in the parish in the winter of 1905-6, relief was granted in 1904-5 to five aged persons, since dead, and to the family of one man in prison.

Two of the cases of widows with family afford striking examples of the futility, if not the actual harmfulness, of granting in such cases small and inadequate doles, unconditionally, and in these instances apparently without inquiry as to the character of mother or home.[1]

No. 206 was receiving relief on the understanding that she had two children at home, though as a matter of fact the elder had been out in service for a year or two. She was herself earning good money as a midwife, her receipts being, however, irregular. Her two sons were earning probably 30s. a week between them, and her boy, still at school, was able to contribute to the family purse by running errands or doing garden work after school hours. The income of the family was therefore considerably in excess of that of the average labourer. Since that date her boy has left school, and relief has been stopped. She has quarrelled with her elder sons, and is now solely dependent on the earnings of her boy of fourteen and her own, which are less than formerly. Her health has improved with this reduction of her income to 7s. or 8s. per week.

1   For the unsatisfactory condition of homes and families of widows in receipt of outdoor relief found in all parts of England as a result of this system see Minority Report of Poor Law Commission 1909 Cd. 4499, p. 753

Index No.	Sex.	Status re marriage.	Age.	Actual Earnings.	Normal Earnings when in Work.	Present or last Occupation.	Health.	Clubs.	Savings.	Character.	Family.	House.	Rent.	Garden.	General Condition: Cleanliness.	Cause of Application for Relief.	Amount of Relief during year 1904-5.	Total Income.
																	£ s. d.	
211.	F.	Widow.	58.	None.		At one time had small farm.	Cripple.			Nothing against her.	1 son at home, malting in winter. 1 son, miner; Wales. 2 daughters in service.	3 rooms.		Garden.	Clean.	Crippled widow.	6 10 0	
210.	F.	Spinster.	67.	None.	7s. per week.	Laundress.	"Afflicted."		Some.	Very respectable.	Living alone.	3 rooms and pantry.		Garden.	Very clean.	"Ill and blind."	2 0 0	
209.	F.	Spinster.	63.	? 6d. per week.		Occasionally does a little washing.	"Afflicted."		?None.	Honest.	Living alone.	5 rooms.		Garden.	Clean.	Not strong.	6 10 0	
194.	F.	Spinster.	26.	? A few pence knitting.			Cripple.			"Passable."	Mother (widow) and sister; needlework, charing and laundry. Brother, labourer.	4 rooms.		Garden.	Clean.	Badly deformed and deaf.	6 10 0	
206.	P.	Widow.	50.	Say 5s.		Midwife.	Moderate.		None.	"Passable."	2 sons in regular work. 1 boy, aged 11.	8 rooms.		Garden.	Untidy.	"Widow and family."	3 18 0	Family income over 30s.
67.	M.	Married.	85.	None.		Labourer (retired).	All right.			Formerly not good.	Wife, charing and laundry work—6s. 3 children; boy of 15 in Warminster.	2 rooms.		Garden.		"Aged."	15 12 0	
65.	M.	Widower.	77.	None.		Stonebreaker, then marketer with donkey-cart.	Poor.			Always very hard-working. Respectable.	Living alone. Stepson scrubs money fortnightly and pays niece 6d. per week to look after him.	2 rooms.		Garden.	Very clean.	"Amputated leg."	7 16 0	Say 4s. 6d.
212.	F.	Widow.	66.	None.			All right.			Respectable.	Illegitimate grandson. Daughter away, did not keep up payments, so P.R. to be reduced.	2 rooms.		Garden.		Widow.	11 14 0	
68.	M.	Widower.	72.	Probably none.	? 12s.	Labourer (retired).	All right but feeble.	Belonged to Corsley Club now broken up.		Respectable.	None.	3 rooms.		Garden.		"Aged."	7 16 6	
11.	M.	Married.	72.	Something from garden and marketing.	?	Market gardener.	Rheumatic.			Hardworking, but drank more than could afford.	Wife. 3 sons in Wales who send money.	3 rooms.		Garden.	Clean.	"Aged."	4 10 0	Say 8s. per week.
208.	F.	Widow.	50.	Probably none.			All right.			Clean and hard-working.	1 daughter, married. 2 sons, labourers, at home. 3 children at home.	4 rooms.		Garden.	Clean.	"Widow and family."	1 9 6	
204.	F.	Widow.	43.	Unknown.		Charing. Takes M. lodger and said to earn money by prostitution.	All right.			Very bad character, said to be prostitute and drinks.	2 sons away. 1 daughter, married. 1 daughter in service. 3 children. M. lodger.	3 rooms and pantry.		Garden.	Dirty and untidy; home neglected.	"Widow and family."	1 2 6	Probably nearly 20s.
70.	M.	Widower.	85.	None.		Labourer (retired).	All right but feeble.	Belonged to Corsley Club now broken up.		Honest. Has only just come on the parish; over 80 years old.	Living alone. 2 sons and 3 daughters who help him.	? 2 rooms.	£2 15s.	Garden.	Clean.	"Aged."	1 11 6	3s. 6d. per week.
127.	M.	Single.	74.	None.		Schoolmaster (retired), now helps tradesman with account-keeping and receives food, &c., in return.	All right; only one leg.			Respectable.	Living alone.	? 3 rooms.		Garden.		"Aged."	1 4 6	
149.	F.	Spinster.	17.	?		Servant to tradesman's wife.	Ill.				Residing with employers.					"Illness of self."	7 6	

Table of Paupers

No. 204 works at charing during the day, neglecting her home and children. She is said to bear a very bad character, and to earn money by prostitution. The children struck the school teachers as coming from an exceedingly poor home, but were clean and tidy as far, they said, 'as the mother can keep them'. The small dole given in this case is quite insufficient to enable the woman to stay at home and look after her children, or to encourage her to take to a more respectable mode of living.

These cases may be compared with those of two old men dependent on poor relief through no fault of their own.

No. 68, in receipt of relief, has no relations who can help him. His next-door neighbour does his washing and odd jobs which he cannot do for himself, and in return he helps to work her garden, lights her fire when she is out, and has promised to leave her his 'few traps' when he dies. This old man, with no other source of income, who worked hard all his life, and is deprived of the results of his thrift in belonging to a club by the break-up of the latter, receives only the inadequate sum of 3s. per week.

No. 70, a very old man in receipt of poor relief, has worked hard as a labourer all his life. He gets about 3s. 6d. per week from the parish, part being contributed by a daughter. His children may, perhaps, give him a little further help.

Probably the majority of aged paupers receive some little additional help from relatives, and their case is at least not harder than that of some others who receive no parish relief.

Provision for the Aged. Non-paupers

THERE ARE MANY more poor old people in Corsley who refuse to apply for parochial relief. There is a very independent spirit among the majority of the inhabitants, and sons and daughters often pinch themselves in order to prevent their old parents from 'coming upon the parish'.

One old man, No. 66, started life as a farm labourer, but after twenty-eight years was crippled with rheumatism. Since then, with the help of his wife and children, he supported himself as a 'market gardener'. Now that the old couple are past work, their children keep them, though most of them are married, with families, and have a struggle themselves to make both ends meet. It is the children rather than the parents who are averse to application for poor relief in this case.

Another old labourer, No. 22, now in poor health, has an invalid wife, a daughter, and a son living with him. He receives much kindness from the farmer who employed him, and is sent money by a daughter living away from home. One of his sons would also send him money if necessary.

An old woman at Chapmanslade, No. 193, widow of a small farmer, is supported by her children, mainly by a married daughter.

Provision has been made for No. 167, the widow of a carpenter who earned £1 per week, as follows:

Two sons each pay 2s. per week; married daughter makes a home for her mother, taking 3s. 6d. of the money for her keep, while the other 6d. goes towards clothing and collection in church on Sundays. In the summer the old lady helps her daughter with the housework, while the latter is busy in her garden, and in return the daughter gives her a share of the profits, amounting to 12s. or 13s., as pocket-money. The family live and feed very well (see Budget 131 on p.233).

Another old widow, No. 179, is too feeble to work, and her sons, having families and inadequate incomes, can help her very little. She refuses to apply to the parish, though accepting a little private charity, and consequently is more than half starved and always in bad health.

Similar cases occur from time to time, considerable privation being undergone in preference to application for outdoor relief; and, in case of illness, those who have once been in a better position will firmly refuse to enter the workhouse, though lacking the most necessary attendance.[1]

Though the amount of poverty in Corsley is not great, the proportion of pauperism is still further reduced by the existence of this spirit among a section of the people.

1   Since the above was written most of these old people have been granted an old-age pension.

14
Corsley Family Budgets

THERE IS IN Corsley no lack of competition for the custom of the labouring classes. The housewife may purchase her groceries either from one of the village shops or from the stores and shops in Frome and Warminster. Various butchers and bakers drive round the parish with their carts, delivering goods to their regular customers. Milk she can obtain from most of the numerous small farms. Beer and ale are supplied by at least eight brewers from Frome and Warminster, whose carmen deliver the casks at the houses. Coal and wood appear to be mainly supplied by one local coal-haulier and timber merchant, and a competitor setting up a few years ago failed to get any custom.

Most of the cottages do the main part of their weekly shopping on Saturday at Frome or Warminster, according to whether they live on the eastern or western side of the parish. During the week they supplement their Saturday's purchases from the nearest village shop, where credit is usually granted them if desired.

It is not, however, necessary for any one to go out to shop. One old man in January, 1906, got most of the necessaries of life from the baker, who brought him bread, butter, and sugar regularly, and sometimes tea. Coal was brought round to him once a fortnight, and so he got all his provisions without leaving the house.

Milk is easily obtainable in all parts of the parish. Nearly all the farmers will sell it to the poor in small quantities. Some send it round to the cottages, but it usually has to be fetched, this being no hardship where the dairy farm-houses are near together and widely distributed over the parish. The usual price of new milk is 3d. per quart, or 1½ d. per pint all the year round. In certain cases, in summer, or by special favour, it is sold cheaper, at 1d. per pint. In the winter it is sometimes scarce locally, and the cottagers may then have difficulty in obtaining it, or may have to send farther for it, and perhaps get short quantity for their money. This is, however, the exception.

The greater number of households, irrespective of the number of persons, take 1d. worth of new milk per day. A few of the more well-to-do families take more than 1d. worth, or taking 1d. worth regularly, supplement it by frequently buying more in the afternoon. A few families take separated or skim milk instead of new, or to supplement it.

The produce of the garden furnishes a large proportion of the food of the people. Potatoes, onions, greens, and other vegetables figure largely in the menu of the poorest households, especially those with many children. Bacon is almost universally eaten. Meat is eaten in all but the very poorest houses at least once or twice a week, and it is an article of daily consumption in the majority of cottages.

At the mid-day dinner-hour in winter the wife or mother is very frequently found preparing a stew with meat, potatoes, and vegetables, if well off, or if poor, of potatoes and cabbage, or potatoes and onions alone. The well-to-do sometimes have hot or cold roast meat, meat pies, chicken, where fowls are kept, etc., by way of variety. They will also have a second course of tarts, pancakes, or other sweets. If poor they will vary the stew of potatoes and vegetables by having bread with bacon, dripping, or pickles, children being sometimes fed on the latter. School-children who cannot return home to dinner take bread with butter, jam, or dripping. The mothers find that meat sent with the children is too often thrown away and wasted. On their return some mothers give the children hot vegetables or meat with their tea, or let them share in an early supper after a tea of bread and butter with jam or cake. Other mothers give nothing further but a plain tea, an inadequate diet for growing children who have a long walk in addition to their school work, and it must be remembered that little milk is taken per head in a large family.

The time and constitution of the meals taken subsequent to the mid-day dinner vary from one household to another. Most of the well-to-do have a good meal of bread and butter, cake, and jam about 4.30, followed by supper later. In some poorer families one meal takes the place of tea and supper. At tea-time one sometimes finds prepared a meal of hot meat or stew, kippers and other fish, jam-tarts, etc., besides jam and cake, and in one very poor family where the mother was out working the tea appeared to consist of bread and jam and the contents of innumerable jars and pots. There has been a great increase in the quantity of groceries consumed by cottagers within the last forty years, since the rise of wages. People dealing with a certain shop would, some thirty years ago, buy 1 oz. of tea or of coffee to last a whole week, and 1 lb. of sugar. Fifteen years later the same families would take ¼ lb. of tea and 3 lbs. of sugar per week.

In the budgets which follow the daily menu shows the form and variety of food eaten in thirteen households taken as examples. The list of articles purchased indicates the amount of the various commodities besides home produce which are available for division among the members of the family, whose number is given. The preliminary remarks should be consulted to see how much cooking is done, in cases where it is not stated whether meals are hot or cold. Nos. 44, 51, 62, and 36 are families where the income is insufficient. Not only is the quantity of nourishing food obtainable by these families inadequate, but the inevitable monotony of the diet is extremely trying, especially when any member of the family is in poor health and not enjoying a good appetite.

It will be seen that some women are much better managers than others. No. 62, for instance, gives a more varied and appetising diet than No. 51, though the poorer of the two.

Nos. 29, 116, and 193 are near the margin of primary poverty. No. 29 is 2d. per head per week below the minimum of efficiency by the regular wage, but this is, no doubt, made up by Mrs. T.'s occasional earnings, and by extra money which T., being a strong and industrious man, can make out of his garden over and above the rent. This diet is an excellent one for the income, owing to Mrs. T.'s cleverness as manager and cook. No. 116, too, yields a fairly varied diet. No. 193 is an old woman who is provided by her children with what they deem necessary, and who depends for cooking, etc., upon relatives residing near. It may here be remarked that probably a few of the very poorest old people, paupers, and others, live almost entirely on bread and butter and tea.

Nos. 46, 20, 206, 117, 105, and 131 are all well above the margin of poverty, having more than 2s. per head over the necessary minimum. The quality of the menu in these cases varies with the competency of the housekeeper. The menu of No. 206, where the manager is not in good health, and possibly given to drink, is very poor when the income of the family is considered. That of No. 105 would probably be more regularly appetising if there were an experienced woman to manage the housekeeping, which is now done jointly by the father and a young daughter. On the whole, however, these diaries show a fairly generous diet, and if the section on poverty be compared, it will be found that the majority of households in the parish can afford to feed in this manner, the exceptions being labourers with several children, and others who for one reason or another are in primary poverty.

The budgets have been arranged as far as can be ascertained in order of poverty, beginning with those with the largest deficit, and proceeding to the family with the largest surplus per head.

[Note: in this edition the budgets have been reproduced as reduced facsimiles taken from the 1909 edition, with the result that in places the page layout and type size are uneven.]

BUDGET No. 44.

Deficiency of Income, 7s. 6d.

Labourer, wife, five children. Wage 15s. All the man's wages are given to the wife.

Regular Expenses.—House-rent, 1s. 6d. per week. Allotment (20 poles), 5s. per annum. Man's Friendly Society, 2s. 5d. per month.

The family take 1d. worth of new milk (less than 1 pint) per day, or when occasionally no new milk is to be had, 1 quart of skim milk.

"Broth" is made of butter, milk, and water.

At the time the diary was being kept the mother was nursing her youngest child, and therefore usually had a supper of quaker oats.

The father and school-children usually carry their dinner with them.

Tea is taken at about 4.15, when the children return.

The children share supper at 6 p.m.

THINGS PURCHASED.

January, 1906. First week.

	s.	d.		s.	d.
½ lb. tea ...	0	8	Forward ...	7	0
3 lb. sugar ...	0	5½	Coal ...	1	2½
1½ lb. butter ...	1	6	Loaf ...	0	2¼
Bacon ...	1	4	Milk ...	0	6½
Quaker oats ...	0	5½	Butter ...	0	4
2 oz. tobacco ...	0	6	Sugar ...	0	2¼
Cheese ...	0	9	Loaf ...	0	2¼
½ lb. lard ...	0	2½	Oil ...	0	2½
¼ lb. suet ...	0	2	Stockings ...	0	6½
Baking powder ...	0	1			
Papers ...	0	2		10	4¾
1 lb. soap ...	0	3	Bread bill ...	3	0
Oranges ...	0	2			
½ lb. currants ...	0	1½	Expenditure during week	13	4¾
1 pt. beer ...	0	2			
	*7	0			

January, 1906. Second week.

	s.	d.		s.	d.
Bread ...	2	6	Forward ...	11	2¾
Oil ...	0	2½	Matches ...	0	1½
Beef ...	1	0	¼ lb. sweets ...	0	1
Milk ...	0	7	Oranges ...	0	3
Coal, 1 cwt. ...	1	2½	Tobacco ...	0	6
Flannelette ...	1	4¼	Pepper ...	0	1½
½ lb. tea ...	0	8	Quaker oats ...	0	5½
3 lb. sugar ...	0	5½	Biscuits ...	0	1
3 lb. bacon ...	1	6	Lard ...	0	2½
2 lb. butter [?] ...	1	0	F. fish ...	0	4
1½ lb. cheese ...	0	9	2 lb. sprats ...	0	2
	11	2¾		13	6¾

* This store was probably purchased on Saturday at Warminster, and the other groceries bought during the following week.

	Breakfast.	Dinner.	Tea.	Supper.
SATURDAY...	Father.—Fried potato, bacon, tea. Mother and Children.—Potatoes and bacon and tea.	Bread, fresh butter, tea.	Bread and butter, tea.	
SUNDAY ...	Parents.—Bacon and tea. Children.—Porridge.	Potatoes, cabbage, boiled bacon, currant and suet pudding.	Bread and butter and cake, tea.	Mother.—Porridge.
MONDAY ...	Father.—Fried potato, bacon, tea. Mother and Children.—Toast and tea. .	Father.—Bread and cheese. School Children.—Bread and butter, tea. At home.—Fried potato, bacon, tea.	Toast and tea.	Potatoes, greens, bacon.
TUESDAY ...	Father.—Fried potato and bacon. Others.—Porridge.	Father.—Bread and cheese. School Children.—Bread and butter. At home.—Porridge.	Toast and tea.	Potatoes, greens, bacon, suet pudding.
WEDNESDAY	Father.—Fried potato, bacon, tea. Others.—Toast and tea.	Father.—Bread and cheese. Others.—Bread and butter, suet pudding.	Toast and tea.	Potatoes, greens, bacon, tea.
THURSDAY...	Father.—Fried potato, bacon, tea. Others.—Broth.	Potatoes and bacon.	Toast and tea.	Potatoes, greens, bacon, tea.
FRIDAY ...	Father.—Fried potato, bacon, tea. Others.—Toast and tea.	Father.—Bread and cheese. School Children.—Bread and lard. At home.—Soup (a present).	Toast and tea.	Potatoes and greens.
SATURDAY...	Father.—Potato, bacon, tea Others.—Broth.	Father.—Bread and bacon. Others.—Soup (a present).	Sprats and tea.	
SUNDAY ...	Fried fish and tea.	Potatoes, greens, beef, suet pudding.	Bread and butter, tea.	Mother.—Porridge.
MONDAY ...	Father.—Fried potato, bacon, tea. Others.—Toast and tea.	Father.—Bread and cheese. School Children.—Bread and butter and tea. At home.—Fried potato, bacon, tea.	Toast and tea.	Potatoes and fried onions.
TUESDAY ...	Father.—Fried potato, bacon, tea.	Father.—Bread and cheese. Children at home.—Fried potato, bacon, tea.	Toast and tea.	6 p.m. : Potatoes and fried onions.
WEDNESDAY	Father.—Fried potato, bacon, tea. Others.—Toast and tea.	Father.—Bread and cheese. School Children.—Bread and butter. Others.—Fried onions, bacon, bread.	Toast and tea.	Potatoes, greens, bacon, tea.
THURSDAY...	Father.—Fried potato, bacon, tea. Others.—Toast and tea.	Father.—Bread and cheese. School Children.—Bread and butter. Others.—Potatoes, bacon, tea.	Toast and tea.	Potatoes, greens, bacon, tea, bread.
FRIDAY ...	Father.—Fried potato, bacon, tea. Others.—Toast and tea.	Father.—Bread and cheese. School Children.—Bread and butter. Others.—Milk broth.	Tea, bread.	Rabbit soup, potatoes, bread.

BUDGET No. 62.

Deficiency of Income, 5s. 4d.

Labourer, wife, six children (eldest boy of 14, youngest an infant). Two older children have left the parish, one child (the second out of nine), died as an infant.

The family of eight live in a three-roomed cottage, which they get rent free, with small garden, from employer.

	s.	d.
Man's wage	13	0
Boy's wage	3	6
	16	6 per week.

The man gets £3 over-money at Christmas, and now and then a rabbit. In summer they are allowed to collect some firewood free.

All earnings are given to the wife. They have no beer, and man keeps no pocket-money. They are better off than a few months ago, before boy began to earn.

EXPENDITURE.

January 6–12, 1906.

	s.	d.		s.	d.
Bread	3	11½	Forward	12	5
Flour	0	5	Mr. N.'s Club	0	3½
Tea	0	8	Mrs. N.'s Clothing Club	0	3
Sugar	0	8	Ellen's ,,	0	2
Bacon	1	6	Eva's ,,	0	2
Cheese	1	2	Cwt. coal	1	1½
Fresh butter	0	7½	Lamp oil	0	4½
Salt butter	0	6	Milk	0	3½
Best lard	0	4	Salt	0	0½
Soap	0	1½	1 doz. boot laces ...	0	2
Fresh pork	1	5	1 reel black cotton ...	0	1
Candles	0	1½	1 card angola	0	1
Pepper	0	1	Wool for mending ...	0	2
Mustard	0	1			
Starch	0	1½	Total expenditure ...	15	7½
Cocoa	0	3½			
Currants	0	2			
Shoe blacking	0	1	The rest was put by for boots.		
Grate polish	0	1			
	12	5			

January 13–19, 1906.

	s.	d.		s.	d.
Bread	3	11½	Forward	13	5
Flour	0	5	Mr. N.'s Club	0	3¼
Tea	0	8	Mrs. N.'s Clothing Club	0	3
Sugar	0	8	Ellen's „	0	2
Bacon	2	0	Eva's „	0	2
Cheese	1	2	1 cwt. coal	1	1½
Fresh butter	0	7½	Milk	0	3½
Salt butter	0	6	Lamp oil	0	4½
Best lard	0	4½	1 reel of thread ...	0	1
Soap	0	1½	2 pieces tape	0	1½
Candles	0	1½	2 yards calico	0	5¼
Soda	0	1½	Boots mended	0	7
Coffee	0	5	Total expenditure ...	17	4
Salt	0	1			
Beef	2	0			
Fish	0	2			
	13	5			

January 20–27, 1906.

	s.	d.		s.	d.
Bread	3	11½	Forward	11	2
Flour	0	5	Mr. N.'s Club	0	3¼
Tea	0	8	Mrs. N.'s Clothing Club	0	3
Sugar	0	8	Ellen's „	0	2
Cheese	1	1	Eva's „	0	2
Pork	1	4	1 cwt. coal	1	1½
Butter	0	7½	Lamp oil	0	4½
Salt butter	0	6	Milk	0	4½
Lard	0	4½	3 yds. flannelette at 3½d.	0	10½
Rice	0	4	Cake	0	4
Baked faggots	0	2	Fish	0	2
Blue	0	1	Total expenditure ...	15	3½
Candles	0	1½			
Suet	0	2			
Cocoa	0	3½			
Soap	0	1½			
Starch	0	1	The rest was put by for boots.		
Pepper	1	1			
Sweets	0	1			
	11	2			

This budget was carefully kept by the wife, and is probably accurate.

Three or four of the children are of an age to attend school, and though they live two miles away the attendance of the three elder ones is very regular. These and the father must take their dinners out with them.

Only ½d. of milk is taken each day, and as this makes bread and milk twice a day no doubt it is skim milk.

Most of the marketing is done in Warminster. The only store in the house worth consideration was potatoes. The man has to work hard for his over-money at Christmas, and sometimes is not in till 8 or 12 p.m. It is probably on these nights only that supper is taken.

	Breakfast.	Dinner.	Tea.	Supper.
SUNDAY ...	Bread and fresh butter, tea, sugar, milk, bread and milk.	Boiled potatoes, pork, cabbage, bread, gravy, currant pudding.	Bread and butter, bread, jam, tea, sugar, milk.	Bread and cheese, cocoa, sugar, milk, bread and milk.
MONDAY ...	Bread and butter toasted, tea, sugar, milk, bread and milk.	Bread and meat, cold pork, tea, sugar, milk, bread and milk.	Boiled potatoes, bacon, cocoa, sugar, milk.	
TUESDAY ...	Bread and fried bacon, tea, sugar, milk, bread and milk.	Bread and cheese, cocoa, sugar, milk.	Bread and fried bacon, fried potatoes, tea, sugar, milk, bread and milk, pepper, salt.	
WEDNESDAY	Bread and butter toasted, tea, sugar, milk, bread and milk.	Boiled potatoes, bacon, bread, cocoa, milk, pepper, salt.	Bread and butter, bread, jam, tea, sugar, milk, bread and milk.	
THURSDAY...	Bread and fried bacon, fried bread, tea, sugar, milk, bread and milk.	Boiled potatoes, boiled bacon, bread, suet pudding, cocoa, milk, sugar.	Bread and butter, bread, jam, tea, sugar, milk, bread and milk.	
FRIDAY ...	Bread and salt butter toasted, bread, dripping, tea, sugar, milk, bread and milk.	Bread and cheese, bread and cold pork, cocoa, sugar, milk.	Boiled potatoes, fried bacon and bread, pepper, salt, tea, sugar, milk, bread and milk.	
SATURDAY...	Bread and fried bacon, tea, sugar, milk, bread and milk.	Boiled bacon, potatoes, with suet dumplings, pepper, salt, onions, cocoa, sugar, milk.	Bread and butter, bread and dripping, tea, sugar, milk, bread and milk.	Bread and fish, cocoa, sugar, milk.

	Breakfast.	*Dinner.*	*Tea.*	*Supper.*
SUNDAY ...	Bread and fried bacon, tea, sugar, milk, bread and milk.	Potatoes, cabbage, beef, bread, gravy, pepper, salt, plain suet pudding.	Bread and butter, bread, jam, tea, sugar, milk, bread and milk.	Bread and cold beef, mustard, salt, coffee, sugar, milk.
MONDAY ...	Bread and butter toasted, bread and dripping, salt, tea, sugar, milk, bread and milk.	Bread and cheese, coffee, sugar, milk.	Cooked potatoes, bacon, pepper, bread, salt, tea, sugar, milk, bread and milk.	
TUESDAY ...	Bread and fried bacon, fried bread, tea, sugar, milk, bread and milk.	Bread and cold beef, mustard, tea, sugar, milk.	Bread and fresh butter, rice pudding, tea, sugar, milk, bread and milk.	Bread and cheese, coffee, sugar, milk.
WEDNESDAY	Bread and salt butter toasted, tea, sugar, milk, bread and milk.	Bread and cheese, tea, sugar, milk.	Boiled potatoes, bacon, bread, pepper, salt, tea, sugar, milk, bread and milk.	
THURSDAY...	Bread and bacon, potatoes (fried), pepper, salt, tea, sugar, milk, bread and milk.	Bread and cold beef, mustard, coffee, sugar, milk.	Boiled potatoes, bacon, pepper, salt, plain suet dumplings, bread, tea, sugar, milk, bread and milk.	
FRIDAY ...	Bread and salt butter toasted, tea, sugar, milk, bread and milk.	Bread and cheese, mustard, coffee, sugar, milk.	Bread and fresh butter, bread and jam, tea, sugar, milk, bread and milk.	Bread and meat, fish, coffee, sugar, milk.
SATURDAY...	Bread and butter toasted, bread and dripping, salt, tea, sugar, milk.	Bread and cheese, mustard, tea, sugar, milk.	Boiled potatoes, fried bacon, bread, pepper, salt, tea, sugar, milk, rice pudding.	
SUNDAY ...	Bread and butter and dripping, tea, sugar, milk, bread and milk.	Boiled potatoes, cabbage, roast pork and gravy, plain suet pudding, bread, pepper, salt.	Bread and butter, cake, tea, sugar, milk, bread and milk.	Bread and cold pork, mustard, cocoa, sugar, milk.
MONDAY ...	Bread and fried bacon, bread and fried bread, tea, sugar, milk, bread and milk.	Bread and cheese, cocoa, milk, sugar.	Bread and butter, rice pudding, tea, sugar, milk, bread and milk.	
TUESDAY ...	Bread and fried bacon, bread and fried bread, tea, sugar, milk, bread and milk.	Bread and cold pork, mustard, cocoa, sugar, milk.	Boiled potatoes, boiled bacon, bread, pepper, salt, tea, sugar, milk, bread and milk.	
WEDNESDAY	Bread and butter, bread and dripping toasted, tea, sugar, milk, bread and milk.	Bread and cheese, cocoa, sugar, milk.	Bread and butter, bread and jam, tea, sugar, milk, bread and milk.	Bread and fried fish, cocoa, sugar, milk.
THURSDAY...	Bread and fried bacon, fried potatoes, tea, sugar, milk, bread and milk.	Bread and cold pork, cocoa, sugar, milk, mustard, salt.	Boiled potatoes and bacon, bread, rice pudding with milk, tea, sugar, milk, bread and milk.	
FRIDAY ...	Bread and butter, tea, sugar, milk, bread and milk.	Bread and cheese, cocoa, sugar, milk.	Bread and butter, bread and jam, tea, sugar, milk, bread and milk.	Bread and cheese, cocoa, sugar, milk.
SATURDAY...	Bread and fried bacon, bread and dripping, tea, sugar, milk, bread and milk.	Boiled potatoes, bacon fried, bread, pepper, salt, cocoa, sugar, milk.	Bread and butter, bread and jam, tea, sugar, milk, bread and milk.	Bread and cheese, cocoa, sugar, milk.

BUDGET No. 51.

Deficiency of Income, 3s. 8d.

Family : Labourer, wife, four children. They live in a three-roomed cottage, and have about 40 poles of potato-ground. The man belongs to a good club. Mother and children belong to a medical club. They belong to a clothing club. The children are all insured.

The mother was expecting her confinement, for which she was saving. One of children at school suffers from chorea.

There is considerable discrepancy in the statement as to the earnings of this man from his employer, his wife, and a third source of information. The wife states that the employer gives 12s. 6d. and pays half the rent. This seems to be an under-statement. Probably the man receives 13s. to 14s. and house and garden rent free, paying rent for his extra land.

The wife states that her husband keeps 1s. for boots, &c., and gives her 11s. 6d. for housekeeping.

They, no doubt, supplement this from sale of garden produce and occasionally they fatten a pig.

They are said always to pay cash for their purchases.

They have about 1 quart of skim milk daily from the employer.

The diary was kept by the wife. It may err by omissions.

EXPENDITURE.

January 12–18, 1907. *First week.*

	s.	d.
3 large loaves	1	1½
½ lb. salt butter	0	6½
¼ lb. lard	0	3
Bacon	0	6
Clothing club	1	0
3 large loaves	1	1½
4 lb. sugar	0	8
¼ lb. tea	0	5
2 lb. rice	0	4
Suet	0	3
Lamp oil	0	4
Soap	0	3
	6	9½

January 19–25, 1907. *Second week.*

	s.	d.
3 large loaves	1	1½
½ lb. salt butter	0	6½
Ox cheek	1	0
3 large loaves	1	1½
Suet	0	3
4 lb. of sugar	0	8
¼ lb. of tea	0	4½
Flour	1	0
Lamp oil	0	4
Soap	0	3
Soda	0	2
	6	10

	Breakfast.	Dinner.	Tea.	Supper.
SATURDAY...	Bread and butter, bread and milk, tea.	At home. — Potatoes, parsnips, bread.	Bread and jam, tea, milk.	Bread and lard, milk and water.
SUNDAY ...	Tea, toast with lard.	At home. — Potatoes, cabbage, bacon.	Bread and butter, tea, milk.	Bread and milk.
MONDAY ...	Bread and butter, tea.	At home.—Bread and bacon (husband). Children's (carried). — Bread and jam.	Toast with lard, tea, milk.	Bread and milk.
TUESDAY ...	Fried potatoes, bread.	At home. — Potatoes, cabbage, bacon. Children's (carried).— Bread and lard.	Bread and butter, tea, milk.	Bread and milk.
WEDNESDAY	Bread and butter, tea, milk.	Baked potatoes, boiled rice. Children's (carried).— Bread and lard.	Bread and jam, tea, milk.	Boiled rice, milk and water.
THURSDAY...	Toast with lard, tea, milk.	Potatoes, boiled onions. Children's (carried).— Bread and jam.	Bread and butter, tea, milk.	Bread and milk.
FRIDAY ...	Fried potatoes, bread, tea, milk.	Potatoes, cabbage, fried suet. Children's (carried).— Bread and butter.	Dry toast, tea, milk.	Bread and milk.
SATURDAY...	Dry toast, tea, milk.	At home. — Potatoes, onion soup.	Bread and butter, tea, milk.	Bread and butter, milk and water.
SUNDAY ...	Dry toast, tea.	At home. — Potatoes, cabbage, ox cheek.	Bread and jam, tea, milk.	Husband out.
MONDAY ...	Fried potatoes, bread, tea.	At home.—Bread and meat. Children's (carried).— Bread and jam.	Bread and lard, tea, milk.	Bread and milk.
TUESDAY ...	Dry toast, tea, milk.	At home. — Potatoes, onion soup. Children's (carried).— Bread and jam.	Dry toast, tea, milk.	Onion soup.
WEDNESDAY	Fried potatoes, bread, tea.	At home. — Potatoes, boiled rice. Children's (carried).— Bread and butter.	Toast, butter, tea, milk.	Bread and meat, milk and water.
THURSDAY...	Butter and toast, tea.	At home. — Potatoes, pea soup. Children's (carried).— Bread and jam.	Bread and butter, tea, milk.	Bread and milk.
FRIDAY ...	Fried potatoes, bread, tea.	At home. — Potatoes, pea soup. Children's (carried).— Bread and dripping.	Bread and butter, tea, milk.	Pea soup, bread.

BUDGET No. 36.

Deficiency of Income, 3s. 6d.

Family: Labourer, wife, son, three children. Some of the family are very delicate. They reside in a five-roomed cottage with a garden.

The man belongs to the Corsley Gathering Club. The son belongs to a good Friendly Society. They insure some of the children, and belong to a medical club and a clothing club.

The father earns 14s., the son 7s. 6d., per week. Of this the father gives 13s., the son 4s., towards housekeeping expenses.

Expenditure.

The regular weekly expenses are stated as follows:

	s.	d.
Insurance: son...	0	3
" Jack	0	2
" Tom	0	1
Club (Jack, 7d. per month)	0	1¾
Clothing club	0	3
Father's club	0	3
Doctor's money...	0	2½
House-rent	3	4*
	4	8¼

Things Bought.

January, 1907. *First week.*

	s.	d.		s.	d.
4 loaves ...	1	6	Forward	8	8½
2 loaves ...	0	9	½ oz. pepper	0	0½
2 lb. of liver	0	4	¼ lb. tea ...	0	4½
½ lb. fat ...	0	2	2 loaves ...	0	9
Milk for week ...	0	7	Bag of flour	0	6
Beef	2	2	A small loaf	0	6
2 lb. cheese	1	4	1 pint of lamp oil	0	1
Bloaters...	0	3	Matches...	0	0½
½ lb. butter	0	6½	Coal	1	0
2½ lb. sugar	0	5	3 lb. bacon	1	9
¼-lb. tin Fry's cocoa	0	7½	Candles ...	0	1½
1 lb. salt...	0	0½		13	10½
	8	8½			

* This is probably given erroneously. Two shillings a week is a more likely figure, but, as the house is two cottages knocked into one, the rent may be somewhat higher than customary.

Things Bought.

January, 1907. *Second week.*

	s.	d.		s.	d.
2 loaves ...	0	9	Forward	8	5
½ lb. butter	0	7½	Milk for week ...	0	7
¼ lb. tea ...	0	4½	4 loaves ...	1	6
Pork	2	0	¼-lb. tin of Fry's cocoa	0	7½
2 lb. cheese	1	4	2 lb. pigs' liver ...	0	8
3 lb. bacon at 7d.	1	9	½ lb. fat ...	0	2
Coal	1	0	3 loaves ...	1	1½
Lamp oil	0	2		13	1
2½ lb. sugar	0	5			
	8	5			

The wife cooks only once or twice a week during the winter. She cooks oftener in summer when potatoes are more plentiful.

The children always take bread and jam or bread and butter to school for their dinner.

The diary was kept by one of the children, and is not perfectly clear and accurate.

	Breakfast.	Dinner.	Tea.	Supper.
SATURDAY...	Bacon, fried potatoes, tea, cocoa, bread.	Pickled cabbage, cocoa, meat, bread.	Bread and butter, tea, bloaters, cake.	Bread and cheese, cocoa.
SUNDAY ...	Bread, bacon, toast, tea, cocoa.	Beef, potatoes, greens, gravy, cocoa.	Bread and butter, tea, cake.	Cocoa, bread and meat.
MONDAY ...	Bread, bacon, potatoes, tea, cocoa.	Pudding, bread, meat, cocoa.	Bread and butter, cake, tea.	Bread and cheese, cocoa.
TUESDAY ...	Bread, bacon, potatoes, tea, cocoa.	Potatoes, greens, beef, cocoa.	Bread and butter, cake.	Bread and cheese, cocoa.
WEDNESDAY	Bread, bacon, potatoes, tea, cocoa.	Bread, beef, pickled cabbage, cocoa.	Bread and butter, cheese, tea, cocoa.	Bread and meat, cocoa.
THURSDAY...	Bacon, vinegar, tea, cocoa.	Fried onions, cocoa.	Bread and butter, jam, tea.	Bread and cheese, tea.
FRIDAY ...	Bread, liver, tea, cocoa.	Boiled beef, soup, potatoes, turnip, onions.	Bread and butter, tea.	Bread and cheese, cocoa.
SATURDAY...	Bread, bacon, potatoes, tea, cocoa.	Bacon, cocoa, bread.	Bread and butter, jam, tea.	Bread and cheese, tea.
SUNDAY ...	Bacon, fried potatoes, tea, cocoa, bread and butter, bread.	Bacon, cocoa, potatoes, greens.	Bread and butter, jam, tea.	Bread and cheese, tea.
MONDAY ...	Bread, bacon, potatoes, tea, cocoa.	Pork, bread, cocoa.	Bread and butter, tea, cocoa.	Bread and butter, tea.
TUESDAY ...	Bread, bacon, potatoes, tea, cocoa.	Pork, tea, bread, apple-dumpling.	Bread and butter, tea.	Bread and cheese, cocoa.
WEDNESDAY	Bread, fried bacon, fried potatoes, tea, cocoa.	Onion soup, tea, bread. Bread and butter, cake, for Willie. Bread and meat for Fred.	Bread, toast, with dripping on it, tea, cocoa.	Bread and cheese, tea.
THURSDAY...	Bread, fried bacon, fried potatoes, tea, cocoa.	Fried liver, onions, bread, cocoa. Bread and meat for Fred. Bread and butter, cake, for Willie	Bread, toast, with dripping on it, tea.	Bread and cheese, tea.
FRIDAY ...	Bread, bacon, potatoes, tea, cocoa.	Bread, onion soup. Bread and butter for Willie. Bread and meat for Fred.	Bread and butter, cake, tea, cocoa.	Bread and cheese, tea.

BUDGET No. 29.

Deficiency of Income, 10d.

Family : Labourer, wife, three children, also girl of eleven years for some meals.

They reside in a three-roomed cottage with large garden (¾ acre) for which they pay £6 per annum. Rent for water, 10s. per annum.

The man belongs to a good club. Mrs. T. pays 3d. a week for each child into savings bank at Corsley School.

Mr. T.'s wage is 15s. He keeps 5s., out of which he pays his club, firewood (buying 40 faggots at a time for 10s.), coal (half ton for 9s. 8d.), ale (5s. per month), and all outdoor expenses, such as food for pigs and fowls. He pays for the clothing of the family out of the profits of garden, pigs, &c.

Mrs. T. receives 10s. per week from her husband for the housekeeping, and she occasionally makes 6d. for washing. During the fortnight the budget was kept she had a present of some liver from their butcher.

Mrs. T. has been a cook and takes pride in her cooking and housekeeping. She cooks every day. Potatoes for breakfast, and meat, potatoes, and pudding for dinner. The children do not like milk puddings so she usually makes tarts, &c. They have cold food in the evening.

They take 1d. worth of milk per day at 1½d. per pint.

All the family are home for the midday dinner. The children do not take supper.

The budget was kept very carefully by Mrs. T. and is probably quite accurate.

December 30, 1905.

STORE IN HOUSE.

Sugar, tea, ¼ lb. cheese, ¾ lb. butter, 1½ lb. bacon, a large loaf, five eggs, two bloaters, flour, currants, jam, pickles, store of potatoes.

EXPENDITURE.

December 30, 1905—*January* 12, 1906.

	s.	d.				s.	d.
12 large loaves	5	0	Forward			13	2
[2 have not been put			¼ lb. tea		...	0	4½
down, but bread bill			½ lb. currants ...		...	1	0½
was 5s.]			Tin mustard ...		...	0	1
3 lb. beef	1	9	Soap		...	0	3
1 lb. butter	1	1½	Rabbit		...	0	6
1 lb. mutton	0	8	Beef		...	1	3
Bloaters	0	3	Lamp oil ...		...	0	4
7 lb. sugar	1	2	Flour		...	0	6
1 lb. lard	0	6	1 lb. mutton ...		...	0	8
1 lb. sultanas ...	0	4	Fish		...	0	3
Egg powder	0	2	Lamp oil ...		...	0	4
¼ lb. peel	1	0½	Butter		...	1	1½
1 lb. 14 oz. cheese ...	1	1	14 days' milk ...		...	1	2
Salt	0	1	Bacon		...	1	2½
			½ lb. tea		...	0	9
	13	2				1 3	0

	Breakfast.	Dinner.	Tea.	Supper.
SATURDAY...	8 a.m. : Tea with milk and sugar, fish, fried potatoes, bread, toast, butter.	1 p.m. : Bacon, potatoes, parsnips, turnips, cabbage.	5 p.m. : Tea, milk sugar, bread and butter, jam.	9 p.m.: Bread and cheese, ale, celery.
SUNDAY	8 30. a.m. : Meat, hot potatoes, bread and butter, tea, milk, sugar.	12 30. : Roast beef, cabbage, potatoes, plum pudding.	5 p.m. : Tea, milk, sugar, bread and butter, cake.	8.30 p.m. : Bread, meat, cheese, pickles, ale.
MONDAY	8 a.m. : Tea, milk, sugar, fried bacon, fried potatoes, bread and butter.	p.m. : Cold beef, potatoes, cabbage, plum pudding.	5 p.m. : Tea, milk, sugar, bread and butter, cake.	9 p.m.: Bread and cheese, pickle, cabbage, ale.
TUESDAY	8 a.m. : Tea, milk, sugar, fried bacon, potatoes, bread and butter.	Stew beef, potatoes, cabbage, turnips.	Tea, sugar, milk, bread and butter, jam.	Bread and cheese, beetroot, ale.
WEDNESDAY	8 a.m. : Tea, sugar, milk, fried bacon, bread and butter, toast.	1 p.m. : Roast mutton, potatoes, cabbage.	5 p.m.: Tea, sugar, milk, bread and butter, cake, toast.	8.45 p.m. : Fried liver, bread, ale.
THURSDAY...	8 a.m. : Tea, sugar, milk, bread and butter, bread and milk.	1 p.m. : Roast mutton, potatoes, parsnips, turnip, boiled apple dumplings.	5 p.m. : Tea, milk, sugar, toast, bread and butter.	9 p.m. : Fish, bread and cheese, ale.
FRIDAY	8 a.m. : Tea, milk, sugar, fried fish, potatoes, bread and butter.	1 p.m. : Fried liver, potatoes, cabbage, boiled rice.	5 p.m. : Tea, milk, sugar, bread and butter, toast.	9 p.m. Cold mutton, bread, pickle onions, ale.
SATURDAY...	8 a.m. : Tea, milk, sugar, fried bacon, bread and butter.	1 p.m. : Hash mutton, potatoes, cabbage.	Tea, milk, sugar, bread and butter, toast, jam.	8.30 p.m. : Bread and cheese, celery, ale.
SUNDAY	8 a.m.: Tea, milk, sugar, fried bacon, bread and butter.	1 p.m. : Roast rabbit, potatoes, parsnips, turnips, apple pudding.	5 p.m.: Tea, milk, sugar, cake, bread and butter.	8.30 p.m. : Cold rabbit, celery, bread, ale.
MONDAY	8 a.m.: Tea, milk, sugar, fish, bread and butter.	1 p.m. Roast beef, potatoes, cabbage.	5 p.m.: Tea, milk, sugar, bread and butter, cake, jam.	8.30 p.m. : Bread and cheese, celery, ale.
TUESDAY	8 a.m. : Tea, milk, sugar, fried bacon, bread and butter.	1 p.m. : Hash beef, potatoes, cabbage.	5 p.m.: Tea, milk, sugar, bread and butter, toast.	8.30 p.m. : Bread and cheese, pickle onions, ale.
WEDNESDAY	8 a.m. : Tea, milk, sugar, fried bacon, bread and butter.	1 p.m. : Cold beef, potatoes, cabbage, jam tart.	5 p.m.: Tea, milk, sugar, bread and butter toast.	8.30 p.m.: Cold beef, beetroot, bread, ale.
THURSDAY...	8 a.m.: Tea, milk, sugar, bread and butter, bread and milk.	1 p.m.: Roast mutton, potatoes, parsnip.	5 p.m.: Tea, milk, sugar, bread and butter, buns, jam.	8 p.m. : Fish, bread, ale.
FRIDAY	8 a.m. : Tea, milk, sugar, bread and butter, fried bacon, potatoes.	1 p.m. : Mutton, potatoes, cabbage.	5 p.m.: Tea, milk, sugar, bread and butter, toast.	9 p.m.: Bread and cheese, pickle onions, ale.

BUDGET No. 193.

Aged widow of small farmer supported by her children. A daughter pays her rent (£5), and sends her bacon, butter, potatoes, or a load of wood, if her own do not last out.

Her children send her money, but not regularly.

One of her nieces and family live near, and look after her.

January 14–21, 1906.

1½ lbs. cooked ham	...	...	...	from daughter.
1 lb. bacon ...	...	...	...	,,
½ lb. fresh butter	...	...	...	,,
½ lb. salt butter ...	...	...	...	,,
2 eggs	...	...	...	,,

		s.	d.
1 lb. sugar		0	2
¼ lb. tea		0	5
⅛ lb. candles			
1 lb. pork		0	8
Beer for two nights		0	2½
Two small loaves		0	4½

January 22–28, 1906.

1½ lbs. pork ...	...	...	...	from daughter.
4 lbs. bacon ...	...	...	...	,,
½ lb. fresh butter	...	...	...	,,
½ lb. salt butter ...	...	...	...	,,

		s.	d.
2 small loaves		0	4½
¼ lb. tea		0	5
1 lb. sugar		0	2

This budget was kept by great-niece, who lives near, and is probably quite accurate.

	Breakfast.	Dinner.	Tea.	Supper.
Monday ...	9 a.m.: Bread and butter, tea.	1 p.m.: Fried bacon, potatoes.	4 p.m.: Toast, buttered, tea.	8.30. p.m.: Bread and cheese, glass of beer.
Tuesday ...	9 a.m.: Bacon, fried potatoes, tea.	1 p.m.: Potatoes, boiled bacon, cabbage.	4 p.m.: Bread and butter, tea.	8.30. p.m.: Bread and cheese, glass of beer.
Wednesday	9 a.m.: Buttered toast, tea.	1 p.m.: Bread and butter, boiled eggs.	4 p.m.: Bread and butter, cake, tea.	8.30. p.m.: Bread and cheese, glass of beer.
Thursday...	9 a.m.: Buttered toast, tea.	1 p.m.: Cold ham, bread.	4 p.m.: Bread and butter, tea.	8.30. p.m.: Bread and cheese, glass of beer.
Friday ...	9 a.m.: Fried bacon, potatoes, tea.	1 p.m.: Boiled potatoes, cold ham.	4 p.m.: Bread and butter, tea.	8.30. p.m.: Cold ham, bread, glass of beer.
Saturday...	9 a.m.: Buttered toast, tea.	1 p.m.: Fried bacon, potatoes.	4 p.m.: Bread and butter, tea.	8.30. p.m.: Bread and cheese, glass of beer.
Sunday ...	9 a.m.: Buttered toast, tea.	1 p.m.: Roast pork, potatoes, cabbage.	4 p.m.: Bread and butter, tea.	8.30. p.m.: Bread, cold meat, glass of beer.

	Breakfast.	Dinner.	Tea.	Supper.
MONDAY ...	9 a.m.: Bacon, fried potatoes, tea.	1 p.m.: Cold pork, boiled potatoes.	4 p.m.: Bread and butter, tea.	8.30 p.m.: Bread and cheese, glass of beer.
TUESDAY ...	9 a.m.: Buttered toast, tea.	1 p.m.: Boiled bacon, cabbage, potatoes.	4 p.m.: Bread and butter, jam, tea.	8.30 p.m.: Bread, cold bacon, glass of beer.
WEDNESDAY	9 a.m.: Fried bacon, bread, tea.	1 p.m.: Fried bacon, potatoes, cabbage.	4 p.m.: Buttered toast, tea.	8.30 p.m.: Bread, cold meat, glass of beer.
THURSDAY...	9 a.m.: Buttered toast, tea.	1 p.m.: Boiled bacon, cabbage, potatoes.	4 p.m.: Bread and butter, tea.	8.30 p.m.: Bread and cheese, glass of beer.
FRIDAY ...	9 a.m.: Fried bacon, potatoes, tea.	1 p.m.: Fried bacon, boiled potatoes.	4 p.m.: Buttered toast, tea.	8.30 p.m.: Bread and cheese, glass of beer.
SATURDAY...	9 a.m.: Fried bacon, bread, tea.	1 p.m.: Cold meat, bread.	4 p.m.: Buttered toast, tea.	8.30 p.m.: Bread and meat, glass of beer.
SUNDAY ...	9 a.m.: Fried bacon, egg, tea.	1 p.m.: Roast pork, potatoes, Brussels sprouts.	4 p.m.: Buttered toast, tea.	8.30 p.m.: Bread and meat, glass of beer.

BUDGET No. 116.

Income Sufficient—on margin of primary poverty.

Family : Market gardener and carrier, wife, two children. Other sons and daughters sometimes at home.

Mr. H. belongs to a good friendly society, paying 3s. 9½d. per month to it.

The receipts vary considerably; 16s. per week is perhaps an average sum.

The school-children come home for their dinner, and there are usually about five persons present for meals.

They take 1d. worth of milk, or about 1 pint, per day from Mrs. H.'s brother. They have meat or soup for dinner most days.

The budget was kept by one of the children, and is not very complete. For instance, it was found that coffee or cocoa is usually taken for supper, and sometimes the parents have porter. This has been omitted in the diary.

EXPENDITURE.

January 7-13, 1907. First week.

	s.	d.
Butter	1	3
Milk	0	1
Sugar	0	4
Starch	0	4
Blacklead	0	2
Flour	0	6
Meat (fresh beef for stewing)	1	6
Club	1	9½
Bread	1	3¼
Milk	0	2
Butter	1	3
*Baking [?]	4	0
Oil	0	6
Soap	0	6
Coals	2	6
Paper	0	4
Oranges	0	6
Sugar	1	0
	18	0

* Possibly bacon.

January 14–20, 1907. Second week.

	s.	d.
Sugar	1	0
Cheese	2	0
Butter	1	0
Lard	0	6
Mutton	2	6
Steak	1	0
Suet	0	8
Candles	0	4
Soda	0	3
Bread	1	6
Flour	0	6
Corn for fowls	1	6
	12	9

January 21–27, 1907. Third week.

	s.	d.			s.	d.
Bread	2	8	Forward	7	11½
3 lb. beef	1	9	Oil	0	4
1 lb. butter	1	2	Powder for washing ...	0	3
Coals	1	3	Corn for fowls	1	6
Wool	1	1½	Milk	0	8
	7	11½			10	8½

	Breakfast.	Dinner.	Tea.	Supper.
MONDAY ...	8 a.m. : Tea, bacon, potatoes, bread and butter, milk, sugar.	1 p.m. : Bread. cold meat, pickles, milk.	4 p.m. : Bread and butter, cake, tea, milk, sugar.	Bread, cold meat, celery.
TUESDAY ...	8 a.m. : Toast, bread and butter, tea.	1 p.m. : Stewed rabbit, carrots, potatoes.	Bread and butter, cake, tea, milk, sugar.	Bread and cheese, butter.
WEDNESDAY	Bread, bacon, porridge, tea, milk, sugar.	Potatoes, cabbage, meat.	Bread and butter, jam, cake, tea, milk, sugar.	Bread and cheese, butter, coffee.
THURSDAY...	8 a.m. : Mutton chops, butter, toast, tea, milk, sugar.	1 p.m. : Soup, carrots, onions, meat, potatoes.	5 p.m. : Bread and butter, fish, tea, milk, sugar.	8 p.m. : Bread, meat, cheese.
FRIDAY ...	8 a.m. : Bread and butter, toast, milk, quaker oats.	1 p.m. : Potatoes, greens, pork, Christmas plumpudding.	5 p.m. : Bread and butter, jam, apple-tart, tea, milk, sugar.	Bread and cheese, butter, pickles.
SATURDAY...	8 a.m. : Bread, toast, butter, bacon, tea, milk, sugar.	1 p.m. : Potatoes, bread, roast pork.	5 p.m. : Bread and butter, jam-tart, tea, milk, sugar.	8 p.m. : Bread and butter, cheese, cocoa.
SUNDAY ...	Steak, bread and butter, tea, milk, sugar.	Potatoes, sprats, roast mutton, plum-pudding.	Bread and butter, jam, plum-cake, scones.	Bread, cold meat, cheese, butter.
MONDAY ...	8 a.m. : Tea, bread and milk, sausages, bread and butter.	1 p.m. : Potatoes, cold meat, mince-pie.	5 p.m. : Bread and butter, cake, tea, jam, milk, sugar.	8 p.m. : Bread and milk.
TUESDAY ...	8 a.m. : Bread, bacon, fried potatoes, tea, milk, sugar.	Potatoes, parsnips, boiled bacon.	Bread and butter, jam, tea, toast, milk, sugar.	Bread and cheese, celery.
WEDNESDAY	Bread and butter, bacon, fried potatoes.	Potatoes, meat.	Bread and butter, tea, milk, sugar.	Bread and cheese.
THURSDAY...	8 a.m. : Bread, bacon, fried potatoes, tea, milk, sugar.	Potatoes, greens, fried bacon.	5 p.m. : Bread and butter, rice - pudding, tea, milk, sugar.	Bread and cheese, butter, coffee.
FRIDAY ...	8 a.m. : Bread and butter, toast, tea, milk, sugar.	1 p.m. : Soup, potatoes, suet-pudding.	5 p.m. : Bread and butter, jam, tea, milk, sugar.	Bread, cold meat, coffee.
SATURDAY...	8 a.m. : Bread and butter, cold meat, tea, milk, sugar.	1 p.m. : Hot potatoes, steak, bread.	5 p.m. : Bread and butter, jam, tea, milk, sugar.	8 p.m. : Soup, bread, meat.
SUNDAY ...	8 a.m. : Bread, meat, butter, tea, milk, sugar.	1 p.m. : Potatoes, greens, roast beef, plum-pudding.	5 p.m. : Bread and butter, apple-tart, tea, milk, sugar.	8 p.m. : Cold meat, cheese, pickles.

BUDGET No. 20.

Income Sufficient + 6s. 4d.

Family : Labourer, wife, one boarded out orphan.

They reside in a six-roomed cottage, rent £4, and rent some land at £2 per annum. They keep pigs.

The husband belongs to a good club. Both man and wife have insured their lives so that if they live to a certain age a sum of money will be paid them.

They take 1 quart of milk, price 3d., daily all the year round.

Weekly receipts for housekeeping :

	s.	d.
From husband	10	6
For orphan	3	6
	14	0

EXPENDITURE.

January, 1907. First week.

	s.	d.		s.	d.
Bread	0	9	Forward	4	7
1 lb. fresh butter ...	1	3	2 lb. bacon	1	4
½ lb. tea	0	10	Beef (brisket, English)	2	6
3 lb. sugar	0	6	Bread	0	7
2 lb. flour	0	4	Bread	0	7
¼ lb. lard	0	4	Mutton (at 7d. lb.) ...	1	7
1 lb. currants	0	4	Camp coffee	0	6
Pepper	0	1	2 cwt. coals	2	6
Salt	0	1	4 sheep's hearts ...	0	10
Mustard	0	1	1 lb. mixed jam ...	0	6
	4	7		15	6

January, 1907. Second week.

	s.	d.		s.	d.
1 lb. fresh butter ...	1	3	Forward	8	1½
Bread	0	9	¼ lb. starch	0	2
½ lb. tea	0	10	2 lb. soda	0	1
3 lb. sugar	0	6	Ball blue	0	1
2 lb. flour	0	4	2 cwt. coals	2	6
¼ lb. lard	0	4	Lamp oil, 2 pts. ...	0	3
1 lb. currants	0	4	2 lb. cheese	1	5
2 lb. bacon	1	4	1 lb. candles	0	6
4 lb. beef (brisket) ...	2	2		13	2
1 lb. soap	0	3½			
	8	1½			

This budget was kept by the wife, and appears to have been very carefully kept in every respect.

	Breakfast.	*Dinner.*	*Tea.*	*Supper.*
SATURDAY...	At 7 o'clock: Bacon, bread and butter, tea.	At 12 o'clock: Cold ham, beetroot, bread, coffee.	At 5 o'clock: Bread and butter, tea.	At 8 o'clock: Bread and butter, cheese, coffee.
SUNDAY ...	At 7 o'clock: Bacon, bread and butter, tea.	At 12 o'clock: Roast mutton, cabbage, potatoes.	At 5 o'clock: Bread and butter, cake, tea.	At 8 o'clock: Cold mutton, bread and butter, coffee.
MONDAY ...	At 7 o'clock: Bacon, bread and butter.	At 12 o'clock: Cold mutton, winter greens, potatoes.	At 5 o'clock: Bread and butter, cake, tea.	At 8 o'clock: Bread and cheese, butter, coffee.
TUESDAY ...	At 7 o'clock: Bacon, bread and butter.	At 12 o'clock: Cold beef, cabbages, potatoes, apple-pudding.	At 5 o'clock: Bread and butter, tea, seed cake.	At 8 o'clock: Bread and cheese, coffee.
WEDNESDAY	At 7 o'clock: Bread and butter, tea.	At 12 o'clock: Sheep's hearts, cabbage, potatoes.	At 5 o'clock: Brea and butter, jam, tea.	At 8 o'clock: Bread and cheese, coffee.
THURSDAY...	At 7 o'clock: Cold beef, bread and butter, tea.	At 12 o'clock: Cold hearts, bread and cheese, milk rice pudding.	At 5 o'clock: Bread and butter, tea.	At 8 o'clock: Bread and cheese, beetroot, coffee.
FRIDAY ...	At 7 o'clock: Bread and butter, tea.	At 12 o'clock: Fried bacon, potatoes, greens, coffee.	At 5 o'clock: Bread and butter.	At 8 o'clock: Sheep's hearts, bread, coffee.

	Breakfast.	*Dinner.*	*Tea.*	*Supper.*
SATURDAY...	At 7 o'clock: Bread and butter, tea.	At 12 o'clock: Bread and cheese, beetroot.	At 5 o'clock: Bread and butter, jam.	At 8 o'clock: Bread and butter, cheese, coffee.
SUNDAY ...	At 7 o'clock: Fried bacon, bread and butter, tea.	At 12 o'clock: Roast beef, cabbage, potatoes.	At 5 o'clock: Bread and butter, currant cake.	At 8 o'clock: Cold beef, bread, coffee.
MONDAY ...	At 7 o'clock: Bread and butter, tea.	At 12 o'clock: Cold beef, potatoes, greens.	At 5 o'clock: Bread and butter, tea.	At 8 o'clock: Bread and cheese, beetroot, coffee.
TUESDAY ...	At 7 o'clock: Fried bacon, bread and butter, tea.	At 12 o'clock: Fried fish (cod), bread, cocoa.	At 5 o'clock: Bread and butter, tea.	At 8 o'clock: Bread and cheese, cocoa.
WEDNESDAY	Bread and butter, tea.	At 12 o'clock: Cold beef, cabbage, potatoes.	At 5 o'clock: Bread and butter, currant cake, tea.	At 8 o'clock: Bread and cheese, cocoa.
THURSDAY...	At 7 o'clock: Fried bacon, bread, tea.	At 12 o'clock: Fried bacon, fried potatoes, bread, cocoa, apple-pudding.	At 5 o'clock: Bread and butter, tea.	At 8 o'clock: Bread and cheese, coffee.
FRIDAY ...	At 7 o'clock: Fried bacon, bread and butter, tea.	At 12 o'clock: Cold beef, fried potatoes, tea, rice milk pudding.	At 5 o'clock: Bread and butter, tea.	At 8 o'clock: Bread and cheese, beetroot, coffee.

BUDGET No. 206.

Income Sufficient + 12s. 2d.

Family : Widow, midwife, only goes out occasionally for the day ; two sons, agricultural wage-earner and carter ; boy of 12.

The family resides in a double cottage of eight rooms, one of the sons paying half the rent, and contributing 4s. per week towards household expenses when away from home. The mother receives 1s. 6d. per week poor relief for her boy, who also earns something unning errands, &c., after school hours. The total family income must average more than 30s. per week, but this is not all contributed to the housekeeping expenses.

The budget was kept by the boy of 12, and the diary of food is probably quite accurate.

The mother has a poor appetite and eats little.

Saturday, December 30, 1905.

STORE IN HOUSE.

2 lb. cheese, butter, 2 lb. bacon, cocoa, store of potatoes.

EXPENDITURE.

First week, December 30, 1905, *to January* 5, 1907.

Saturday :
    ¼ lb. tea.
    ½ lb. cocoa.
    ½ lb. salt butter.
    4 lb. sugar.
    3 large loaves.
    3 lb. mutton.
    2 lb. salt fish.
    Milk, 1d.
Sunday :
    Milk, 1d.
Monday :
    1 large loaf.
    Milk, 1d.

Tuesday :
    Chole of bacon, 1s.
    Milk, 1d.
    3 large loaves.
Wednesday :
    Milk, 1d.
    ½ lb. butter.
    2 lb. sugar.
Thursday :
    3 large loaves.
    Milk, 1d.
    1½ lb. bacon.
    ¾ lb. cheese.
Friday :
    Milk, 1d.

Second week, January 6–12, 1906.

Saturday :
    Milk, 1d.
    2 lb. bacon.
    3 lb. cheese.
    ½ lb. butter.
    Pot of jam.
    1 lb. dripping.
    ½ lb. bongalia tea.
    4 lb. sugar.
    3 lb. beef.
    3 loaves.
    1 lb. meat cuttings.
    3d. fresh herrings.
    Cake, 4d.
Sunday :
    Milk, 1d.

Monday :
    Milk, 1d.
    2 large loaves.
Tuesday :
    Milk, 1d.
    3 large loaves.
Wednesday :
    Milk, 1d.
    ½ lb. cocoa.
    2 lb. sugar.
    2½ lb. beef.
    3d. bloaters.
Thursday :
    Milk, 1d.
    3 large loaves.
Friday :
    1 lb. sugar.
    ½ lb. butter.

	Breakfast.	Dinner.	Tea.	Supper.
SATURDAY...	Taken out.—Toast with butter, cold tea.	Taken out.—Bread and cheese, cold tea.	At 6 o'clock : Fish, tea, bread.	At 9 o'clock (mother and myself): Bread and milk. At 10 o'clock (two brothers) : Bread and cheese, cocoa.
SUNDAY ...	At 8 o'clock (all together) : Fish, tea.	At 1 o'clock (all together) : Potatoes, greens, mutton, pudding.	At 5 o'clock (all together) : Bread and butter, tea, cake.	At 9 o'clock (all together) : Bread and cheese, celery, cocoa.
MONDAY ...	At 7 o'clock (two brothers) : Fried bacon, bread, tea. At 8 o'clock (mother and myself) : Toast, tea.	Taken away.—Bread and cheese, cold tea. Mother and myself.— Bacon and potatoes at 1 o'clock.	At 5 o'clock (mother and myself) : Bread and butter, tea. At 6 o'clock (two brothers) : Bacon and fried potatoes, tea.	At 10 o'clock (two brothers) : Bread and cheese, cocoa. At 8 o'clock (mother and myself) : Bread and butter, tea.
TUESDAY ...	Two brothers (taken away) : Bread and meat, cold tea. At 8 o'clock (mother and myself) : Dry toast, tea, bread and butter, tea.	Two brothers (taken away) : Bread and cheese, cold tea. At 1 o'clock (mother and myself) : Fried bacon, bread.	At 5 o'clock (mother and myself) : Bread and butter, tea. At 6 o'clock (two brothers) : Stewed meat, onions, turnips, parsnips, potatoes.	At 9 o'clock (mother and myself) : Cup of tea. At 10 o'clock (two brothers) : Bread and cheese, cocoa.
WEDNESDAY	At 8 o'clock (mother and myself) : Fried bacon, bread. At 7 o'clock (two brothers) : Fried bacon and potatoes, tea.	At 1 o'clock (mother and myself) : Stewed meat, bread. Two brothers (taken away) : Bread and cheese, cold tea.	At 5 o'clock (mother) : Bread and butter, tea. At 6 o'clock (two brothers) : Potatoes, greens, pig-meat, tea.	At 9 o'clock (mother and myself) : Bread, soup, cow-heel.[1] Two brothers supper out.

[1] Brought home by one of the sons as a delicacy for his mother, who was ill.

	Breakfast.	Dinner.	Tea.	Supper.
THURSDAY...	At 8 o'clock (mother and myself) : Dry toast and tea, bloaters, bread, tea. At 7 o'clock (two brothers) : Fried bloaters, tea.	At 1 o'clock (Mother and myself) : Soup and bread. Two brothers (taken away) : Bread, meat, cold tea.	At 4 o'clock (mother and myself) : Bread and butter, tea. At 6 o'clock (two brothers) : Fried potatoes and bacon, tea.	At 8 o'clock (mother and myself) : Soup. At 9 o'clock (two brothers) : Bread and cheese, cocoa.
FRIDAY ...	At 8 o'clock (mother and myself) : Bread and butter, tea. Two brothers (taken away) : Cold meat with cold tea.	Mother and myself : Fried bacon, potatoes, cocoa. Two brothers (taken away) : Bread and cheese, cold tea.	At 4 o'clock (mother) : Bread and butter. Myself away. At 6 o'clock (two brothers) : Bacon, potatoes, tea.	At 8 o'clock (mother and myself) : Bread and milk. At 9 o'clock (two brothers) : Bread and cheese, cocoa.
SATURDAY...	At 8 o'clock (mother and myself) : Dry toast, tea, potatoes, bacon. At 7 o'clock (two brothers) : Bacon, eggs, bread, tea.	Two brothers (taken away) : Bread and cheese, cold tea.	At 4 o'clock (mother and myself) : Bread and butter, tea. At 6 o'clock (two brothers) : Bread, fried meat, tea.	At 9 o'clock (mother and myself) : Fish, bread, cocoa. At 10 o'clock (two brothers) : Bread and cheese, cocoa.
SUNDAY ...	At 8 o'clock (all together) : Bread, fish, tea.	At 1 o'clock (all together) : Potatoes, greens, beef.	At 5 o'clock (all together) : Bread and butter, cake, tea.	At 9 o'clock : Bread, meat, cocoa, for us all.
MONDAY ...	Two brothers (taken away) : Meat and bread, cold tea. At 8 o'clock (mother and myself) : Bacon, bread, tea.	Two brothers (taken away) : Bread and cheese, cold tea. Myself : Bread and jam at school. Mother : Fried potatoes, bread, cocoa.	At 6 o'clock (all together) : Tea, toast.	At 9 o'clock (mother and myself) : Bread and milk. At 10 o'clock (two brothers) : Bread and cheese, cocoa.
TUESDAY ...	Two brothers : Bread, meat, cold tea. At 8 o'clock (mother and myself) : Fried bacon, bread.	At 1 o'clock (myself) : Bread and dripping. Mother : Bread, meat, cocoa. Two brothers (taken away) : Bread and cheese, cold tea.	At 5 o'clock (mother) : Bread and butter, tea. Myself out. At 6 o'clock (two brothers) : Potatoes, stew.	At 9 o'clock (mother) : Bread and butter, cocoa. At 10 o'clock (two brothers) : Bread and cheese, cocoa.
WEDNESDAY	At 8 o'clock (mother) : Bacon, fried potatoes. At 7 o'clock (two brothers) : Bacon, potatoes, tea.	Brother : Bread, meat, cheese, cold tea. Mother : Soup. Myself : Bread and jam at school.	At 4.30 (mother) : Bread, fish. At 6 o'clock (myself and two brothers) : Potatoes, cabbage, meat, bread, tea.	Mother and myself : Beef, bread. At 10 o'clock (two brothers) : Bread and cheese, cocoa.
THURSDAY...	Mother and myself : Bread and butter, tea. Two brothers (taken away) : Bread and butter, cold tea.	Mother : Soup. Myself : Bread and dripping at school. Two brothers (taken away) : Bread and meat.	At 5.30 (all together) : Fried bacon, onions, bread.	Mother : Bread, meat, cocoa. Myself : Bread and cheese.
FRIDAY ...	Two brothers (taken out) : Bread, meat, cold tea. Mother and myself : Bread and butter, tea.	Two brothers : Bread and cheese, cold tea. Mother : Bread and soup. Myself : Bread and jam.	Mother : Bread and butter, cold tea. Myself away. Two brothers : Vegetables, bacon.	Myself away. At 9 o'clock (mother and two brothers) : Onion broth.

BUDGET No. 46.

Income Sufficient + 14s. 8d.

Family: Labourer, wife, son (artisan), two children, aged mother-in-law.

The family live in a four-roomed cottage and have a garden and allotment. They pay £5 per annum rent.

Father and son belong to good friendly societies. Man and wife are insured, the money to be paid to survivor on death of either. The children pay money into Corsley School savings bank.

The man's wage is 14s., out of which he keeps 1s. "Sunday money," paying 13s. to his wife for housekeeping. The son, who is earning good wages, pays 8s. 6d., or less than half, to his mother. Total available for housekeeping, 21s. 6d.

The wife and other children do not go out to work, but some garden produce is sold.

Expenditure.

Mrs. J. pays ready money for everything. She pays the baker one week and the grocer the next.

She usually buys per week seven or eight 4-lb. loaves, and two joints of meat, about 6 lb. and 4 lb., and takes 1d. worth of milk per day.

The family do not as a rule take their meals all together.

They eat meat every day, and eat more meat now than they did before the eldest son began to earn money. The children always have a little meat for tea or supper.

Mrs. J. gives the following account of their usual menu :

Breakfast.—Bacon or toast. Son sometimes has porridge. Children occasionally bread and milk. Formerly they always had bacon for breakfast, but they are now tired of it and often have toast instead.

Dinner.—Father and son take dinner out with them—always bread, meat, and cheese. The children take dinner to school, bread and butter or bread and jam. Mrs. J. sometimes keeps some vegetables hot for the children when they come home from school.

Tea.—All except the two men take tea, with cake, bread, butter, and jam.

Supper.—Father and son, and sometimes the children, "if they fancy it," take supper. Meat and vegetables, bread and cheese.

BUDGET No. 131.

Income Sufficient + 10s. 8d.

Family : Labourer in Frome, wife, wife's mother (three adults). Five-roomed cottage with large garden.

Mrs. J. is a careful manager, buying her groceries monthly at a Working Men's Co-operative Store, and receiving a half-yearly dividend on the money expended. She is careful not to waste any of the fat from the meat, which can be utilised for making cakes or stock for soup. She buys in a small cask of beer, so that her husband may have his pint for supper without going to the public-house. When the couple married they had a little capital left after furnishing their cottage, and they have made it a rule always to pay ready money for all purchases, thus getting them cheaper.

The following is an average of the amount of food-stuffs used weekly :

20 lb. bread.	2¾ lb. sugar.
5½ lb. fresh meat.	6 oz. tea.
1 lb. salt meat.	2 lb. flour.
1½ lb. butter.	8 pints milk.
¾ lb. cheese.	8 pints ale.

Blacking, blacklead, ink, &c., cost about one farthing per fortnight.

Other expenses are collection at church, 3d. per week ; newspapers, 2d. per week ; magazine, 1d. per month ; 1s. annually to Home Missions and 1s. 6d. to the Bell-ringers.

Mr. J.'s ordinary wage is 17s. He keeps 1s. 6d. of this for the Amalgamated Weekly Club, tobacco, and pocket-money.

Mrs. J. pays £2 per annum into the Oddfellows Club, which ensures a weekly sum during illness, with medical attendance and medicine.

The following diary of purchases and food was kept by Mrs. J. herself during January, 1907, and is, no doubt, quite accurate. They live, she says, much more cheaply in the summer, requiring less meat and hot soup, and saving coal by the use of an oil-stove.

	s.	d.
Money received from husband	15	6
„ „ „ mother	3	6
	19	0

EXPENDITURE.

January 14–21, 1907. *First week.*

	s.	d.		s.	d.
Monday :			Forward	8	9
1 cwt. coal	1	3	Saturday :		
Soap 3d., soda 1d.,			6 oz. tea	0	7½
starch and blue 1d.	0	5	2¾ lb. sugar	0	6
2½ lb. collar of beef...	1	3	1 lb. bacon	0	9
3 2-lb. loaves... ...	0	6¾	¾ lb. cheese	0	6
Tuesday :			1 oz. pepper ½ lb. salt	0	1¼
Clothing club ...	1	0	2 lb. flour	0	4
Wednesday :			8 pts. milk	0	8
6 kippers	0	6	8 pts. dinner ale ...	0	10
1 lb. pork	0	8	Biscuits 1d., ¼ lb. cur-		
Thursday :			rants 1d.	0	2
3 2-lb. loaves... ...	0	6¾	Rice 1d., 3 eggs 3d.	0	4
Friday :			Whiskey	0	3
1½ lb. fresh butter ...	1	10½	Peppermint	0	0½
½ gal. lamp oil and			4 2-lb. loaves ...	0	9
1 lb. candles ...	0	8	2 lb. 2 oz. pork ...	1	4
	8	9		15	11¼

In hand for collection, papers, rent, club, clothing, 3s. 0¾d.

January 22–28, 1907. *Second week.*

	s.	d.		s.	d.
Monday :			Forward	11	0
2 cwt. coal	2	6	Saturday :		
Soap 3d., soda 1d.,			1 oz. peppermint and		
starch and blue 1d.	0	5	¼ lb. salt	0	1¼
3 2-lb. loaves... ...	0	6¾	2 lb. flour	0	4
Tuesday :			8 pts. milk	0	8
2 lb. pork, salted ...	1	4	8 pts. dinner ale ...	0	10
Thursday :			Suet 1d., carroway		
4 2-lb. loaves... ...	0	9	seeds ¼d.	0	1¼
½ bullock's check ...	0	7½	Gin and peppermints	0	1½
Friday :			7 eggs...	0	6
1½ lb. fresh butter ...	1	10½	3 lb. roasting beef for		
Saturday :			Sunday	2	0
3 2-lb. loaves ...	0	6¾		15	8
6 oz. tea	0	7½			
2¾ lb. sugar	0	6			
1 lb. bacon	0	9			
¾ lb. cheese	0	6			
	11	0			

In hand for collection, papers, rent, club, and clothing, 3s. 4d.

	Breakfast.	Dinner.	Tea.	Supper.
MONDAY ...	Husband.—6 a.m. : Hot tea with milk and sugar, bread and butter. 8.30 a.m. : Cold tea, bread and butter. Mother and myself.— 6 a.m. : Hot tea. 8 a.m. : Hot tea, bread and butter.	Husband.—12.30 p.m. : Cold roast pork, bread, mince-pies, cold tea, cheese. Mother and myself.— 12.30 p.m. : Hot stewed beef and onions, boiled celery, parsnips, potatoes, apple-tart.	Husband.—6 p.m. : Hot stewed beef and onions, boiled celery and potatoes, hot tea with milk and sugar. Mother and myself.— 4 p.m. : Hot tea with milk and sugar, bread and butter, cake.	Husband.—8 p.m. : One pint of beer, three thin lunch biscuits. Mother and myself.— 8 p.m. : half pint of beer, six biscuits.
TUESDAY ...	Husband.—6 a.m. : Hot tea, bread and butter. 8.30 a.m. : Hot bacon, one egg, bread, cold tea. Mother and myself.— Hot tea with milk and sugar. 8.30 a.m. : Hot bacon, bread, hot tea with milk and sugar.	Husband.—12.30 p.m. : Cold roast pork, bread, mince - pie, cheese, cold tea. Mother and myself. — 12.30 p.m. : Hot stewed pork, onions, boiled celery, potatoes, bread, apple-tart.	Husband.—6 p.m. : Hot stewed pork, boiled onions, turnips, potatoes, hot tea with milk and sugar. Mother and myself.— 4 p.m. : Hot tea with milk and sugar, bread and butter, cake.	Husband.—8 p.m. : One pint of beer, two biscuits. Mother and myself.— 8 p.m. : Two glasses hot peppermint, bread and butter.
WEDNESDAY	Husband.—6 a.m. : Hot tea with milk and sugar, bread and butter. 8.30 a.m. : Hot fried bacon, and bread, cold tea. Mother and myself.— 6 a.m. : Hot tea with milk and sugar. 8.30 a.m. : Bread and butter, strawberry jam, hot tea with milk and sugar.	Husband.—12.30 p.m. : Cold stewed beef, bread, mince-pie, cold tea. Mother and myself.— 12.30 p.m. : Hot roast pork, boiled greens, potatoes.	Husband.—6 p.m. : Hot roast pork, boiled greens and potatoes, hot tea with milk and sugar. Mother and myself.— bread and butter, cake, hot tea with milk and sugar.	Husband.—8 p.m. : One pint of beer. Mother and myself.— 8 p.m. : One glass of beer, one wineglass of whiskey and water, bread and butter.
THURSDAY...	Husband—6 a.m. : Hot tea, bread and butter, 8.30 a.m. : Bread and butter, toasted kipper, cold tea. Mother and myself.— 6. a.m. : Hot tea. 8.30 a.m. : Bread and butter, two kippers, toasted, hot tea with milk and sugar.	Husband.—12.30 p.m. : Cold pork, bread, cheese, cold tea. Mother and myself.— 12.30 p.m. : Cold beef, pickled onions, bread, rice-pudding, baked and stewed apples.	Husband.—6 p.m. : stewed beef and onions, boiled turnips and potatoes, baked rice-pudding, stewed apples. Mother and myself.— 4 p.m. : Bread and butter, cake, hot tea with milk and sugar.	Husband.—8 p.m. : One pint of beer. Mother and myself.— 8 p.m. : Two small glasses of beer (or ¼ pint), bread and butter, cheese. (The above means one piece of bread and butter for mother, one piece of bread and cheese for myself.)
FRIDAY ...	Husband—6 a.m. : Hot tea, bread and butter. 8.30 a.m. : Toasted kipper, bread and butter, cold tea. Mother and myself.— 6 a.m. : Hot tea. 8.30 a.m. : Toasted kipper, bread and butter, hot tea.	Husband.—12.30 p.m. : Bread and cheese, pickled onions, cold tea. Mother and myself.— 12.30 p.m. : Boiled bacon, greens, potatoes, boiled apple-dumplings.	Husband.—6 p.m. : Boiled bacon and greens, boiled potatoes, boiled apple dumpling, hot tea. Mother and myself.— 4 p.m. : Bread and butter, cake, hot tea.	Husband.—8 p.m. : One pint of beer.
SATURDAY...	Husband.—6 a.m. : Hot tea, bread and butter. 8.30 a.m. : Hot fried bacon, one egg, and bread, cold tea. Mother and myself.— 6 a.m. Hot tea. 8.30 a.m. : One boiled egg, bread and butter, cold boiled bacon, bread, hot tea.	Husband.—1.40 p.m. : Hot roast pork, potatoes, greens, stewed apples. Mother and myself : 1.40 p.m. : Hot roast pork, potatoes, greens, stewed apples.	Husband.—5.15 p.m. : Bread and butter, celery, cake, jam-tarts, hot tea, milk, sugar. Mother and myself.— 5.15 p.m. : Bread and butter, celery, cake, jam-tarts. Hot tea, milk, sugar.	Mother and myself.— 8 p.m. : One glass of beer, wineglass of whiskey and water, two pieces of bread and butter.
SUNDAY ...	Husband.—5.30 a.m. : Hot tea, bread and butter. 8.30 a.m. : Bread and butter, cold tea. Mother and myself.— 5.30 a.m. : Hot tea. 8.30 a.m. : Bread and butter, hot tea.	Husband.—12.30 p.m. : Cold roast pork, bread, jam turnover. Mother and myself.— 1 p.m. : Cold roast pork, bread, hot apple-tart.	Husband.—6.15 p.m. : Hot fried bacon, two eggs, bread, one pint of beer. Mother and myself.— 4 p.m. : Bread and butter, cake, hot tea.	Husband. — 8.15 p.m. : One pint of beer. Mother and myself. — 8.15 p.m. : One small glass of beer, one wineglass of whiskey and water.

	Breakfast.	Dinner.	Tea.	Supper.
MONDAY ...	Husband.—6 a.m.: Hot tea, bread and butter. 8.30. a.m.: Bread and butter, cold tea. Mother and myself.—6. a.m.: Hot tea, 8.30. a.m.: Fried bacon, bread, hot tea.	Husband.—12.30 p.m.: Cold roast pork and bread, jam turnover, cold tea. Mother and myself.—12.30 p.m.: One poached egg, bread and butter, bread and cheese, one glass of beer, apple-tart.	Husband.—6 p.m.: Hot pork, greens, potatoes, apple-tart, hot tea. Mother and myself.—4 p.m.: Bread and butter, cake, celery, hot tea.	Husband.—8 p.m.: One pint of beer Mother and myself.—8 p.m.: Two glasses of hot peppermint, two pieces of bread and butter.
TUESDAY ...	Husband.—6 a.m.: Hot tea, bread and butter, 8.30 a.m.: Fried bacon, one egg, bread, cold tea. Mother and myself.—6 a.m.: Hot tea. 8.30 a.m.: Bread and butter, hot tea.	Husband.—12.30 p.m.: Cold roast pork and bread, jam turnover. Mother and myself.—12.30 p.m. Hot stewed pork, and onions, boiled celery and potatoes, stewed apples.	Husband.—6 p.m.: Hot stewed pork, onions, boiled celery and potatoes, hot tea. Mother and myself.— 4 p.m.: Bread and butter, cake, hot tea.	Husband.—8 p.m.: One pint of beer. Mother and myself.—8 p.m.: Two glasses of peppermint, bread and butter.
WEDNESDAY	Husband.—6 a.m.: Hot tea, bread and butter. 8.30 a.m.: Hot fried bacon, one egg, bread, cold tea. Mother and myself.—6 a.m.: Hot tea. 8.30 a.m.: Fried bacon and bread, hot tea.	Husband.—12.30 p.m. Cold stewed pork and bread, jam turnover, cold tea. Mother and myself.—12.30 p.m.: Cold stewed pork, bread, boiled apple-dumplings.	Husband.—6 p.m.: Boiled vegetable marrow, potatoes, fried bacon, boiled apple-dumpling, hot tea. Mother and myself.—4 p.m.: Bread and butter, cake, hot tea.	Husband.—8 p.m.: One pint of beer. Mother and myself.—8 p.m.: Two glass of beer (or ⅜ pint), two pieces of bread and butter.
THURSDAY...	Husband.—6 a.m.: Hot tea, bread and butter. 8.30 a.m.: Bread and butter, cold tea. Mother and myself.—6 a.m.: Hot tea. 8.30 a.m.: Bread and butter, hot tea.	Husband.—12,30 p.m.: Cold stewed pork, bread and cheese, one pint of beer. Mother and myself.—12.30. p.m.: Hot stewed bullock's cheek, onions, parsnips, potatoes, and suet-dumpling.	Husband.— 6 p.m.: Hot stewed bullock's cheek, onions, parsnips, potatoes, suet-dumpling and large cup of hot soup. Mother and myself.—4 p.m.: Bread and butter, blackberry jam, hot tea.	Husband —9 p.m.: One glass hot beer. Mother and myself.—8 p.m.: Two glasses of hot peppermint, one piece of bread and cheese, one piece of bread and butter.
FRIDAY ...	Husband.—8 a.m.: Ho fried bacon, two eggs, bread and hot tea. Mother and myself.—8 a.m.: Hot fried bacon and bread, hot tea.	Husband.—12.30 p.m.: Hot stewed bullock's cheek, bread and half a pint of hot soup. Mother and myself.—12.30 p.m.: Hot stewed bullock's cheek, onions, parsnips, potatoes, and suet-dumplings.	Husband. — 6 p.m.: Hot stewed bullock's cheek, onions, parsnips, potatoes and suet-dumpling. Mother and myself.—4 p.m.: Bread and butter, blackberry jam, hot tea.	Husband.—9 p.m. One glass of hot beer. Mother and myself.—8 p.m.: One breakfast cup of bread and milk, one glass of hot peppermint, one piece of bread and butter.
SATURDAY...	Husband.—8.30 a.m.: Hot fried bacon, one egg, bread, hot tea. Mother and myself.—8.30. a.m.: One boiled egg, bread and butter, hot tea.	1.40 p.m.: Hot stewed bullock's cheek, onions, parsnips, and potatoes, with hot suet-dumplings.	5.30 p.m: Bread and butter, cake and jam, hot tea.	8.30 p.m. Two glasses of beer, one glass of gin and water, one piece of bread and butter and two pieces of bread and cheese.
SUNDAY ...	8.30 a.m.: Fried bacon and bread, two eggs, bread and butter, hot tea.	1 p.m.: Hot roast rib of beef, greens, potatoes hot apple-tart, two glasses of beer.	4 p.m.: Bread and butter, cake and blackberry jam, hot tea.	8.30 p.m.: Cold roast rib of beef, bread, and pickled onions, cold apple-tart, two glasses of beer, one wineglass of gin and water.

BUDGET No. 105.

Income sufficient + 14s. 4d.

Shoemaker, daughter, two sons (artisan and labourer), one out of work. Earnings uncertain, but do not average " anything like " 10s. per week. Pig-keeping helps, and one son contributes 7s. per week to the housekeeping. The father usually does the family marketing as the daughter is inexperienced, and does not buy so economically. The family appears to be in quite comfortable circumstances. The father does not belong to a club. One son belongs to a good friendly society. The daughter insures her father.

1d. worth of milk is purchased every day ; amount obtained varies with the season.

The daughter cooks every day—sometimes twice a day.

EXPENDITURE.

January 7–13, 1906.	s.	d.	*January 14–20*, 1906.	s.	d.
Milk	0	7	Sugar	0	6
Mutton chops	0	10	Pepper...	0	3
Pork	2	0	Butter	0	7½
Cheese	1	0	Cheese...	1	10
Fish	0	8	Bacon	2	0
Sugar	0	8	Fish	0	9
Tea	1	0	Loin of mutton and		
1 lb. butter	1	3	mutton chops ...	4	0
Ham	3	0	Milk	0	7
			Tea	1	7
	11	0	Bread	0	4½
				12	6
			Bread bill " bonfire night " (Nov. 5th) to Jan. 14th	1 0	0½
			£1	12	6½

This budget was nominally kept by the daughter, but she was absent part of the time, so it is possible that strict accuracy was not observed in filling in from memory. The father estimated that over 17s. worth of provisions were consumed during each week, though the amount purchased (omitting the bread bill) does not appear so large.

	Breakfast.	Dinner.	Tea.	Supper.
MONDAY ...	8.30 a.m.: Tea, milk, bread, boiled bacon.	None.	4 p.m.: Toast, bread and butter, honey.	8 p.m.: Potatoes, cabbage, boiled bacon.
TUESDAY ...	8 a.m.: Tea, milk, bread and butter, boiled bacon.	12 o'clock. Potatoes, sprouts, roast mutton.	5 p.m.: Bread and butter, tea, milk.	9 p.m.: Bread and cheese, Father, brandy and water.
WEDNESDAY	8 a.m.: Tea, milk, bread, bacon.	1.30 p.m.: Mashed potato, beef, bread.	5 p.m.: Bread and butter, cake, tea, milk.	9 p.m.: Bread and cheese, cocoa, milk, mutton.
THURSDAY...	8.30 a.m.: Tea, milk, bread, bacon, egg.	1.30 p.m.: Potatoes, sprouts, bread, mutton.	5 p.m.: Tea, milk, butter, bread, jam.	9 p.m.: Bread and cheese, beef, pickled cabbage, cocoa, milk.
FRIDAY ...	8.45 a.m.: Tea, beef, marmalade, milk.	2 p.m.: Tea, bread and butter, milk.	None.	Potatoes, stew, bread, soup.
SATURDAY...	8.15 am.: Tea milk, bread, bacon.	1.45 p.m.: Bacon fried potatoes, bread, tea, milk.	6 p.m.: Milk, tea, toast, honey.	9.30 p.m.: Bread and cheese, pickles, butter, cocoa, milk.
SUNDAY ...	8.45 a.m.: Tea, milk, bread, fish, vinegar.	12.30 p.m.: Potatoes, sprouts, bread, pork.	4.30 p.m.: Tea milk, bread and butter, toast, jam.	9 p.m.: Bread and cheese, pickles, glass of beer.
MONDAY ...	8.30 a.m.: Tea, milk, bread, toast, bacon.	1 p.m.: Potatoes, cabbage, pork, bread.	5 p.m.: Tea, milk, bread and butter.	9.15 p.m.: Bread and cheese, glass of beer.
TUESDAY ...	8 a.m.: Tea, milk, bread, ham, fried potatoes.	12.30 p.m.: Bread and cheese, pickles, coffee, milk.	4.30 p.m.: Tea, milk, bread and butter, honey.	8 p.m.: Potatoes, cabbage, bread, ham.
WEDNESDAY	8 a.m.: Tea, milk, bread, bacon.	1 p.m.: Potatoes, cabbage, bread, ham.	4. p.m.: Tea, milk, bread and butter.	9.15 p.m.: Bread and cheese, beer.
THURSDAY...	8 a.m.: Coffee, milk, bread, fried bacon.	1 p.m.: Mashed potatoes, bread, boiled bacon.	5.30 p.m.: Tea, milk, bread and butter, toast.	9 p.m.: Bread and cheese, butter, cocoa, milk.
FRIDAY ...	7.45 a.m.: Tea, milk, bread, butter, ham.	12.30 p.m.: Bread and cheese, butter, roast onions.	4.30 p.m.: Tea, milk, bread and butter.	7.30 p.m.: Potatoes, cabbage, bread, bacon.
SATURDAY...	8 p.m.: Tea, milk, bread and butter, toast.	1.30 p.m.: Potatoes, cabbage, bread, bacon.	6 p.m.: Milk, tea, bread and butter, honey.	9.15 p.m.: Cocoa, milk, bread, fish.
SUNDAY ...	8.45 a.m.: Tea, milk, bread and butter, fish	1 p.m.: Potatoes, sprouts, mutton, bread.	4.30 p.m.: Tea, milk, bread and butter, honey, cake.	9.15 p.m.: Bread and cheese, milk, cocoa, beer.

BUDGET No. 117.

Income ample.

Family: Father (retired artisan), mother (midwife), two sons (artisans, but when out of work, market-gardeners jointly with father), daughter (does housework and earns some money gloving).

Total income of family not given, and was, no doubt, uncertain, as sons were out of regular work, but the family were probably quite comfortably off.

The father and eldest brother belonged to a good club, but father was resigning his membership. The youngest brother was not in a club.

Rent for cottage, large garden, and common for fowls and pigs, £10 per annum.

Milk taken :—½d. one day, 1d. the next, delivered at door, and sometimes a 1d. worth from another farmer during the day. Average 1d. per day. Price 1½d. per pint.

Corsley Family Budgets

January, 1907. First week.

	s.	d.
Money received from son	8	0
" " " "	8	0
" " " daughter	5	0
	21	0

EXPENDITURE.

	s.	d.		s.	d.
2½ lbs. 2 oz. beef	1	9	Forward	10	7
1½ lbs. mutton	1	1½	Soap	0	3
1½ lbs. cheese	1	0	Starch	0	2
1½ lbs. butter	1	10½	Blue	0	0½
Bacon	0	10	Coal	2	6
3 lbs. sugar	0	6	12 small loaves	2	3
¾ lb. tea	1	6	Flour	0	3
Cocoa	1	3	Rabbit	0	8
Oil	0	6		16	8½
Candles	0	3			
	10	7			

Second week.

	s.	d.
Beef	3	3
Fresh herrings	0	6
Kippers and haddock	1	3
Extract of beef	1	3
Biscuits	0	6
1 lb. butter	1	3
	8	0

The regular weekly expenses of the family, besides food, clothing, &c., were as follows:

	s.	d.
Doctor (club)	0	2½
Club	0	9½
Insurance	0	4
*Rent (?)	0	6
Garden (?)	0	3
Coal (paid fortnightly)	1	10½

This budget was kept by the daughter, and probably the diary of meals is fairly accurate, though the list of things bought appears to be very incomplete, and there is some confusion in the statements as to expenses.

* Possibly these sums were put by weekly towards rent paid quarterly. The total rent cannot have been less than 3s. 6d. to 7s. weekly, and the statement that it was £10 per annum is probably accurate.

	Breakfast.	Dinner.	Tea.	Supper.
SATURDAY ...	8.30 (No. of persons to breakfast, five) : Bacon, bread and butter, tea. 9.30 (Father's breakfast): Cold mutton, cocoa.	1 o'clock : Bread and cheese, cocoa. Father's dinner : Bread and butter, boiled egg.	4 o'clock : Buttered toast, tea.	9 o'clock: Bread and cheese, quaker oats, cocoa.
SUNDAY ...	8.30 Bacon, toast, tea. 9.30 (Father's breakfast): Bread and butter, boiled egg, cocoa.	1 o'clock : Boiled rabbit, ham, potatoes, turnip, carrots, jam tart, tea.	4 o'clock : Bread and butter, toast, tea.	9 o'clock: Bread and cheese, pickles, cocoa, beer.
MONDAY ...	8.30 Bacon and eggs, tea, bread and butter. 9.30 (Father's breakfast) : Cocoa, bread and butter, boiled egg.	1 o'clock : Cold rabbit, ham, bread, cup of tea, jam tart. Father had cocoa, and one cup before dinner.	4 o'clock : Bread and butter, cake, tea.	9 o'clock : Bread and cheese, tea. Father had mutton chop, cocoa, and had two cups of cocoa in the afternoon.
TUESDAY ...	8.30 Bacon and fried potatoes, bread and butter, tea. 9.30 (Father's breakfast) : Mutton, cocoa.	1 o'clock : Roast beef, Brussels sprouts, potatoes.	Bread and butter, jam, tea.	Bread and cheese, pickles, cocoa. Father had three cups of cocoa between meals to-day.
WEDNESDAY	8.30 Bacon and fried potatoes, bread and butter, tea. 9.30 (Father's breakfast): Cold mutton, cocoa.	1 o'clock : Cold beef, bread, tea. Father had cold mutton, cocoa.	4 o'clock : Bread and butter, jam, tea.	9 o'clock : Bread and cheese, pickles, cocoa.
THURSDAY...	8.30 Bacon and fried bread, tea. 9.30 (Father's breakfast) : Bread and butter, boiled egg, cocoa.	1 o'clock : Potatoes and stew, beef, carrots, onions, tea, biscuits.	4 o'clock : Bread and butter, toast, tea.	9 o'clock : Bread and cheese, tea. Father had cold mutton, cocoa.
FRIDAY ...	8.30 Bacon and fried potatoes, tea. 9.30 (Father's breakfast) : Bread and butter, boiled egg, cocoa.	1 o'clock : Fried bacon, eggs, bread, tea.	4 o'clock : Bread and butter, jam, tea.	9 o'clock : Rabbit, potatoes, turnip.
SATURDAY...	8.30 : Fried bacon, bread and butter, tea. 9.30 (Father's breakfast): Bread and butter, boiled eggs, cocoa.	1 o'clock : Fried bacon, bread and cheese, cocoa. Father's dinner : A mutton chop, cocoa.	4 o'clock : Bread and butter, toast, tea.	9 o'clock : Fresh herrings, bread and cheese, beer, cocoa.
SUNDAY ...	8.30: Bacon, bread and butter, tea. 9.30 (Father's breakfast) : Mutton chop, cocoa.	1 o'clock : Roast beef, Brussels sprouts, potatoes.	4 o'clock : Bread and butter, jam.	9 o'clock : Cold meat, cocoa.
MONDAY ...	8.30: Bacon, fried potatoes, tea. 9.30 (Father's breakfast) : Cold mutton, cocoa.	1 o'clock : Potatoes, cold meat, tea.	4 o'clock : Bread and butter, toast, tea.	9 o'clock : Bread and cheese, beer, cocoa.
TUESDAY ...	8.30: Bacon, fried potatoes, tea. 9.30 (Father's breakfast) : Cold mutton, cocoa.	1 o'clock : Potatoes, stew, beef, carrots, onions. 2 o'clock : Cup of tea.	4 o'clock : Bread and butter, jam, tea.	9 o'clock : Bread and cheese, cocoa.
WEDNESDAY	8.30: Buttered toast, tea. 9.30 (Father's breakfast) : Cold mutton, cocoa.	1 o'clock : Bread, cold meat, pea-soup.	4 o'clock : Bread and butter, jam, tea.	9 o'clock : Bread and cheese, cocoa.
THURSDAY...	8.30 : Bacon, fried potatoes, tea. 9.30 (Father's breakfast) : Bread and butter, boiled eggs, cocoa.	Bread and butter, boiled eggs, tea.	4 o'clock : Buttered toast, tea.	9 o'clock : Bread and butter, kippers, tea.
FRIDAY ...	8.30: Bacon, fried potatoes, tea. 9.30 (Father's breakfast) : Bread and butter, kipper, cocoa.	1 o'clock : Bread and butter, haddock, tea.	4 o'clock : Buttered toast, bread and butter, tea.	9 o'clock : Bread and cheese, cocoa.

Friendly Societies or Sick Benefit Clubs

IT WILL HAVE been noticed in the family budgets that club money is often put aside every week. Nearly every working-class householder and most of the young men belong to a benefit society, to secure medical attendance and a weekly allowance in case of their own illness, and burial money on the death of themselves or their wives. Thirty-two families were specially questioned as to membership of clubs. In only three cases was it found that the head or principal male wage-earner of the family had no club. The first case was that of a man in receipt of a good pension, who therefore did not need it; the second was a shoemaker, his life being insured by his daughter. The sons of these two men belonged to clubs. The third exception was a man who for some reason in the history of his character or health was refused admittance to the better clubs, and thought the local public-house clubs not worth joining.

In two cases one or more sons living at home with their parents had not joined a club, though their fathers belonged to one. In most families all adult males belonged to a friendly society. These 32 families give a total of 39 men in clubs and 7 men without a club. The 32 householders or principal male wage-earners were 18 labourers, 7 artisans, 4 market gardeners, 1 shopkeeper, 1 brickmaker (on own account), and 1 shoemaker.

A more complete census would probably give much the same results, it being a rare thing to find a Corsley man who does not belong to a sick benefit society.

For more than a century village clubs have existed in Corsley, and these were in a thriving condition at the middle of the nineteenth century. During the last fifteen years branches of the Ancient Shepherds and of the Wilts Working Men's Conservative Benefit Society have been established here; and the old local dividing clubs, being unrenewed by young blood, have fallen more or less into decay. The oldest of these clubs, which lingered on into the twentieth century, was the Corsley Walking Club, broken up in June, 1905.[1] If, as alleged, this club had been founded 107 years before, it was not the first to exist in Corsley.[2] It derived its name from the practice of the members walking round the parish in procession at Whitsuntide, headed by their banner and with a band. Forty years ago there would be 200 men in the procession. They first attended service at the church, then they walked to Corsley House, proceeding thence to Corsley Heath, where the fair was still held at this time. They dined at the public-house and then marched to Lane End and back; after which they were supposed to spend £1 at the public-house. The club-room was built on to the house opposite the Cross Keys Inn, with a separate outside stairway. The club box was stolen or broken into once or twice, and some fifty years ago the members purchased a strong one, bearing the date of 1817, and an inscription stating that it was the property of the Broad and Narrow Weavers' Society, this Society in connection with Shepherds' cloth mills at Frome being broken up at that time.

In about the year 1855 the membership was 230, the practice of belonging to a club being evidently fairly general even in those days of low wages. In 1905, when the club was broken up, only about twelve members remained, most of them being aged men, some of whom were forced to come upon the parish in consequence. About 10s. per head remained to be divided up.

The Corsley Gathering Club, another of the old dividing societies, is still in existence, having about 22 members in the winter of 1905-6. It provides medical attendance and an allowance for twelve weeks in sickness; 1s. is paid on the death of a member by each of the

1   See *Warminster and Westbury Journal*, June 17, 1905.
2   See MS. Corsley Parish Accounts, April, 1789.

others to the widow. The money is divided up every three years. Most of the members of this club are old men.

The Corsley Mutual Provident Society, or Baptists' Club, founded in 1891, is on much the same lines. It throve at first, but has been reduced lately by the competition of the branches of larger clubs lately established in Corsley. In the winter of 1905-6 it had a membership of 22.

Another old parish club, the Working Men's Benefit Society, meets at the 'Three Horse Shoes', Chapmanslade. Particulars of membership have not been ascertained.

This concludes the list of the local parish clubs, so far as can be discovered, though it is not beyond the bounds of possibility that another similar institution may linger in some nook or corner of the parish.

We now come to the new clubs, on county or national basis and established on sound financial principles. The first of these to set up a branch in Corsley was the Loyal Order of Ancient Shepherds, established here in 1893. This branch now has 23 adult and 15 juvenile members resident in Corsley. It aims at providing for its members in sickness and death, and paying old age pensions to those who live to require them.[1] The other new club is the Wiltshire Working Men's Conservative Benefit Society, a non-political club. The Corsley branch was started in 1900. The Society aims at providing for members in sickness and death, and acts as a savings fund. In December, 1905, it had 40 adult members, 3 being women, and 2 juveniles. Only the members of these branch clubs actually residing in Corsley have been enumerated. They also have members residing in other parishes.

The hundred or more persons who constitute the membership of these various clubs by no means include all the men who belong to a friendly society. Many Corsley men belong to the Hearts of Oak, the Oddfellows, and the Foresters, these having no local branch in the

1   See manifesto of the Society.

parish. Most of the men who have migrated from some other parish or district belong to the branch of some club in the locality from which they have come. The exact number belonging to clubs is therefore unknown, but undoubtedly a large estimate should be allowed for members of clubs or branches outside Corsley. Out of 30 men who gave particulars of the club or branch they belonged to, 21 belonged to a Corsley club or branch, 9 to clubs or branches not in Corsley. These were: Hearts of Oak, 1; Foresters, 3; Oddfellows, 3; Warminster branch of Shepherds, 1; the local club of a neighbouring parish, 1. These figures are not, however, sufficient for any statistical conclusions.

Some of the people of Corsley insure themselves, their children, or their parents, but the practice is not very general and amount of insurance is usually very small.

Twenty-three children belonged to the Corsley School Savings Bank in January, 1906, some of whom brought their money regularly, some irregularly. The younger children usually draw it out at intervals. The elder girls keep it in till they leave school, when, no doubt, it helps to provide a clothing outfit for going out to service.

Medical Attendance

MOST OF THE men of Corsley are provided with medical attendance and medicines free by their clubs. Twenty-seven families of labourers, artisans, and market gardeners and women householders, taken at random, were questioned as to medical attendance in case of illness of the women or children. Seven of these, including three laundresses and four families of labourers, belonged to the Medical Club of a Warminster doctor, who, for the payment of 4s. 4d. a year per head for each adult and less for a child, attends in case of illness and provides medicines free. All members of the Medical Club spoke of the kindness and attention which they receive from their doctor.

Four widows were attended and received medicines free from the parish doctor. One of these had belonged to his club, but, on becoming a widow was told that she was no longer to pay a subscription. The only extra expense to members of the Medical Club, and the only charge to those receiving attention free, is any incurred in sending for medicines.

The remaining families were 7 labourers, 3 artisans, and 4 women (laundress, baker, charwoman, and needlewoman with a small property). In these cases the women and children of the family made no provision for medical attendance, but when requiring it paid the usual doctor's fees; 5s. per visit and medicines extra appears to be the customary charge when a doctor is sent for specially, he usually having to drive three or four miles to see a patient in Corsley. Less is charged when the patient attends at the doctor's house. One woman owed £12 after her mother's illness and death. A man had to pay 13s. for three visits and medicine in the illness of his wife.

There are many doctors in Frome and Warminster who attend the poor. They usually allow some time to elapse before asking for settlement of their accounts, and these appear to be often paid in instalments.

In the summer of 1906 it became possible, by the establishment of the Cley Hill Nursing Association, for the people of Corsley to make provision for good nursing in case of sickness. By paying an annual subscription, beginning at 2s. for a labourer, 3s. for an artisan, and rising to 10s. for a large farmer, subscribers are provided with a trained nurse at the same rate per week during sickness. Much of the nursing is still done by local midwives, of whom some account has been given in the section on Women's Work.

15

Ancestry and Children of Corsley

THE READER, IF he refers to the form of inquiry given on p. 135-6, will see that information was asked from every householder as to the birthplace and occupation of himself, his father, and his two grandfathers, his wife's birthplace, the total number of children born to him, distinguishing those still living from those since dead, and finally the present place of abode of his living children. Particulars as to the occupations of all his children over school age were also noted on the forms.

In the present chapter the information thus collected is analysed. In the great majority of cases information was duly obtained respecting the man, his wife, and children. In a fair number the birthplace and occupation of the father, and sometimes one grandfather, was also stated, and in a comparatively few instances particulars for father and both grandfathers were remembered, and the form fully filled up.

All this information is, of course, liable to natural errors from inaccuracy of memory, and from the tendency which many people have to magnify the social position of their family, especially that of their ancestors. The history of some of the present inhabitants shows it to be a common thing for a man to follow many occupations in succession or simultaneously, and in such a case his descendant naturally elects to think of, and dwell on, that one which affords him the most satisfaction; thus, while in a few instances a man has stated that his father started as a labourer, and after a time became a shopkeeper, or acquired a small farm, the majority in such a case have probably simply returned their ancestor as shopkeeper or farmer; and, while some have stated that the father or grandfather 'kept a few cows', which suggests that this was only one of two or more occupations, others, descendants of such small holders, have no doubt set down 'farmer' without qualification.

The result of this is that the number of farmers among the ancestry is probably exaggeratedly large – or at least many of the farms were extremely small, and the farming rather a bye-industry than a main occupation.

Again, in tabulating results, it has usually been necessary, where two or more occupations are set down for one person, to select one of these. In such cases the occupation which seemed the more important has been chosen, so that throughout the tendency is in the direction of calling a man an independent worker, or employer, rather than a wage-earner, when, in fact, simultaneously or in succession he has been both.

With regard to the children, there are a few omissions, and perhaps also some mis-statements. It is likely that some of the children who died in infancy were omitted, and though in nearly all cases the parents appear to have been very frank in giving information, one or two in lunatic asylums or in prison may have been left out. Memory also sometimes failed with regard to the children. One man, for instance, with a long family, after consulting his wife as to the total number, was unable for some time to recall the names and account for them all. It was often necessary to consult the family Bible before a list of the children could be made out, and where this was not kept posted up, sometimes neither wife nor husband could remember the age or year of birth of their children. In stating occupations of children the present occupation only is given, and no account is therefore taken of the fact that some of the men residing here have previously served in the Army. While the following figures do not therefore claim perfect accuracy, they are, taken altogether, a fairly good indication of the origin and migrations of the people, and the degree in which children tend to follow the occupations of their parents among the inhabitants of Corsley.

Average Size of Families in Corsley

W E HAVE PARTICULARS of the children born, and now living or dead, in 195 out of the 220 households of Corsley.

No papers were filled up for the gentlemen's houses, the clergyman, Congregational minister, nor schoolmaster; the police-constable has also been omitted in this classification; particulars are missing for two or three farmers, and one artisan and publican; and a few other papers were not filled up owing to illness or absence.

The 195 householders are of all ages, and some are sons of other householders, and thus come twice into the classification as both parents and children.

The total number of children stated to have been born to these 195 householders is 742, and of these 660 are still living and 92 dead. Many of the latter died in middle age, being children of the oldest living inhabitants of Corsley.

The following is a summary of those born to householders of various occupations:

Occupation.	No. for which Particulars.	No. un-married.	No. married without Children.	No. with Children.	Total No. Children born.	No. still living.	No. dead.	Average No. of Children born per Family. where any.	Percentage of Total dead.
Farmers	28	3	8	17	68	65	3	4	4'6
Market gardeners and marketers ..	9	—	2	7	47	46	1	6'7	2'1
Labourers	32	—	5	27	126	112	24	4'6	21'4
Carters	12	—	2	10	53	50	3	5'3	6'0
Dairymen or cowmen	8	—	1	7	37	34	3	5'3	8'8
Miscellaneous agricultural	8	—	1	7	33	27	6	4'7	22'2
Retired labourers, &c.	9	—	2	7	40	31	9	5'7	29'0
Head gardeners, coachmen, groom-gardeners	7	—	1	6	27	24	3	4'5	12'5
Keepers, &c.	3	—	—	3	28	27	1	9'3	3'7
Manual workers residing in Corsley, but working elsewhere	3	—	1	2	14	9	5	7'0	55'5
Miscellaneous, residing in Corsley, retired from work elsewhere	8	1	2	5	18	15	3	3'6	20'0
Tradesmen and dealers	5	—	—	5	28	23	5	5'6	21'7
Independent workers (brickmaker, saddler, and 2 shoemakers)	4	—	2	2	21	21	—	10'5	0'0
Artisans	22	—	2	20	79	70	9	4'0	8'86
Women householders	37	7	3	27	123	106	17	4'5	16'0
	195	11	32	142	742	660	92	5'2	12'3

In the following table the last two columns of the preceding are arranged in order according to the average number of births per family to each occupation.

	Average No. of Children born per family, where any.	Percentage of Total dead.
Miscellaneous, retired from work, not in Corsley	[1] 3·6	[2] 20·0
Farmers	4·0	4·6
Artisans	4·0	8·86
Servants (head gardeners, coachmen, grooms)	4·5	12·5
Women householders ...	4·5	[2] 16·0
Labourers	4·6	21·4
Miscellaneous—agriculture ...	4·7	22·2
Carters	5·3	6·0
Dairymen or cowmen... ...	5·3	8·8
Tradesmen and dealers ...	5·6	21·7
Retired labourers	5·7	[2] 29·0
Market gardeners	6·7	2·1
Persons working elsewhere ...	7·0	55·5
Keepers	9·3	3·7
Independent workers	10·5	0·0

All the 195 householders with the exception of 4 farmers, one being retired from another parish, and 7 women are, or have been, married. One or two other unmarried male householders are omitted, since particulars were not obtained. A large proportion of the married farmers are childless, because the class includes several labourers who, having no children, were able to save sufficient capital to take a small farm. The average number of children born in each farmer's family is small, being 4, but the number of these surviving is large, only 4.6 per cent having since died, though some middle-aged and a few old people are included in the class. Among the artisans there are only two childless couples. The average number of births per family is

1 Possibly the small number of children returned for this group is due to some of the forms being incompletely filled up.

2 These groups contain many old persons and therefore have an abnormally large percentage dead.

4, like that of farmers, and the percentage of deaths is also not large. Gardeners and coachmen have slightly larger families and also more deaths. But when we come to labourers and miscellaneous agricultural workers, we find only a slightly larger average of births per family, but a greatly increased number of deaths, and since the retired labourers, including most of the aged, are given separately this indicates an unnecessarily high infantile mortality rate and a wastage of human life. Carters and dairymen show a higher percentage of births and a low rate of deaths, the latter being probably mainly due to a lower average age among carters and cowmen than among labourers; it might also be partly the result of the higher rate of wages among the former, and facilities for obtaining milk among the latter, producing a lower death rate for the young children.

But the most remarkable fact that comes out of these figures is the high number of births and very small proportion of deaths in the seven market gardeners' families, there being 6.7, as compared with 4.0 children born on the average, and less than half as many dying as in the farmers' families, while there are 6.7 as compared with 4.6 born, and only about one-tenth as many dying as in labourers' families.

It must be borne in mind that the number of families in most of these groups is too small to afford reliable statistical results, since one or two exceptional cases are sufficient to alter the whole, and these figures must only be taken for what they are worth. The average number of children born per family to, the total of 142 families with children is 5.2.

Birthplace and Migrations of Corsley People

SOME PARTICULARS AS to birthplace have been obtained from 198 householders, and the results are given in a table. Out of 198 householders, including 36 women, 107 were born in Corsley and 58 in the neighbourhood, while 33, or 16.6 per cent, were born more than twenty miles from the parish.[1] Particulars are given of 167 grandfathers. Of these, 76 were born in Corsley, 63 in the neighbourhood, and 28, or 16.6, not in the neighbourhood. Presumably a large proportion of those, either grandfathers or fathers, of whom their descendants could tell nothing, were of Corsley descent, migration being an event which would probably be remembered in the family. Out of 159 fathers of whom particulars were given, 90 were Corsley born, and 45 were born in the neighbourhood, while 24, or nearly 15.1 per cent were strangers.

Of the male householders 12 gave no particulars as to the birthplace of their wives, a few of them being unmarried. We have particulars therefore respecting the wives of 150; 65 had married women of Corsley birth, 50 had married wives from the neighbourhood, and 35, or 23.3 per cent, had married strangers. Some of the men, not of Corsley birth, residing here are married to women born in the parish, there being frequently a family connection which induced persons born elsewhere to migrate here.

The 198 householders, including widows, have 456 living sons and daughters over school age. Of these, 200 are residing in Corsley and 256 are residing elsewhere. The latter include many who, though their parents are now inhabitants of Corsley, were born before they came here, and who therefore may never have been in the parish. We shall see presently what proportion of males and females have left the place, and what kind of occupations they are following.

---

1   Known places within a radius of twenty miles have been included as 'near Corsley', but as many of the localities were unknown these may have been wrongly grouped; the error in this case will generally be in the direction of making too many 'strangers'.

Occupation	ADULT CHILDREN Migrated elsewhere	ADULT CHILDREN Residing in Corsley	WIVES Unstated, or Man not married	WIVES Not born in Neighbourhood	WIVES Born near Corsley	WIVES Born in Corsley	HOUSEHOLDERS Unstated	HOUSEHOLDERS Not born in Neighbourhood	HOUSEHOLDERS Born near Corsley	HOUSEHOLDERS Born in Corsley	HOUSEHOLDERS Total Number
Farmers	16	24	9	3	11	5	—	4	10	14	28
Market gardeners and marketers	20	16	—	—	2	7	—	—	2	7	9
Labourers	34	33	—	4	7	21	—	2	6	24	32
Carters	9	12	—	1	5	6	—	—	5	7	12
Dairymen or cowmen	13	5	—	1	4	3	—	2	4	2	8
Miscellaneous agricultural	11	5	—	4	3	1	—	5	2	1	8
Retired labourers	16	12	1	—	2	6	—	1	2	6	9
Head-gardeners, coachman, grooms, groom-gardeners	13	5	—	5	2	—	—	3	2	2	7
Keepers, &c.	9	3	—	2	1	—	—	2	1	—	3
Manual workers residing in Corsley, but working outside parish	2	3	—	1	3	1	—	—	2	3	5
Miscellaneous residing in Corsley — retired from work outside parish	12	3	2	3	2	2	—	1	3	5	9
Tradesmen and dealers	12	10	—	—	—	5	1	—	1	3	5
Independent workers (brickmaker, saddler, naturalist, 2 shoemakers)	10	9	—	2	2	1	—	2	1	2	5
Artisans	22	16	—	9	6	7	—	7	6	9	22
Women householders	57	44	—	—	—	—	—	4	11	21	36
	256	200	12	35	50	65	1	33	58	107	198

PRESENT Occupation	FATHERS Unstated	FATHERS Not born in Neighbourhood	FATHERS Born near Corsley	FATHERS Born in Corsley	GRANDFATHERS Unstated	GRANDFATHERS Not born in Neighbourhood	GRANDFATHERS Born near Corsley	GRANDFATHERS Born in Corsley
Farmers	5	3	9	11	21	5	21	9
Market gardeners and marketers	1	1	—	7	10	—	2	6
Labourers	3	2	5	22	43	4	7	10
Carters	1	—	4	7	13	—	4	7
Dairymen or cowmen	1	2	4	1	11	3	2	—
Miscellaneous agricultural	3	2	2	1	10	4	2	—
Retired labourers	1	—	3	5	9	—	4	5
Head-gardeners, coachman, grooms, groom-gardeners	2	1	2	2	9	—	3	2
Keepers, &c.	—	2	1	—	6	—	—	—
Manual workers residing in Corsley, but working outside parish	1	—	3	1	8	—	—	2
Miscellaneous residing in Corsley — retired from work outside parish	1	1	2	5	4	2	5	7
Tradesmen and dealers	2	—	—	3	5	—	1	4
Independent workers (brickmaker, saddler, naturalist, 2 shoemakers)	—	2	1	2	6	2	—	2
Artisans	3	7	3	9	28	5	4	7
Women householders	15	1	6	14	47	3	8	14
	39	24	45	90	230	28	63	76

Occupation of Ancestry and Children

THERE ARE MANY gaps in the particulars returned as to occupations of fathers and grandparents, and in considering those stated, it must be remembered that only one, and that usually the one which bestows most social distinction, is given where several may have been followed in succession or simultaneously. The particulars for the children profess to be complete, except where specially noted, and 202 forms were sufficiently filled in to include here.

Farmers: 29 farmers, for whom there are particulars, are for convenience divided arbitrarily into two groups, the first containing 12 larger, the second 17 smaller farmers. In the first group 13 fathers or grandfathers are returned; 9 of these are farmers, 1 a publican and brewer, and 1 a weaver or woollen manufacturer.

There are in these farmers' families 6 sons over school age. One of these is an independent farmer, the other 5 are helping on their fathers' farms. The 8 daughters are all living at home or with a farmer brother.

In the second group of 17 smaller farmers particulars are given of 15 grandfathers, viz.: 2 farmers, 1 clothier and farmer, 1 coal-haulier and farmer, 1 shopkeeper, 1 cloth-manufacturer, 1 worker in cloth factory, 1 weaver, 1 poultry dealer and hawker, 1 dairyman, 1 woodman, 1 shepherd, 2 carpenters, and 1 tailor. The occupations of 16 of the fathers are: 6 farmers, 1 farmer and blacksmith, 1 market gardener, 1 shopkeeper, 1 coal-haulier, 1 faggoter, 1 shepherd, 1 gardener, 1 labourer, 1 shoemaker, 1 tailor.

There are 13 sons grown up in this group; 5 are helping their fathers, 1 is in America, 1 farmer and artisan, 1 school attendance officer, 2 railway clerks, 1 gardener, 1 barman, 1 carter. Thirteen daughters are: 3 married, 6 at home including a school-teacher, a dressmaker, and a glover, 4 in domestic service.

Market gardeners or Marketers: We have particulars of 9 market gardeners or marketers. These have stated the occupation of 7 grandfathers, viz.: 1 market-gardener, 1 weaver, 1 shoemaker, 1 worker at limekiln, 1 carpenter, and 2 labourers. The occupations of their fathers were: 1 farmer, 1 maltster, 1 dyer, 1 independent blacksmith, 1 shoemaker, 1 carter, 3 labourers.

Among the families of market gardeners, there are 18 male and 18 female children over school age. The occupations of the males are: 1 motor-driver, 1 in cycle works, 2 blacksmiths, 3 miners in Wales, 1 milk-carrier, 1 oilman, 1 wood-carver, 1 gardener, 5 labourers, 2 masons' labourers. The 18 females are: 7 married, 3 at home, two of whom are dressmakers, 7 in domestic service, 1 barmaid.

Labourers: There are particulars for 33 labourers. These were able to remember the occupations of 19 grandfathers, viz.: 4 labourers, 4 carters, 1 shepherd, 1 thatcher, 1 head gamekeeper, 2 small farmers or market gardeners, 2 shoemakers, 1 weaver, 2 dyers, 1 carrier. Twenty-six have given the occupations of their fathers. These are 15 labourers, 2 carters, 1 thatcher, 5 farmers,[1] a market-gardener, 1 working for auctioneer, 1 coal-haulier, 1 did not work much, but was supported by wife or mother.

There are among the labourers' families 36 male and 34 female children over school age. The occupations of the males are: 15 labourers, 4 carters, 2 gardeners, 1 woodman, 1 market gardener with mother, 2 timber hauliers, 1 milkman, 1 baker's assistant, 1 blacksmith, 1 mason, 1 wood-carver, 1 miner, Westbury iron-works, 1 footman, 2 soldiers, 1 sailor, 1 out of work. The females are: 15 married, 7 at home, including one dressmaker, and 12 in domestic service.

Carters: We have particulars for 12 carters. These have returned the occupations of 10 grandfathers, viz.: 1 carter, 3 labourers, 2 farmers (one small farm and donkey-cart), 2 tailors, 1 butcher, 1 blacksmith.

---

1   One of these is still living in the parish, and is a brickmaker, who rents about three acres of land, which he works as a by-occupation.

The fathers of 11 carters were: 2 carters, 4 labourers, 2 painters, 1 collier, 1 village postmaster, 1 publican.

There are 9 male and 12 female children over school age among the families of the 12 carters. The occupations of the males are: 2 labourers, 1 road-mender, 1 indoor milkman, 1 cellarman's assistant, 1 mason's labourer, 1 blacksmith, 1 engine-driver, and 1 out of work. The females are: 2 married, 1 at home, and 9 in domestic service.

Cowmen: There are particulars for 6 cowmen. The occupations of 4 grandfathers are: 1 dairyman, 1 woodman, 1 thatcher, and 1 groom. The fathers of 5 of them were: 1 cowman, 3 labourers, 1 thatcher.

There are 3 male and 6 female children over school age among the families of the 6 dairymen. The occupations of the males are: 1 dairyman and 2 labourers. The females are: 5 married and 1 at home, an invalid.

Employed in Agriculture with higher Wages: There are 4 men, 2 being dairymen, 1 a woodman, and 1 a thatcher, who receive higher wages or rates of payment than other agricultural workers. These have given particulars of 7 grandfathers, viz.: 3 farmers, 1 woodman, 1 thatcher and innkeeper, 1 weaver and 1 woodman, 1 'independent'. Their fathers were: 1 dairyman, 1 woodman, 1 thatcher, and 1 worker in Frome iron-works.

These 4 families have 5 male and 11 female children over school age. The occupations of the males are: 1 gardener, 1 soldier, 1 sailor, 1 apprentice in outfitter's shop, and 1 clerk. The females are: 2 married, 2 at home (one learning dressmaking), and 7 in service.

Miscellaneous Agricultural: There are 8 miscellaneous agricultural workers for whom we have particulars. These give the occupation of 3 grandfathers as 1 gardener, 1 carpenter, and 1 dyer. The fathers of 5 were 2 labourers, 1 woodman, 1 timber-merchant and 1 market gardener.

There are among these 8 families 4 male and 5 female children over school age. The occupations of the males are: 1 farmer in

America, 1 coal-merchant, 1 in police-force, 1 cowman. The females are: 2 married, 2 at home, 1 in domestic service.

Gamekeepers: There are 3 gamekeepers or keepers' labourers; 1 of these, however, was out of work at the time the inquiry was made. The fathers of these 3 men were: 1 gamekeeper, 1 dairyman, and 1 labourer.

They have 4 male and 7 female children over school age. The occupations of the males are: 1 gamekeeper, 2 labourers, 1 baker's assistant. The 7 females are: 2 married, 4 in service, and 1 living with a sister.

Retired Labourers: We have particulars for 9 retired labourers, including a mole-catcher, a stone-breaker and two who became respectively a small farmer and a market gardener. These give the occupations of 7 grandfathers as 5 labourers (two with a query), 1 weaver, and 1 who rented the limekiln on Cley Hill. The fathers of 8 were: 3 labourers, 1 shepherd, 1 sawyer, 1 worker at limekiln, 1 market gardener, and 1 soldier.

Among the families of these 9 labourers are 13 male and 14 female grown-up children still living. The occupations of the males are very various, viz.: 1 labourer, 1 market gardener, 1 market gardener and blacksmith, 1 gamekeeper, 1 brickmaker, 1 worker in malthouse, 1 coal-miner, 1 engine-driver, 1 mason, 1 plumber, 1 messenger in country town, 1 doing odd jobs, 1 unknown. The 14 females are 9 married, 2 living at home (1 a laundress), 3 unstated.

Head Gardeners, Coachmen, and Grooms: We have particulars for 6 head gardeners, coachmen, grooms, or groom-gardeners. Four grandfathers of these men were: 1 employed in iron-works at Frome, 1 in dye-works, 1 a tailor, 1 a groom. The fathers of 5 were: 1 foreman in woollen factory, 1 farmer, 1 shoemaker, 1 labourer or thatcher, 1 labourer.

There are among these 6 families 12 male and 5 female children over school age. The occupations of the males are: 1 gardener, 1 market gardener, 1 labourer, 1 in motor works, 2 on railway, 2 in glove factory,

1 grocer, 1 grocer's assistant, 1 caretaker, 1 wheelwright's apprentice. The females are: 2 married, 1 at home, 2 in domestic service.

Miscellaneous working elsewhere: There are 5 miscellaneous manual workers employed outside the parish. Six grandfathers of these men were: 3 labourers, 2 carters, 1 shepherd. Their fathers were: 3 labourers, 1 carpenter and odd man, 1 platelayer G. W. R.

One family has 2 male, another 3 female children over school age. The occupations of the males are: 1 gardener and 1 labourer. The 3 females are in domestic service.

Miscellaneous retired from Work elsewhere: There are particulars for 8 men who are retired and living in Corsley, having worked elsewhere. The occupations which were followed by these men are: 1 farmer, 1 baker and grocer, 1 house decorator, 1 engineer and publican, 2 factory workers, 1 policeman, 1 signalman. They state the occupations of 11 grandfathers to have been: 4 farmers, 1 market gardener, 1 pig-butcher, 1 'business', 2 weavers, 2 labourers. The fathers of 7 were: 2 farmers and 1 who helped his sister with her farm, 1 baker and grocer, 1 card-spinner in factory, 1 lime-burner, 1 labourer.

The occupations of children are in one case unstated. Among the remaining families are 6 male and 8 female children still living. The occupations of males are; 3 colliers, 1 quarrier, 1 assistant in co-operative warehouse, 1 in post-office. The 8 females are all married. Probably none of the sons and daughters of this group were born or brought up in Corsley.

Tradesmen and Dealers: There are particulars for 5 tradesmen or dealers, including a builder and wheelwright, a grocer and baker, a coal and timber merchant, a shopkeeper and a plumber and builder, who gives no particulars of ancestry. The tradesmen return 4 grandfathers as 1 butcher, 1 woodman, 1 gardener, and 1 labourer. The fathers of 4 were; 1 gardener, 1 grocer and baker, 1 labourer, and 1 blacksmith.

The 5 families have 9 male and 12 female children over school age. The occupations of the males are: 1 plumber, 1 helping father, 1 farmer, 1 assistant schoolmaster, 3 coachmen, 1 carter, 1 unstated. The females are: 8 married, 2 at home, 2 keeping shop, 1 unstated.

Independent Workers and Miscellaneous: There are particulars for 8 families, 5 being independent workers, viz: 1 brickmaker on own account, 1 saddler, 1 naturalist or bird-stuffer, 2 shoemakers, and 3 miscellaneous, viz.: 1 assistant clerk of works, 1 police-constable, 1 brickmaker and small farmer. These return 7 grandfathers as 1 coal-haulier, 1 head gamekeeper, 1 brick and tile maker, 1 mason and builder, 1 shoemaker, 1 shepherd, and 1 soldier. The fathers of 6 were: 1 brick and tile maker, 1 brickmaker, 1 shoemaker, 1 woodman and engine-driver, 2 labourers.

One of these men has not stated what his children are doing. The 7 families have 14 male and 16 female grown-up children. The occupations of the males are: 3 brickmakers, helping father, 1 collier, 1 plumber, 1 painter, 1 gasfitter, 1 engine-fitter, 1 estate carpenter, 1 carter, 4 labourers. The females are: 4 married, 5 at home, including one who goes out as a daily servant, and 7 in domestic service.

Artisans: We have particulars for 21 artisans. These give information about 18 grandfathers, whose occupations were: 1 farmer, 1 kept a cow or two, 1 rented limekiln, 1 publican, 2 blacksmiths, 1 sawyer, 1 plasterer and tiler, 2 boot or shoemakers, 1 butcher, 1 dyer, 1 carter, 1 cowman, 1 woodman, 2 labourers, 1 emigrated to America. The fathers of 19 were as follows: 2 blacksmiths, 1 mason, 1 plasterer and tiler, 2 carpenters, 2 wheelwrights, 2 sawyers, 1 shoemaker, 1 butcher, 1 publican, 1 woodman and afterwards farmer, 2 carters, 1 cowman, 2 labourers.

Among the 21 families are 20 male and 17 female children over school age. The occupations of the males are: 2 carpenters, 1 carpenter-builder, 1 blacksmith, 1 painter, 1 bricklayer, 1 apprentice painting, 2 engineers, 1 working in malthouse, 1 coachman, 1 groom, 1 baker, 1 carter, 6 labourers. The females are: 5 married, 2 at home, including a laundry-worker and an imbecile, 8 in domestic service.

Women Householders: The remaining section, 'Women Householders', contains the widows and children of so miscellaneous an assortment of workers that it is not worth while to analyse here the occupations pursued by their children, sufficient indication of these being given by the table on p. 260.

The following is a summary of occupations pursued by the children of male householders in Corsley, which may be compared with those of their fathers in Chapter 10; 166 male householders are included in this inquiry, but a large number have no adult children.

OCCUPATIONS OF SONS OF MALE HOUSEHOLDERS OF CORSLEY.

Farmers	12[1]
Market gardeners	3
Labourers, inclusive	55[2]
Gardeners, coachmen, and grooms	14
Tradesmen or tradesmen's assistants	14[3]
Artisans	26[4]
Engineers	8[5]
Railway clerks	3
Miners	10[6]
Soldiers	3
Sailors	2
Abroad or emigrated	2
Domestic service	2
Assistant-schoolmaster	1
Clerk	1
Post-office	1
School attendance officer	1
Working in malthouse	2
Glove factory	2
Police force	1
Barman	1
Wood-carver	1
Caretaker	1
Messenger, country town	1
Odd jobs	1
Out of work	2
Unknown or unstated	2
Total	172

[1] Including several sons helping their fathers.
[2] This includes all the agricultural employments.
[3] Including three timber-hauliers, one helping father, one coal-merchant, one grocer, one baker, the rest being assistants.
[4] Including three brickmakers helping their father and two apprentices.
[5] These are either in motor or cycle works, or motor or engine drivers.
[6] Including colliers, quarriers, miners, and employees in iron-works.

OCCUPATIONS OF DAUGHTERS OF MALE HOUSEHOLDERS
OF CORSLEY.

Married	74
Living at home	42[1]
In domestic service	66
Barmaid	1
Unstated	4
Total	187

The following is a summary of the occupations of the children of 36 women householders.

OCCUPATIONS OF SONS OF WOMEN HOUSEHOLDERS OF CORSLEY.

Farmers	3
Market gardeners	3[2]
Labourers	17
Gardeners, coachmen, and grooms	5
Artisans	7
Miners	1
Soldiers	2
Abroad or emigrated	3
Odd man	1
Signalman	1
Inspector of water-works	1
Labourer, gas-works	1
Malting	3
	48

OCCUPATIONS OF DAUGHTERS OF WOMEN HOUSEHOLDERS OF
CORSLEY.

Married	25
Domestic service	16
At home	11
Shop-assistant	1
	53

[1] Ten of these follow some occupation, such as dressmaking or laundry-work.

[2] One of these is helping his mother.

This gives a total of 460 adult children from 202 families, 4 being included which were omitted from the table of ancestry on p. 252.

That table shows that of 456 children over school age and still living, born to 198 of the householders of Corsley, 200 are now residing in the parish, while 256 are living elsewhere. Having viewed in detail the occupations which these persons are following, it will be interesting to consider more generally what becomes of Corsley's sons and daughters. From the appended table on p. 252 it will be seen that more than half the 219 males have remained in the parish, 121 being still in Corsley, while 98 have left. These 121 are many of them married and themselves householders. Of the 98 who have left, 51, or about half, are living in a town, mining districts and moderate-sized market towns being both included. 34 have migrated to other country districts, and are chiefly working in agriculture, or in the service of country gentlemen. 7 are in the Army or Navy, and it may be noted that many of the present residents of Corsley have previously passed some period in the Army. 6 are abroad or in the Colonies. It will be noticed that it is the sons of people of a higher social status than that of agricultural labourer who chiefly find their way to the towns; gentlemen's servants, artisans, and market gardeners furnishing a larger proportion than the labourers, carters, and cowmen. The sons of these latter, when they leave the parish, migrate more to other country districts, or enlist in the Army. Of the 237 females, only 79 remain in Corsley, while 158 are residing elsewhere. About 26 of those still living in Corsley are married, while over 70 of those living elsewhere in town or country are married. 53 are living at home, many of these being laundresses, dressmakers, or glovers. 82 are in domestic service, ranging from 'generals' to housekeepers in large houses. Most Corsley girls on leaving school go out as general servant or nurse-maid to a farmer's wife, or to a tradesman in one of the neighbouring small towns. After a year or two they usually migrate to the larger towns, still as general servants, or else they enter a gentleman's house as scullery-maid or between-girl. Sooner or later the majority find their way into a middle or upper class household, and they remain in domestic service until they marry. It will be seen from the table that the exodus of females is much greater than that of males, there being exceedingly few well-paid occupations available for women in the parish, as was shown in the section on Women's Work (pp. 159-64).

The following table shows the migrations of the adult children belonging to the 198 households referred to in the table of ancestry on p. 252.

MIGRATION OF CHILDREN OVER SCHOOL AGE.

Occupation of Father.		Adult Children residing in Corsley.		Adult Children migrated to a Town.[1]		Adult Children migrated to other Parts of Country.		In Army or Navy.	Abroad, or emigrated.	
		M.	F.	M.	F.	M.	F.		M.	F.
Farmers		12	12	4	4	2	5	—	I	—
Market gardeners, or marketers		11	5	5	6	2	6	—	—	I
Labourers		22	11	4	14	6	7	3	—	—
Carters		12	—	—	6	1	2	—	—	—
Dairymen or cowmen		2	3	1	7	2	2	1	—	—
Miscellaneous agricultural		2	3	—	6	1	2	1	—	I
Retired labourers		7	5	5	9	1	—	—	I[2]	—
Head gardeners, coachmen, grooms		4	1	6	2	2	2	—	I	—
Keepers, &c.		2	1	—	7	2	—	—	—	—
Miscellaneous, working outside parish		2	1	—	2	—	—	—	—	—
Miscellaneous, retired from work, not in Corsley		—	3	6	6	—	—	—	—	—
Tradesmen and dealers		5	5	—	3	4	5	—	—	—
Independent workers (brickmaker, saddler, shoemaker) ...		6	3	—	2	2	6	—	—	—
Artisans		9	7	7	3	4	8	—	—	—
Women-householders		25	19	13	24	5	10	2	3	—
		121	79	51	101	34	55	7	6	2

[1] Under the heading of Town are included market towns and mining districts as well as the Metropolis and other large cities.
[2] Unknown.

16

Social Life in Corsley

SOCIAL LIFE IN Corsley centres round the family or household, round clubs for games and recreation, and the public-houses, and round the churches or chapels of the various religious denominations. Family life has already been considered from an economic point of view; we may now regard it in its purely social aspect, together with various forms of recreation, and with the religious life of the community.

In a scattered parish, such as Corsley, where many of the houses are situated in lonely lanes, the family is naturally inclined to live a more isolated life than in villages where even on a dark winter's night the street forms a sociable meeting-place; and although Corsley is well provided with public-houses – and it cannot be said that these are unattended – yet most of the married men prefer to have their cask of beer at home, taking a glass after supper with their wives, rather than turn out habitually into the dark muddy lanes which have to be traversed before they reach the haunts of men.

The reading-room at Corsley Heath is very little frequented except by those living in its near vicinity. The total number of members in the winter of 1905-6 was thirty.

When inquiries as to the population were being made during the winter of 1905-6, many of the visits were paid between 6 and 7.30 p.m. At this time the whole family would almost invariably be found at home, grouped round the fire, or where there were children they might be seated round the table playing some game. At Christmas-time not uncommonly a small Christmas-tree for the children would be standing in the corner of the room. A large proportion of the young people of Corsley quit the parish on leaving school; but the young men who remain very frequently take up some hobby, such as fretwork, photography, or music, with which they employ their evenings quite happily at home. The few young girls who stay with their parents usually complain that it is 'dull', especially in the winter, when they often go out very little. These remarks naturally apply more to the smaller hamlets of Corsley than to Chapmanslade, where a real village exists, with a somewhat different type of social life, and where the parishioners of Corsley join with those of Westbury, on the other side of the way, in getting up concerts, dances, and other festivities during the winter months. Music is the fashion here, too, and Chapmanslade has its own brass band, composed of local musicians.

But even in other parts of Corsley a few occasions for social gathering occur in the course of the winter. Of late years most successful and popular dramatic entertainments have been given at the school by the children of the parish, under the tuition of the master and mistress. Occasionally, too, a concert is got up at the reading-room. Such entertainments are always largely attended.

Evening services at the chapels take out some of the older people, and there is probably a little visiting of each other in the evening among the more well-to-do.

But while part of the people appear to be almost puritanical in their lives, it must be admitted that there are some families who regularly frequent the public-house. It is not the custom for sons living at home to pay more than 7s. or 8s. per week to their parents, unless in exceptional cases. A few sons living with parents consequently get into the habit of working only part time, and thus take to loafing ways, working on odd jobs not more than two or three days a week, much to the distress of the parents. Those young men who, working regularly, occupy their leisure with performance on a musical instrument, or some such hobby, usually save a good deal of money. Others, though spending a considerable part of their earnings on beer and tobacco, yet manage to save something. A remaining section spend all they get on food and drink, or dissipation in the neighbouring towns, to the neglect sometimes of their recognised liabilities to relatives. These people, mostly unmarried men, described by a native of Corsley as 'sillylike', thinking, she says, of nothing but what they eat and drink, and going to the public-house in the evening for a 'lark', form the chief clientele of the public-houses. It was not found possible to ascertain the amount of beer consumed in Corsley, for while some keepers of public-houses were good enough to furnish particulars, others declined to do so, and a large amount of beer is also taken direct from the brewers by the cottagers and others. It cannot, however, be doubted that the average consumption per head is somewhat large. At Christmas-time, 1905, notes were made of persons in the six public-houses of Corsley, including one situated a few yards outside the parish, with the following results:

	December 25th.		Present.
No. 1	...	9 p.m.	...	8 men, 2 wives.
No. 2	...	9.30 p.m.	...	11 men, 4 strange women. Singing.
No. 3	...	9.50 p.m.	...	13 men, 1 wife, also 10 strangers, male and female. Gramaphone and singing.
	December 26th.		
No. 1	...	7.30 p.m.	...	15 men.
No. 2	...	8 p.m.	...	17 men.
No. 3	...	8.30 p.m.	...	17 men, with 5 wives or daughters, 4 strangers, male and female. Gramaphone.
	December 27th.		
No. 1	...	9 p.m.	...	10 men.
No. 2	...	10 p.m.	...	5 men, one with wife and daughter from Frome.
No. 3	...	9.30 p.m.	...	14 men. Concertina and tambourine playing.
No. 4	...	8.15 p.m.	...	6 persons. Talking of coming election.
No. 5	...	9 p.m.	...	4 persons. Talking about Ireland, one of the company being bound there.
No. 6	...	7.45 p.m.	...	4 persons. Playing bagatelle.

December 28th.

No. 1 ... 9.30 p.m. ... 8 men.
No. 2 ... 9.30 p.m. ... 8 men.
No. 3 ... 6 p.m. ... 9 men.
No. 4 ... 8 p.m. ... 7 persons. Talking of agriculture.
No. 5 ... 7 p.m. ... 2 persons. Playing darts.
No. 6 ... 9 p.m. ... 6 persons. Playing bagatelle.

December 29th.

No. 4 ... 9 p.m. ... 5 persons. Playing darts.
No. 5 ... 9.30 p.m. ... 1 person. Drinking.
No. 6 ... 9 p.m. ... 6 persons. Playing bagatelle.

December 30th.

No. 1 ... 7 p.m. ... 4 men.
No. 2 ... 7.30 p.m. ... 2 men. The landlord gave free drinks, 8.30 to 10 p.m., to finish up the Christmas holidays.

No. 3 ... 8 p.m. ... 5 men.

December 31st.

No. 1 ... 9 p.m. ... 8 men.
No. 2 ... 8 p.m. ... 9 men.
No. 3 ... 9.40 p.m. ... 6 men.

January 1st.

No. 4 ... 9.30 p.m. ... 3 persons. Playing darts.
No. 5 ... 8 p.m. ... 8 persons. Playing darts.
No. 6 ... 8.30 p.m. ... 2 persons. Drinking only.

January 2nd.

No. 4 ... 9 p.m. ... 1 person. Drinking.
No. 5 ... 9.45 p.m. ... 2 persons. Playing darts.
No. 6 ... 9.15 p.m. ... 4 persons. Playing bagatelle.

January 3rd.

No. 4 ... 8.45 p.m. ... 10 persons. Talking of the coming election.
No. 5 ... 8 p.m. ... 4 persons. Playing dominoes.
No. 6 ... 9.15 p.m. ... 8 persons. Playing bagatelle and talking of the coming election.

January 6th.

No. 4 ... 8.30 p.m. ... 5 persons. Talking of shooting pigeons, there being a shooting match in the village.
No. 5 ... 8 p.m. ... 10 persons. Playing darts and talking of coming election.
No. 6 ... 9 p.m. ... 9 persons. Playing bagatelle—some only drinking.

It is not to be supposed that this census, taken at Christmas-time, and when also an election was looming in the near future, is in any way typical of the ordinary attendance, which is probably considerably smaller at a less festive season. Moreover, besides the number of persons noted as 'strangers', many names are included of persons not residing in Corsley, though well known to some of the inhabitants. An investigation at this time, however, showed the kind of amusement which was sought in these houses, games such as 'darts' or bagatelle probably taking an even more prominent place at a season when exceptional entertainments such as gramaphones and singing were unprovided. But no doubt, though the number who go merely to 'soak' may not be numerous, a considerable amount of liquor is consumed by the players, or conversationalists, as well as by the less sociable drinkers.

The main amusement at Corsley on holidays during the winter is football, in which many of the men take part, while the women and girls, and older men, will often go to watch. In the winter of 1905-6 there were 48 members of the Corsley Football Club. The talk at public-houses, etc., during the winter months is mainly of football, unless an election or some such exceptional excitement should claim a share of attention. After a match men of all ages may be found going up, when the day's work is over, to learn the result.

For the mothers of Corsley a weekly recreation is provided in the mothers' meeting, held at the Reading Room by a lady of the parish.

So much for the winter. In summer the inhabitants and visitors, or lodgers are to be seen about in the roads and lanes till after dusk, and the household is no longer so isolated and self-contained as during the winter months. Cricket forms the chief occupation and amusement of the men, after their work is over. In 1906 there were 42 members of the Corsley Cricket Club.

While most of the natives of Corsley are known to each other, and display a friendly interest in one another's concerns, especially

Temple and the Longleat Woods

when united by the bond of mutual religious sect, it appears to be difficult for a newcomer to make friends or even acquaintances. A young farmer's sister after being over a year in the parish had made acquaintance with no farmers' daughters, or other young girls, and cottagers' wives who have been only a year or two in the place usually tell one that they have made no acquaintances. The Corsley people, on the other hand, will tell you that these newcomers have only recently arrived and that they know nothing of them.

The distinction between the inhabitant of Corsley descent and the stranger in the land, in the minds of the former, is probably something far deeper than the outsider has any notion of. Nevertheless, memory does not go back very far. Many inhabitants could not tell whether their own grandfathers were natives of the place, and a couple of generations is therefore sufficient to establish an old family.

The religious groups into which the people of Corsley assort themselves have already been alluded to. There is firstly the Church of England, with the parish church of St. Margaret and the smaller church of St. Mary at Temple. Two services are usually held at each on Sunday by the Rector, in addition to occasional week-day services, and Sunday School is held at St. Margaret in the afternoon. A good attendance at the morning service at the parish church would number about 100 persons, including children and the choir. The evening services are more fully attended.

The Wesleyan community at Lane End has on Sunday preaching services, morning and evening. These are usually taken by lay preachers from the neighbourhood, and occasionally a travelling preacher attends. The congregation numbers as a rule about 70 at each service. Prayer-meetings or preaching services are also held on Tuesday evenings. Sunday School is held twice on Sundays, and the Wesleyan community give their children a school treat from time to time.

The Baptists at Whitbourne have their chapel, with an organ, and an adjoining room where Sunday School and prayer-meetings are held. The chapel is surrounded by a burial-ground, and beyond that is a deep tank for use in the rite of baptism. The Baptists, like the Wesleyans, give treats to the children attending their school.

At Chapmanslade members of the Church of England, Congregationalists, and Baptists are provided with churches and chapels within the parish of Westbury or Diltons Marsh.

The bond of union between members of each Nonconformist community appears to be close, the members taking a keen interest in one another, and the more well-to-do exercising much kindness toward the poorer members when these are ill or in trouble.

On Sundays, when the holiday cannot be devoted to cricket or football, many of the parishioners take walks about the lanes, and groups of young men are usually found standing at the cross-roads, dressed usually in black coats and bowler hats. The people of both sexes usually go out carefully dressed on a Sunday, and all who are seen on the roads appear to possess good clothes.

It remains to notice the execution of public business in Corsley. The Parish Council, having eleven members, besides the Rector as

Chairman and the Clerk, meets four times a year. The members are mainly farmers and tradesmen, with one or two artisans. The proceedings are conducted with a fair degree of formality, but a good deal of conversation in undertones goes on between the farmers during the meetings. Keenness is shown by some of the members in the detection of possible flaws in the modes of procedure adopted, and all, or nearly all, are alert to find means to avoid expenditure of the ratepayers' money. On the whole the Council appears anxious to carry out conscientiously the work entrusted to it. Since the first formation of a Corsley Parish Council under the Act of 1894 the matters which have been chiefly dealt with by this body are the formalities and necessary arrangements for conducting the business of the meetings, the parochial charities, the repair, etc., of footpaths, the state of the roads, the establishment of a postal-telegraph office and second delivery of letters in Corsley, Chapmanslade water supply, arrangements for celebration of the Diamond Jubilee, and the expression of congratulation or condolence with important persons connected with the parish, or members of the Council.

17

Conclusion

HAVING ENDEAVOURED TO give a faithful description of Corsley as it was in 1905-6, perhaps the writer may be allowed to summarise briefly the conclusions to which she was forced during the course of her investigations, and the subsequent analysis of their results – conclusions some of which were entirely at variance with the preconceived notions she had formed from twelve years' superficial acquaintance with the parish and its inhabitants.

One is accustomed to think of the labourers of Wilts and Dorset as the worst paid and most poverty-stricken class in rural England. Looking therefore to find poverty in a Wiltshire village, it was no small surprise to the investigator to discover that the majority of the inhabitants were in quite affluent circumstances, and that only about one-eighth of the households had an income insufficient, with wise and careful management, to procure food and clothing adequate in quantity and quality to keep all the members in full health and vigour, or, as Mr. Rowntree expresses it, to maintain efficiency.

This prosperity of the majority of the families was found to be due to two main causes, the one highly satisfactory and promising for the future, the other of a more dubious nature.

First and foremost, this prosperity results from the distribution of land in the parish, from the good gardens attached to each cottage, the abundance of allotment land, the number of small holdings and the ease with which these are newly formed and obtained by any one in a position to rent them from the principal landlord of the parish.

The advantage resulting from this easy access to the land cannot be overrated. Not only do many families derive a living entirely from gardening on their own account, but nearly all have one or other of these occupations as a bye-industry. The wage-earning labourers and artisans are nearly all market gardeners, and a few of them farmers; the publicans and the various functionaries of the parish are likewise in most instances farmers or gardeners. Moreover, the land is quite elastic in its fertility, and a family left with no other resource can by concentrating all their efforts on one cottage garden make a hard living from this alone.

The second cause of prosperity is a negative one, namely absence of children. Many of the farmers are childless couples, who were able to save out of a low labourer's wage, and thus become small capitalists. There are market gardeners, too, who come under this category, though not so shown in the table on p. 248 (Chapter 15) as a man often remains nominally a labourer, while a considerable part of his time and the whole of his wife's is in reality devoted to gardening.

The reverse side of the prosperity which appears so striking when the household is taken as the unit is, however, discovered when we examine more minutely into the various data collected and tabulated in Chapters 14 and 15.

We find in the first place that from the insignificant one-eighth of the households in primary poverty, two-fifths, or nearly half, of all the children in the parish are drawn, and that only one-third of all the children are in households above the line of secondary poverty.

In the second place it becomes clear when the mortality figures are compared that a huge wastage of human life occurs among the descendants of agricultural labourers, this being the class that passes through periods of primary poverty. This wastage would seem to be mainly due to infantile mortality or deaths during later childhood.

In the third instance it was plainly shown when the school reports were compared that the children from homes in primary poverty often reveal evident marks of insufficient nutrition of brain and body, most of the children characterised by the teachers as dull and lazy coming from these homes, or from those in secondary poverty, and be it noted that the comparison is largely with similar labouring families where either because the elder children are already at work, or the family is comparatively small, the income per head is larger, for with very few exceptions all agricultural wage-earners who have several children pass in turn through a period of primary poverty, and the condition is characteristic of the class in Corsley, and not due to any avoidable fault of any particular family.

In striking contrast to the agricultural wage-earning families is the extraordinary vitality displayed by the children of market gardeners. It is shown by the table on p. 248 (Chapter 15) that the total number of children born to 27 labourers was 126, or an average of 4.6 per family, and that of these 24, or 21.4 per cent, were since dead, although the children of aged retired labourers were not included.

The same table shows that 7 market gardeners' families had produced 47 children, or an average of 6.7 per family, and that of these 47 of all ages, only one, or 2.1 per cent, had since died.

There were, therefore, 2.1 less children born on the average in the family of a labourer than in that of a market gardener, and in these smaller families the death rate was just ten times as great.

It has often been pointed out by writers on infantile mortality that the true gravity of a high rate lies not so much in the numerical loss of population as in the fact that when conditions are such as to produce a large proportion of deaths among infants, these conditions also inflict an unmeasured injury on the constitution of those infants who succeed in surviving.

It may, therefore, be surmised that not only do these children of market gardeners live, while the children of labourers die, but that if a careful examination could be made into the life history of these children, they would be found on the average more vigorous, healthy, and intelligent than those men and women who, born in labourers' households, had passed through the ordeal of 'survival of the fittest'.

An examination of the occupations being followed by the children of various groups given on pp. 253-8 shows at least that the sons of market gardeners are in the main following skilled trades and those of labourers unskilled occupations.

The greatest vitality of all is shown in the families of a brickmaker on his own account, and a shoemaker, who with a total of 21 children born have lost not one

The true cause of this difference is obscure. Does the independent worker, gardener or handicraftsman, succeed by some means in avoiding the deadly grip of poverty at the period when his numerous young family are all dependent on him, or is he merely more skilful in averting its pressure upon his offspring? These questions the present writer cannot attempt to answer; she can merely state such facts as the inquiry brought to light.

Besides the families containing 122 persons where want was caused by the presence of a number of children too young to earn a living, there were 11 households in Corsley, comprising in all only 22 persons, in primary poverty, owing to old age or widowhood. Some of this poverty will have been alleviated by the granting of old age pensions, and nearly the whole of it would have been abolished had not several old people been forced to seek relief from the guardians a few years since when the old Corsley Walking Club broke up, thereby becoming disqualified under the present law for receiving State pensions.

Notwithstanding the peculiar gravity of the incidence of poverty in Corsley, which falls, as we have seen, mainly upon the children, there is much hopefulness in the fact that the machinery already exists for its alleviation when local authorities awake to the fact that the conditions of child life need special care and supervision in the country districts of England as well as in the towns.

By exercising the care for school children, which Acts of Parliament have made a duty in part compulsory, in part optional, of the local education authority, and by extending various municipal and charitable experiments which aim at reducing infant mortality, successfully at work in certain urban districts, to country places such as Corsley, the greater part, if not all, of the child poverty might be prevented, and with finer results here than in the towns where mere poverty is only one of many evil conditions to be contended with.

When these unsatisfactory conditions of child life shall have been abolished it may confidently be expected that Corsley, in common with other rural parishes, will bring up an increased number of sons and daughters, more healthy, vigorous, and efficient than their elder brothers and sisters of the past, and ready to renew the less generous blood of the towns, or to recruit the Army and Navy; perhaps, too, more attractive occupation may be provided for the girls as well as the boys, and with a well-adapted education there seems no reason why women should not again take a share in agriculture, and so we may find a larger number of natives remaining in the parish, applying an intensive cultivation, which its soil can well bear, and in their turn bringing up the healthy and vigorous sons and daughters who were regarded by Elizabethan statesmen as the mainstay of national wellbeing.

Appendices

APPENDIX I

RECORDS RELATING TO CORSLEY

(A) MEDIEVAL AND STUART RECORDS.

Grant of the Manor of Corsley to the House of Studley.

"*Inspeximus* and confirmation of a charter of Godfrey de Craw-cumb giving to St. Mary and the house of Stodleg and the nuns there, in frank almoin, the manor of Corsleg, saving the King's service, and the advowson of the chapel of the manor, which was already given to William de Hydemuston ; and the said prioress and house shall support two chaplains celebrating divine service daily for the souls of the said Godfrey and Joan his wife, one chaplain to celebrate daily a mass of St. Mary (celebrabit singulis diebus de Sancta Maria) and the other for the faithful departed. Witnesses, Sir Robert de Muscegros, Henry de Capella, Hugh Giffard, Godfrey de Skydemor, William Bastard, Richard de Ansy, Nicholas de Haveresham, John de Elsefeld, Roger de Craunford, John de Esses, and William de Hydemeston, steward of the said Godfrey.

April 12, 1245, Westminster."[1]

The manor remained the property of this religious house until its dissolution in the reign of Henry VIII.[2]

---

[1] Cal. Charter Rolls Hen. III. vol. i. p. 283.
[2] See William H. Jones, " Domesday for Wilts," p. 209, quotation from " Nomina Villarum " A.D. 1316, Harl. MS. 6281, p. 231 ; and Gairdner, " Letters and Papers of the Reign of Hen. VIII." A.D. 1536, vol. x. p. 526, and A.D. 1537, vol. xii. I, p. 143.

An inquisition made in the Hundred of Warminster in the reign of King Edward III. declared that—

"Item the hamlet of Corsley used to be in the hands of the King's predecessors of the (present) King, belonging to the manor of Warminster, until the King Henry aforesaid gave it to one Henry Dodeman, Norman; which hamlet the Prioress of Studley now holds of the gift of Godfrey Cracumbe in alms.

"Item the Prioress of Studley holds half a Knight's fee of the King in chief in Corsley in demesne.

"Item the Prioress of Studley has gallows (&) assize of bread and beer in Corsley by charter of King Henry father of the present King.

"Item the Prioress of Studley has warren at Corsley by Charter of King Henry father of the present King."[1]

The origin and ownership of the other manors which now form part of the parish remain in obscurity pending the publication of the Victoria County History, but the greater part appear to have been in the hands of various religious houses. Thus the manor of Godwell and Chapmanslade belonged to the Abbey of St. Mary, Stanley, Wilts,[2] prior to the Dissolution, when it was granted to Sir Edward Bainton.[3]

In 1337 William de Littleton bequeathed eighty-one acres of land in Great Corsley, Warminster, and Smalebrook to the Convent of the House of Lepers of St. Mary, Maiden Bradley.

"Licence for the alienation in mortmain to the prior and convent of the house of lepers of St. Mary, Maydenbradelegh, in satisfaction of 60^s of the 10^l yearly of land and rent which they have the king's licence to acquire, of the following, which are of the yearly value of 43^s 10^d as appears by the inquisition; by Master William de Littleton, a messuage, 76 acres of land, 5 acres of meadow and 6^s of rent, in Great Corselegh, Wermenstre, and Smalebrook, and by John Danyel, chaplain, and Reginald le Palmere, six messuages, 12 acres of land and 5 acres of wood, in Maydenbradlegh and Hulle Deverel." Oct. 9, 1337. Tower of London."[4]

---

[1] Extracts from Rotuli Hundredorum, vol. ii. 276 (Record Commission), translated from the Latin.

[2] See Wilts Archæological Magazine, vol. xv. p. 25.

[3] Gairdner, "Letters and Papers of the Reign of Hen. VIII." A.D. 1537, vol. xii. part i. p. 143.

[4] Cal. Patent Rolls, Oct. 9, 1337, vol. 1334–1338, p. 540.

The manor of Whitbourne was sold in 1544, on the dissolution of the Monastery of Maiden Bradley, together with lands in Bugley, Corsley, and Whitbourne, also belonging to the Monastery, to Ric : Andrewes and John Howe for the sum of £1,094. 3. 2.,[1] and it was probably the prior of this house who is mentioned in the following extent of the fourteenth century.

" *Whyteborne. Extent of the same.* [Sept. 30, 1364.]

" Extent of the Manor made on Monday after the festival of St. Michael, in the 38th year of the reign of King Edward III.

" A court with a small piece of land (or garden *Curtilagium*) is worth yearly after deductions [value not given].

" And at Whitborn a court with curtilage.

" There are 34 acres of land in 7 crofts.

" Also in the field of (?) Chadinhangre are 25 acres of land.

" Also on the Lygh 3½ acres.

" Also in the field of Cly 28 acres.

" Also at Bykenham a half-acre.

" Also there are 3½ acres of meadow.

" Also one acre of wood, which is worth in pasture . . .

" Also the lord prior can have and hold there 4 farm-horses and 12 oxen, 12 cows, 250 sheep.

" John de Vake holds in fee two messuages at the rent of 18d. And must do suit at the court of the lord, and must do homage and all other services.

" Henry de Frenshe holds in fee 1 messuage and 3 acres of land at the yearly rent of 6s., and must do all services as the aforesaid John Vake does.

" *Tenants in villenage* (*bondagio*). Thomas Pykenet holds at the will of the lord one messuage and 7 acres of land at the rent of 3s.

" Adam Frenshe [holds] one messuage and 2 acres of land.

" J Forester [holds] 2 messuages and 4 acres of land.

" Edwardus Carpenter holds land and a tenement in Whiteborn for the term of his life, at a yearly rent of 40s., to be paid at the 4 terms of the year.

" Walter [Deye][2] holds manor land and a tenement of Grendon for the term of his life. Rent, 53/4." [3]

---

[1] Gairdner, " Letters and Papers of the Reign of Hen. VIII." A.D. 1544, vol. xix. Part I. p. 629.

[2] Name supplied from p. 2 of MS.

[3] MS. Extent of the Manor of Whyteborne 38 Ed. III., at Long-

In 1415 a papal bull was obtained granting licence for burial in the Corsley churchyard and full parochial rights. This is translated in Hoare's " Modern Wilts" as follows : [1]

" From the Register of Bishop Hallam 1415. License for sepulture to Corsley, which before that time buried at Warminster, by a papal bull.

" ' Johannes Episcopus servus servorum Dei' to his beloved children of both sexes dwelling in Corsley and the hamlets adjoining. 'Whereas the church of Corsley before this time was parochial in all respects except only the above right, the Pope, on account of the distance and bad roads in winter, now permits them to bury in the Church-yard of Corsley, and delegates John Cosham, Prior of Bruton, to carry his bull into execution.'

" WILLIAM FOVENT, then Vicar of Warminster."

Although the Pope had granted his licence, distinct parochial rights do not appear to have been actually and fully obtained for Corsley until the incumbency of William Woolfe, who was appointed to the benefice in 1505.

The following account of the church is found in the record of the Corsley Perambulation of 1754.

" *An Abstract of the Church Book of Corsley, wherein are set down and recorded divers Things appertaining to the s*[d]. *Church and Parish.*

" 1636

" First the Church of Corsley was sometime a Chappell called S[t]. James's but by a Composition made between Dr. Bennett Vicar of Warminster and S[r]. W[m]. Woolfe Rector or Custos of Corsley, it was made a Parish Church of itself & the s[d]. S[r]. W[m]. & his successors were to pay yearly to y[e]. s[d]. D[r]. Bennett and his Success[r]. £1 6s. 8d., as by the s[d]. Composition in writing remaining among

---

leat House. Transcribed by Canon Christopher Wordsworth by kind permission from the Marquis of Bath and translated by Miss S. E. Moffat.

[1] Sir Richard Colt Hoare, " History of Modern Wilts," Hund. of Warminster, p. 64. The original papal bull is among the papers belonging to Corsley Church.

the Writings in the Parish Church of Corsley at large doth appear." [1]

Besides the Chapel of St. James, which seems to have become the parish church of St. Margaret, there were, according to Sir Richard Colt Hoare, also many endowed chapels in Corsley. [2]

One of these, Kington Court Chapel, or Little Corsley Chapel, on the site of the house now known as Cley Hill Farm, remained till the Reformation. [3] This chapel is said to have belonged anciently to the Kingston family, and afterwards to St. John's Hospital, Wilton. [4] The Commissioners in 7 Edward VI. found at this chapel 3 bells, a chalice or cup worth 7d., and some plate, which were to be safely kept to the King's use. [5]

An interesting seating order, comprising a plan of Corsley Church, dated 1635, and showing the name of the occupier of each seat, is among the parish records. The document runs as follows :—

"CORSLEY CHURCHE IN THE COUNTIE OF WILTES.

"The order and manner of placeing of the SEATES within the parish of Corsley by the Right worshipful MARMADUKE LYNN Doctor of the Civill lawe and Chancelor of the Diocese of Sarum in the Countie aforesaid the twenty sixe day of July Anno Dñi 1635 where the said Chancelor did order and appoint HENRY TEDBURY AND WILLIAM GODSELL CHURCH WARDENS And Stephen Holwey John Smith and Anthony Raxworthie their ASSISTANTS to settle and place every MAN and WOMAN in their several seates who were settled and placed accordinglie, as by the Churchbooke and also by this Mappe appeareth as ffolloweth vidzt

THE NORTH CORNER off the bodie
of the Church
SIR THOMAS THYNN Kᵗ.
FOR HIMSELF AND HIS LADY

---

[1] Corsley Perambulation, 1754, in Longleat Estate Office.

[2] Sir Richard Colt Hoare, " History of Modern Wilts," Hund. of Warminster, p. 64.

[3] *Ibid.* Also *Wilts Archæol. Mag.* x. p. 273.

[4] *Wilts Archæol. Mag.* x. p. 273.

Ibid. xii. p. 265.

[The Nave of the Church]

	The piller			Sir Thomas Thynn	Sir Thomas Thynn	Sr. Thomas Thynn
John Stevens ats Shepherd	Maurice Litlecot	Henrye Tedbury	George Turner	Marie Lambe	Robert Rymell
John Crosse	John Nevill	Anthony Rackesworthie	John Smith	Henry Feltham	Thomas Chace
John Barens	Singer	William Holwey	Robert Hopkins	William Raxworthie	Widdowe Dredge
William Smith ats Singer	James Watts	John Carr	Thomas Hill	Robert Knight	William Chace
	John Kennell	Richard Carpenter	Thomas Eyres	Thomas Holweye	John Watts
William Smith ats Singer	William Smith ats Singer	John Knight	Tobie Lambe	Robert Carpenter	John Withie
Stephen Crooch	William Downe	Anthony Rackesworthie	Michael Ewestice	John Williams ats Clarke	Hugh Holwey
The Fonte		Robert Hopkins	Thomas Mines	Edward Adlam	Henry George

WOMENS SEATES

Thomas Hill wives seate	Robert Rymell wives seate	John Stevens ats Shepherd wives seate	Mathew Chandler wives seate	John Carrs wives seate	Robert Knight wives seate
George Turner		John Turner	Henry Feltham	Anthony Rackesworthy	Richard Carpenter
James Watts	John Kennell	Thomas Chace	John Watts	John Knight	John Holwey
John Withie	Christopher Hill	George Turner	Lewes Abraham	Widdowe Cloude	John Hopkins
Robert Watts		William Smith ats Singer	William Smith ats Singer	John Watts	Edward Daniell
			Thomas Mines	Widdowe Paine	Stephen Crutch
John Rogers	John Laurence	Alexander Knight	John Beacham	John Baylie	Robert Minetie

The Vicars wives seate
for the Vicarage

The Farmers wife of Clyhill
for the Farme

MENS SEATES

Nichs Gibbins	Edward Couch	Humphrie Adlam
John Gratewood	Robert Hill	William Hooper
Peter Queile	John Turner	George Paine
Richard Dunnen	Christopher Dunnen	John Hunt
John Hooper	Anthony Coombes	Arthur Gaye
William Hancocks	Robert Watts	Henery Wates
HUNTENHULL	farme	CLYHILL
		Farme

WEOMENS SEATES

for Huntenhull Farme

John Carrs wives	Thomas Eyres wives seate	Thomas Allwood
Michael Ewestice wives seate	Robert Hopkins wives seate	Widdowe Dredge
Whiteborne Temple	Robert Hooper	John Nevill
Humphrie Adlam	Stephen Holweye	Roger Trolloppe
Nichs Dibbins	Anthony Coombs	John Rogers John Barens

CHANCELL DOORE	S^r. Thomas Thynn	THE SOUTH CORNER of the bodie of the Church

SIR THOMAS THYNN

Thomas Carr	. Mathewe Chandler .	Fields Courte
M^r. John Holweye	M^r. John Holweye	M^r. John Holweye

THE VICARS SEATE   } Pull-
....   NICHO : FITZHUGH   } Pitt
    Clearck   And the.......................................

THE CLEARCKS SEATE   · Robert Hooper
John Meare   John Hopkins   John Watts
Whiteborne Temple   Richard Carpenter   William Godsell
Lewes Abraham   George Turner   Stephen Holwey
Edward Danyell   Roger Trolloppe   Michael Ewestice

WOMENS SEATES

William Godsells wives seates | Mr. John | wives seates
                                Holweyes
Robert Hills   Arthur Gayes   William Raxworthies   Henry Tedbury
wife   wife   wife   wife
                                                    The Porch

WEOMENS SEATES

John Williams   Richard   John Hoopers   Feilds Court
als Clarke   Carpenters wife   wife   seate for the
wives seate   woman
Elenor Meares   Mary Lambs   Maurice Litlecots John Smithes
seate   seate   wives seate   wives seate
Wardes   William Holweys   Widdow Carpenters Peter Queile
                 wives   seate   wives seate
John Holweyes   John Bayly   Henry George   Thomas Holweys
wives seate   wives seate   his wives
                                    seate
William Claces   Robert Hopkins   Goodwife Francis   William Smith
wives seate   als Singer
John Kennell   William Watts   William Downe   John Singer
                     Widdowe Greene."

(B) LIST OF INCUMBENTS AND PATRONS AT CORSLEY 1250–1902.

Until 1485, when the predecessor of William Woolfe was appointed, the presentment is often noted as being either to the Chapel of Corsley, or to the Church (E.). Without further evidence it is not very clear whether there were usually two incumbents of Corsley up to this date, or whether the Chapel and Church alluded to are one and the same.

A.D.	Incumbent.	Patron.
1250	Thomas de Corsleya.	Prioress of Studley.
1306	William de Porter.	„
„	Walter de Parco.	„
1309	Nicholas de Hulprintune.	William de Lye.
1316	Richard Spakeman.	„
„	Walter de Stoville.	„
1326	William de Petresfeld.	E. „
1333	John *dictus* de Bathon de Cirencester.	Capella Corslegh Will' Hasard de Malmsbury.
1338	John le Vake of Corsley.	{ Capella. John, son of William de Lye.
1348	William le Forester.	E. John de Lye.
1348	Joseph Southcote.	
1378	Henry Langham.	E. Robert Lye.
1394	John Guynterel.	E. Robert Leghe.
1396	John Bryd.	„
1397	John Rome.	
1425	Thomas Wyddyngton.	E. Richard de Lye.
1430	Thomas Bonar.	„
1433	John Butler.	„
1439	John Fitz-Richard.	{ Capella. Nicholas Upton and other feoffees of Richard Lye.
1441	Nicholas Druell.	ditto.
1441	William Warmyll.	
1453	Richard Dyring.	{ Capella Thomas Tropenell and other feoffees of Robert Lye.
¹ 1454	Richard Gartham.	ditto.
1485	William Say.	E. Robert Ley de Corsley.
1505	William Wolf.	„
1524	William Benet, jun.	Richard Powton, Gen.
1539	John Swynerton.	
1555	Thomas Scott.	John Gly . . . Yeoman.
1563	William Harrington.	John Thynne, Knight.
1576	Henry Schawe.	„
1579	John Cutlett.	„
1908	Nicholas Fitzhugh.	{ Joanna, widow of John Thynne of Longleat.

¹ Last presentation to the chapel.

	Incumbent.	Patron.
A.D.		
1625	Robert Nevill.	
1660	John Yarner.	
1667	Richard Jenkins.	James Thynne, Knight.
1668	Thomas Aylesbury.	
1725	Richard Moody.	{ Thomas, Viscount Weymouth.
1736	Lionel Seaman.	,,
1738	William Colville.	,,
1764	John Lacy.	,,
1768	Millington Massey.	,,
1774	William Slade.	,,
1783	Thomas Huntingford.	Lord Weymouth.
1787	Isaac Huntingford.	,,
1830	R. C. Griffith.	,,
1845	James H. Waugh.	,,
1886	Richard E. Coles.	,,
1902	John T. Kershaw.	,,

(C) PURCHASES OF SIR JOHN THYNNE IN CORSLEY PARISH, SIXTEENTH CENTURY.[1]

The following extracts from Hoare's " History of Modern Wilts " show how extensive were the purchases of Sir John Thynne in the parish of Corsley in the sixteenth century.

"Extracts from Inquisition Roll taken at the death of Sir John Thynne, the elder, of his manor lands with their yearly value. . . .

". . . Maner. de Hunthill, alias Huntenhull, cum pertinen' in Com. Wiltes, ten. de quo vel de quibus ignoratur, et val. p. ann^m. £21. . . .

"Manerium de Corsley, cum pertinen ac domus mansionalis ejusd. Joh'is Thynne mil. una cum dominicis terris, et parcus de Corsley jacen. et existens in Warminster et Corsley, in praed Com. Wiltes. ten de D'na Reginâ in cap. per 20^am part 1 feod. mil. et val. darè p. ann^m. £15. 12s.

" Dominium sive Manerium de Whitborne et Whitborne Temple cum suis pertinents in dicto Com. Wiltes, ten. de D'na Regina in cap. per 20^am part. 1 feod, mil. et valet darè p. annum £4. 18s.

*   *   *   *   *

---

[1] See Hoare, " History of Modern Wilts," Hundred of Heytesbury, pp. 74–78.

" Boscus vocat. Norridge Woods, jacen. et existen. in Warminster et Upton Scudmore, ten. de D'na Regina. 10ˢ. &c.

" Extracts Inquisition Roll, taken at the death of Sir John Thynne the elder (original at Longleat).
" Terræ, Maneria, et Possessiones Johannis Thynne, Wilts. Manor of Hunthill, alias Huntenhull, &c., £21.

* * * * *

" Manor of Corsley, with the *domus mansionalis* of John Thynne, together with the park at Corsley, &c., £15. 12s.
" Demesne or Manor of Whitborne and Whitborne Temple, &c., £4. 18s.
" Norridge Woods, in Warminster and Upton Scudmore, 10s.

* * * * *

" Lands, &c., &c., in Whitburne Temple &c., £2. 2s. 2d.

* * * * *

" Lands, &c., in Warminster, Bugley, &c., £5. 11s.
" Lands, &c., in Corsley, 4/1

* * * * *

" One tenement in Bugley, held of Lord Audley, £1. 6s. 8d."

Extract from MS. list at Longleat of purchases made by Sir John Thynne the elder.
The Manors of Whitborne and lands in Bugley and Corsley, Co. Wilts. Bought of Richard Andrews, de Hayles, Co. Gloucester, anno regni Henry VIII 36°, who had them by grant from the said king in the same year. They had been part of the possessions of the Monastery of Mayden Bradley, Co. Wilts."

Sir John Thynne died in 1580.

APPENDIX 2

EXTRACTS FROM MS. CORSLEY OVERSEERS' ACCOUNTS

THE following is a summary of the expenditure on poor relief from May till October, 1729, and some full extracts from the list of " Extraordinaries " are also given.

During these months an average of thirty persons was in receipt of regular relief, the amount given varying from 1s. to 12s. per month, in different cases.

Expenditure on Poor, May 2 to Oct. 2, 1729.

Month.	Regular Relief.	Extraordinaries.
	£ s. d.	£ s. d.
May 2nd	6 1 6	8 18 10
May 29th	7 7 6	11 15 10
July 4th	7 2 6	5 18 3
July 31st	7 2 6	9 18 4
September 4th ...	6 18 0	6 19 9
October 2nd ...	6 15 6	6 19 6
Total, 6 months ...	41 7 6	50 10 6

Total expenditure on poor relief for six summer months : £91. 18s. od.

	Extraordinaries.	1729, May 2nd.
		£ s. d.
	The Wido Benet in yᵉ smalpox	1 0 6
	Mosis Withy for Rent of a loome	0 7 0
	John Napes wife for to by threed	0 1 0
	Elisabeth West for keeping Grace Bartlets children	1 0 0
	Mary Udil for qureing John Udiel's wife's	0 5 0
	Washing John Bartlet (regular pauper)	0 1 0
	Ester Tusdays expences	0 15 6
	Suzan Coleses house rent (regular pauper) ...	0 10 0

1729,
May 29th.
£ s. d.

Paeid for Briches for Will Langford (regular
pauper) ... ... o 3 8
Paeid for a shurt and making for Will Langford o 2 10
John Saey for Moses Withey's loome ... ... o 8 0
for careing Moses Withey Loome home ... ... o 5 0
5 eles of doules for Wid Holawaey's children
(regular pauper) ... ... o 6 9
for making 5 shifts ... ... o 1 4
John Haines's house rent (regular pauper) ... 1 15 0
Ann Pickford for Nap's family ... ... o 4 0

Extorernieryes.

1729,
July 4th.
£ s. d.

betay Clarke in yᵉ smalpox ... ... o 15 0
John Nap for a discharge & to by the children
bread ... ... o 12 0
Shift for Wid. Brown ... ... o 2 10
for feching Elisabeth withey home (regular
pauper) ... ... o 3 4
Sara Hunt for waishen John Bartlit (regular
pauper) ... ... o 2 0
Expenses for moving Mary Holoway ... ... o 3 6
For feching a warint for Samuel Dunin ... ... o 1 4
Ann pickford for house Rent for Naps ... ... o 2 6

Extorernieryes.

1729,
July 31st.
£ s. d.

too dozen of Read for Ales Gatood ... ... o 11 0
For thatching of ales Gratood (regular pauper)
house & Loft and naiels ... ... o 16 0
Richard Whitaker for bilding ales Gratood's house o 5 0
Wid. Turner for her family in yᵉ smalpox ... o 19 0
Mary Martin in yᵉ smalpox ... ... o 19 0
Issack Singer for building ales Gratoods house
& for timber 1 16 0
Ann pickford for keeping John Napes children
(two entries making) 1 16 0

<table>
<tr><td></td><td></td><td colspan="3">1729,</td></tr>
<tr><td>*Extraordinaries.*</td><td></td><td colspan="3">September 4th.</td></tr>
<tr><td></td><td></td><td>£</td><td>s.</td><td>d.</td></tr>
<tr><td>Mary Marten in the smalpox. ... ...</td><td></td><td>1</td><td>3</td><td>0</td></tr>
<tr><td>(various items of clothing and shoes for paupers)</td><td></td><td></td><td></td><td></td></tr>
<tr><td>Mary Udiel for keeping Mary Martin's chield</td><td></td><td></td><td></td><td></td></tr>
<tr><td>   and tending them both ... ...</td><td></td><td>1</td><td>5</td><td>0</td></tr>
</table>

<table>
<tr><td></td><td></td><td colspan="3">1729,</td></tr>
<tr><td>*Extraordinaries.*</td><td></td><td colspan="3">October 2nd.</td></tr>
<tr><td></td><td></td><td>£</td><td>s.</td><td>d.</td></tr>
<tr><td>Francis Mines his wages ... ...</td><td></td><td>0</td><td>12</td><td>6</td></tr>
<tr><td>George Biffen to send his Dafter to London ...</td><td></td><td>0</td><td>10</td><td>0</td></tr>
<tr><td>for careing of Mary Martin's goods ... ...</td><td></td><td>0</td><td>5</td><td>0</td></tr>
<tr><td>Ann Pickford for keeping John Naps children</td><td></td><td></td><td></td><td></td></tr>
<tr><td>   2 wickes ... ...</td><td></td><td>1</td><td>16</td><td>0</td></tr>
<tr><td>A paier of stockins for John Bartlet (regular</td><td></td><td></td><td></td><td></td></tr>
<tr><td>   pauper) ... ...</td><td></td><td>0</td><td>1</td><td>0</td></tr>
</table>

<table>
<tr><td></td><td colspan="3">1729</td></tr>
<tr><td></td><td colspan="3">[December 2nd].</td></tr>
<tr><td></td><td>£</td><td>s.</td><td>d.</td></tr>
<tr><td>Booft of Timithey Bodman a pice of cloth 34</td><td></td><td></td><td></td></tr>
<tr><td>   yards att 1ˢ. 9ᵈ. yard ... ...</td><td>2</td><td>13</td><td>10</td></tr>
</table>

APPENDIX 3

EXTRACTS FROM CENSUS REPORTS RELATING TO CORSLEY

PARISH OF CORSLEY. AREA 2,580 ACRES.

Year.	Inhabited Houses.	Uninhabited Houses.	Building.	Population.
1801	—	—	—	1,412
1811	—	—	—	1,352
1821	—	—	—	1,609
1831[1]	—	—	—	1,729
1841	351	28	2	1,621
1851[2]	334	17	—	1,473
1861[3]	303	24	—	1,235
1871	283	22	1	1,196
1881[4]	266	21	—	1,019

CIVIL PARISH OF CORSLEY. AREA 3,056 STATUTE ACRES

	Inhabited	Uninhabited	Building	Population
(1881[5]	268	21	—	1,023)
1891	236	26	8	926

		Uninhabited Houses. Occupied.	Unoccupied.	
1901	219	7	25	824

[1] 1831. About two hundred persons are stated to have emigrated within the last three years.

[2] 1851. In consequence of the discontinuance of a large cloth factory, several families have removed to other parishes in search of employment.

[3] 1861. "The decrease of population in the parish of Corsley is attributed to emigration. Many cottages have been pulled down" (Census Report, 1861, p. 667).

[4] Census Report, 1881, vol. ii. p. 253.

[5] Census Report, 1891, vol. ii. Transfers made from Corsley to Warminster of part of Bugley, and from Norton Bavant to Corsley. Census report says that a population of seventeen was transferred in both cases, so total population of Corsley not affected.

APPENDIX 4

EXTRACTS FROM MS. FARMING ACCOUNTS OF MR. JOHN BARTON

On October 18th, 1804, the farm stock was valued as follows:

	£	s.	d.
Old wheat in two Ricks, 130 Sacks at 40ˢ/-	260	0	0
Do. in Barn 24 Doˢ at 40ˢ/-	52	0	0
New Wheat in two Ricks 90 Doˢ at 40/-	180	0	0
Old Barley in Rick 16 Qʳˢ at 40/-	32	0	0
New Dº in two Ricks 30 Dᵒˢ at 40/-	60	0	0
Old Oats in Rick 16 Qʳˢ at 30/-	24	0	0
New Dº in one Rick 30 Qʳˢ at 30/-	45	0	0
Old Beans in Granary 10 Sacks at 26/-	13	0	0
New Dº in Rick 15 Sacks at 26/-	19	10	0
Peas in Rick 20 Sacks at 25/-	25	0	0
Peas in Granary 8 Dº at 25/-	10	0	0
Clover seed, two sacks in Granary ...	20	0	0
Wool in Granary	31	0	0
Vetches in Granary—5 sacks	5	5	0
Six Cows at 15£	90	0	0
Two yearling Cows	12	0	0
Seven Cart Horses	125	0	0
Colt, two years old	23	0	0
Colt, sucking	7	0	0
Poultry	10	0	0
120 Ewes for Stock at 1 gā	126	0	0
40 Dº for Sale at 1£	40	0	0
Two Rams	4	0	0
50 chilver Lambs at 17/-	42	10	0
44 Wedder Dº at 16/-	35	4	0
Two fatting pigs	8	0	0
3 sows and 14 young pigs	16	0	0
Waggons, Harness, &c.	80	0	0
Bills due for work with Cart Horses ...	8	0	0
Potatoes	10	0	0
Rent of potatoe ground	4	0	0
Grass Seeds sown 31 acres at 1£ ...	31	0	0
Wheat bought for Seed and paid for ...	15	13	0
Dº from Mr. Barter for wool ...	31	0	0
Due for Bills for poultry, Hay, &c. at Warmʳ	10	17	4
Dº at Corsley	42	16	10
To Hay there being 72 Ton, and which is supposed more than a usual quantity by 22 ton	80	0	0
	1,575	2	0

LIST OF REFERENCES TO CORSLEY

Hoare, Sir Richard Colt, History of Ancient Wilts, Hundred of Warminster. London, 1812-21.
Jones, William H., Domesday for Wilts. 1865.
Calendar Charter Rolls, Hen. III., vol. i., p. 283.
Rotuli Hundredorum (Record Commission), vol. ii., p. 276.
Calendar Patent Rolls, vols. 1334—38, p. 540.
MS. Extent of Manor of Whitbourne, 1364, in possession of Marquis of Bath.
Gairdner, Letters and Papers of Reign of Hen. VIII., vols. xii., xix.
MS. Wilts Quarter Sessions Records.
Hist. MS. Commission. Various Collections, i. 1901. Wilts Quarter Sessions Records.
Calendar State Papers, Domestic, Chas. I., vols. 1631—33.
Proceedings Court of Chancery, Haynes *v.* Carr. Chas. I. H. H. 69.
MS. Bayliffe's Account of Corsley Manor, 1634, at Longleat Estate Office.
MS. Certificates in Corsley Parish Chest.
MS. Indentures in Corsley Parish Chest.
MS. Examinations of Applicants for Relief in Corsley Parish Chest.

MS. Papers relating to bastardy cases in possession of C. N. Phipps, Esq.

MS. Corsley Overseers' Accounts, 1729—41, 1747—55, 1769—1836.

Enclosure Agreement of 1742, at Longleat Estate Office.

MS. Corsley Survey, 1745, at Longleat Estate Office.

MS. Corsley Perambulation in 1754, at Longleat Estate Office.

MS. Corsley Workhouse Accounts, 1774—1801.

Workhouse Insurance Policy, c. 1774, in Corsley Parish Chest.

MS. Corsley Churchwardens' Accounts, 1782, *et seq.*·

MS. Corsley Vestry Minutes.

Warminster and Corsley Enclosure Award, with Maps, 1783, at Longleat Estate Office, and at Office of Clerk of the Peace, Devizes.

MS. Minutes of Manor Courts, Corsley, Huntenhull, &c., at Longleat Estate Office.

Davis, T., General View of the Agriculture of Wilts, 1794, and second edition, 1813.

Hoare, Sir Richard Colt, History of Modern Wilts, Hundred of Warminster and Hundred of Heytesbury. London, 1822-44.

Census Reports.

MS. Barton Farming Accounts, 1801—11, and 1828—36, at Corsley House.

Abstract Poor Returns, 1815.

MS. Account Book of Mr. Sparey, 1821.

Cobbett, William, Rural Rides, 1825.

MS. Terrier of Corsley, 1828, among parish records.

Scrope, Paulet, Extracts of Letters, from poor persons who emigrated last year to Canada and the United States. Printed for the information of the labouring poor in this country. London : Chippenham [printed], 1831.

Report Charity Commission, 1834, vol. xxviii.

Report Poor Law Commission, 1834, vol. xiii., Appendix B1, vol. xiv., Appendix B1, Part III., Appendix C.

Second Annual Report Poor Law Commission, 1836, vol. i.

Warminster and Westbury Journal, June 17, 1905.

Lea, J. Henry, The Lyes of Corsley. [To be published in America.]

Wiltshire Archæological Magazine, vols. x., xii., xv., xvi., xix., xxii., xxiii., xxvi.

Daniell, John, History of Warminster. Simpkin, Marshall & Co., London : Warminster [printed], 1879.

Doël, W., Twenty Golden Candlesticks. Trowbridge, 1890.

Tuck, Stephen, Wesleyan Methodism in Frome. Frome, 1837.

MS. Corsley Parish Registers.

Various documents and papers relating to the parish in the care of the Rector or of the Clerk to the Parish Council.

MS. Corsley Wesleyan Methodist Chapel Baptismal Register.

Corsley ~ a Hamlet Parish in Wiltshire
by
Brian Short

IN 1905 A student at the London School of Economics received a suggestion from Sidney and Beatrice Webb that she should continue her studies in economic history and social science by pursuing an in-depth study of her parish in which she was living. The result was the fine study of Corsley in Wiltshire by Maud Davies, *Life in an English Village,* which was completed some five years prior to the Valuation and published in 1909. The timing of the study thus provides an interesting example of how previously published material can be re-examined in order to draw on the Valuation material to support or possibly expand on the original – in this case a pioneering sociological study.

The Valuation Books yielded the hereditament numbers within the larger Corsley ITP [income tax parish] that related to Corsley civil parish. Since the Wiltshire County Record Office did not accept Form 37, the examination was confined largely to the Field Books. These were mostly completed in detail, although in the case of the larger hereditaments, the descriptions are usually missing, with references being made to the 'file', or to the 'schedule' attached to Form 37. Thus the information for Cley Hill Farm of nearly 450 acres, tenanted by Richard Oxford from Lord Bath, was in 'Note Book 759 p.17'. Descriptive material was commonly attached to Form 37, and once again the detrimental effects of non-acceptance of the latter are demonstrated. One difficulty that arose on close examination of the Field Books was that much of the field survey for the Valuation was actually carried out in 1914, making this a late valuation, and leaving a gap of nine years between the two sources.[1] In an internal memorandum in 1912 it was stated of Mr W. T. Howes, District Valuer of the Salisbury District under whose responsibility Corsley lay, that: 'He does not inspire that degree of enthusiasm in his staff . . . and the District is one of the most backward in the Division of Central West.'[2] However, a large proportion of the Provisional Valuations in this area were being objected to, and this was undoubtedly slowing down the operation.

Corsley civil parish is today perhaps overshadowed by its well-known neighbour, Longleat House, on its southern boundary. The parish is on the western border of Salisbury Plain, near the Somerset border, and comprises nine separate hamlets with smaller clusters of buildings, and although Corsley itself is the location for the parish church, most of the population were living in 1905 at Chapmanslade, a village bordering on other parishes also, and along the western and southern borders of the parish (map, p.48 above).

The Field Books included 349 hereditaments, but three of these (nos. 83, 195 and 197) were labelled as 'cancelled' in the Field Books, presumably being incorporated elsewhere; another was the main road; and five were included in adjoining parishes for valuation purposes. Thus 340 hereditaments within the civil parish were actually detailed in the Field Books. In the case of smaller hereditaments the data seem full and detailed, and the comparison of information on cottage property with that supplied by Davies is easily fulfilled.

The area of these hereditaments was 2920 acres 2 roods 2

1   Wiltshire County Record Office, Domesday Books, Register 126 Corsley and Upton Scudamore ITP (Warminster Division); PRO IR 58/73332-5, Field Books for Corsley ITP, Wiltshire. For Cley Hill Farm see PRO IR 58/73333, Hereditament no. 110.

2   PRO IR 74/148, 361-2.

perches according to the Field Books. This compared with an acreage of 3,056 according to Davies and the 1911 Census. The few small hereditaments without stated areas presumably account for most of the difference, although discrepancies between the boundaries of the civil parish and the 'hereditament' parish should not be discounted.

Landownership was superficially fragmented between forty-seven different owners. However, all but one owned between them a mere 310 acres. The exception was Lord Bath, resident at Longleat, who owned some 2,610 acres in the parish. Table 10.11 shows the distribution of landownership. Several of these 'owners' were in fact copy, life or lease holders of Lord Bath, so that ultimately his potential influence was probably even greater than the figures suggest. Table 10.12 shows that the majority of hereditaments were owned on a freehold basis.

Owner-occupation was unusual. Apart from Lord Bath, who occupied 360 acres of his own land, and the Church, there were only twelve people occupying their own property. The owner of Corsley House, B. W Davis, occupied some 60 acres of his own land, and A.W. Parish was an owner-occupier of 12.5 acres. The remaining owner-occupiers were cottagers with only a few roods of land.

The various properties were let on a variety of tenancy terms. Davies stated that: 'Some of the old cottages are still let on a lease of lives, but ordinary yearly or weekly tenancies have during the last forty years been gradually substituted for this old system as the lives fall in'. But the Field Books showed only four weekly tenancies, with yearly and longer tenancies (leases for lives?) providing the great bulk (Table 10.13).

These figures may conceal extensive sub-letting on a weekly basis, but this seems unlikely as the valuers tended to indicate sub-letting where it occurred. The conclusion must be that Davies overstated the extent of weekly letting, and this is borne out by a study of the length of residence. Table 10.14 shows that many tenants had occupied their premises for a considerable time. This is known

Table 10.11 *Ownership structure in Corsley, Wiltshire*

Area (acres)	No. of owners
<0.25	11
0.25 to 0.9	22
1 to 4.9	6
5 to 24.9	4
>25	5
Total	48

Source: PRO, Field Books IR 58/73332–5.

Table 10.12 *Types of tenure in Corsley, Wiltshire*

Type of Tenure	Hereditaments
Freehold	264
Leasehold	26
Lifehold	10
Copyhold	7
Not stated	33
Total	340

Source: PRO, Field Books IR 58/73332–5.

Table 10.13 *Tenancy terms in Corsley, Wiltshire*

Period	No. of hereditaments
Weekly	4
Fortnightly	1
Quarterly	24
Half-yearly	11
Yearly	127
Leases over one year	51
Not stated	21
Total	339

Source: PRO, Field Books IR 58/73332–5.

Table 10.14 *Length of occupation in Corsley, Wiltshire*

Period (years)	No. of hereditaments
<1	1
1 to 4.9	66
5 to 9.9	42
10 to 24.9	84
>25	9
Total	202

Source: PRO, Field Books IR 58/73332–5.

Table 10.15 *Hereditaments in Corsley, Wiltshire (by unit size)*

Area (acres)	No. of hereditaments
<0.25	79
0.25 to 0.9	97
1 to 4.9	26
5 to 24.9	31
25 to 49.9	10
50 to 99.9	9
100 to 299.9	4
>300	2
Total	258

Source: PRO, Field Books IR 58/73332–5.

Table 10.16 *Rooms in 'cottages' in Corsley, Wiltshire (according to the Field Books and to Davies)*

	No. of cottages		No. of cottages	
No. of rooms	(Field Book)	%	(Davies)	%
1	2	1.5	—	—
2	4	3.0	8	4.9
3	64	47.8	51	30.9
4	33	24.6	45	27.3
5	17	12.7	33	20.0
6	12	9.0	18	10.9
Not stated	2	1.5	—	—
>6	—	—	10	6.1
Total	134		165	

·*Source:* PRO, Field Books IR 58/73332–5; Davies, *Life in an English Village* (London 1909), 133.

Table 10.17 *Condition of cottage accommodation in Corsley, Wiltshire*

Condition	No. of cottages
Poor	8
Moderate	38
Fair	45
Good	1
Not stated	44
Total	136

Source: PRO, Field Books.

because owners, notably Lord Bath, frequently returned the date of commencement of the tenancy on Form 4, and this was transcribed into the Field Books. The base date for the table is 1 October 1910, and only those hereditaments having the relevant information are included.

The overall impression is one of comparative stability of occupancy in the parish, although Davies argued that this was true only for part of the population, and that the rest were constantly moving. The table does not contradict this, since it could easily be the case that those tenants of less than five years' occupancy comprised this 'floating' population.

This hamlet-dominated parish was characterised by large numbers of small and medium holdings. Although Table 10.15 gives no indication of multiple occupation of hereditaments, it is clear that amongst those hereditaments having relevant information, large farms were in a minority. Moreover, the table demonstrates that a substantial number of 'large gardens' of up to 1 acre were attached to many houses. Some surprising details were sometimes given by the valuer, for example Ellen White's 'good pear tree' on the front wall of her house and the medlar tree on the small lawn in front of the house at Leigh (Lye) Green. The findings on holding size accord fairly well with Davies' figures. She made no attempt to analyse all land holdings, but gave details of the holdings of 'farmers'. Thus she also found only two farms larger than 300 acres, and three between 100 and 300 acres.[1]

Housing conditions in Corsley varied widely. Davies found it impossible to draw a sharp distinction between cottages and houses, and it is equally difficult to do so from the Field Book data. She calculated that there were about 165 'cottages' in the parish, and examined the amount of living accommodation in them. A similar exercise follows to compare her findings with those drawn from the Field Books, for which attention is confined to those inhabited buildings that the valuer described as 'cottages', numbering 134 in total. Table 10.16 shows the results of this analysis.

Davies found that only about one-third of the cottages had three rooms. In the present smaller sample, the figure is almost 50 per cent, and there are thirteen more in absolute terms, although fewer four- and five-roomed cottages were found. The increase in the number of three-roomed cottages may reflect a genuine increase in the years after Davies' study, but may also be due to different methods of counting. Davies counted 'rooms' while the present reexamination counted 'living rooms', and the two clearly may not be identical. In addition, valuers' comments make it plain that landings were frequently used as bedrooms. Where this was the case, they have been included as a room, but changes in use of the landing with new tenants, or life-cycle changes in household composition, could easily therefore affect the number of 'rooms' identified in a house. Nevertheless, both the present analysis and Davies' survey show that housing was cramped in Corsley before the Great War.

The condition of the cottages, according to the Field Books, accords well with Davies' statement that they were 'on the whole'. . . neither specially good nor specially bad . . .' Table 10.17 shows that the valuers described the majority as being of 'moderate' or 'fair' condition. But the fact also that just one cottage could be classed as

1   PRO IR 58/73332, Hereditament no. 65.

'good', out of the ninety-two for which such an adjective is given, is grounds for believing that she was perhaps a little too willing to gloss over some of the deficiencies. She states at one point that 'There is a fair proportion of really good cottages, mainly owned by residents in the parish.' There is little to underpin such a statement from the Field Books. There had certainly been some changes since her survey: Albert Garratt occupied a half-acre property at Leigh Green (Lye Green on the Ordnance Survey map [reprinted on p.48]) which had been an 'old cottage in poor repair' and which had been pulled down around 1909. Part only now (October 1914) remained, being covered by corrugated iron and used as a store. Others, such as Hereditament no.80 at Huntenhall Green, were described as 'ruinous' and 'void', or fit only to be pulled down.[1]

Cottages were stated in the Field Books to be almost all built of stone-rubble and brick, with thatch and/or tile roofs being about equally common. The block of cottages at 79-82 Lane End had been completely reroofed with tiles in early 1914, since the old thatch had been rather poor. Water supply was mentioned only infrequently, and was apparently usually obtained from wells, often shared by adjacent cottages. Only one, 25 Whitbourne Hill, had no water nearby, and James Sims, the unfortunate tenant, had to fetch it nearly a half-mile. The cottage was, however, rent-free.[2] On the other hand, a number had taps as part of the 'estate supply'.

Only five cottages were said to have had stables, one a cowpen, and thirteen were said to have had pigsties. Davies noted that 'some' cottagers kept pigs, and it is doubtful whether the stated number of pigsties gives a full picture of the extent of cottage pigkeeping. Nevertheless, it suggests that the 'cottager's pig' was far from ubiquitous in Corsley in 1910. The Field Books also give land use data on a field-by-field basis for a number of hereditaments, and this material

1   PRO IR 58/73332, Hereditament nos.3, 48, 80.

2   *Ibid.,* Hereditament nos. 40-4 and 13.

confirms Davies' statement that agriculture was predominantly pasture-based .

As well as this work on housing, which could be broadened out by complementing her Chapter XI on 'Houses and Gardens in Corsley', one could also elaborate on Chapter X, for example 'Who the Corsley people are, and how they get their living', by offering details of farms, tradespeople's premises and the conditions of their workshops etc. Thus, her anonymous 454 acre farm, the largest in the parish, was described as: Arable and grass. Wheat, oats, beans, sold Frome and Warminster markets. Calves reared. Sheep. Butter-making. Sometimes milk sold. 10 regular [Men and Boys employed, including sons or other relatives].'

This could be none other than the 448 acre Cley Hill Farm. As noted above, the information for this farm was said to be in a separate notebook, but nevertheless it was certainly possible to identify this property, and Richard Oxford, the tenant of Lord Bath. It is also possible to add that the farm ('one of the historical houses of the parish') was held on a yearly tenure and had been so held since Michaelmas 1904, for a rent of £346.

The farm had been sold previously on 25 December 1903 for £8,500, including all the timber. The hereditament was also valued with six others, one being the sporting rights of Lord Bath, and the others including four houses in the hamlet of Chips (or Landhayes), presumably tied cottages, also belonging to Lord Bath.[1] Similarly Davies' anonymous 255 acre holding can be equated with Manor Farm, built for Sir John Thynne in the early seventeenth century. We are told that the farm was: '25 acres arable, the rest grass. Dairy. Milk sold in London. Grow enough wheat to supply own straw, and roots for own supply, 7 [workers].' The hereditament, actually surveyed at 255 acres 1 rood 37 perches, was held from Lord Bath by A. E. James on a yearly tenancy which dated back to Michaelmas 1900, for

1　PRO IR 58/73333. Hereditament nos. 108, 110-15.

which he paid £307 10s. Four tied cottages were also included in the same valuation, occupied by Messrs Clements, Snelgrove, Harris and Cowley.[1]

Tradesmen's premises have descriptions too. John Pearce was the occupier of several properties from Lord Bath, including Hereditament no. 238 on a thirty-year lease from Michaelmas 1887 at £10, which included a timber shed with a travelling saw, movable steam engine and others carpenters' tools, wheelwright's shop, painting shop, a smithy and various storerooms. Davies mentions painters, carpenters and wheelwrights, a blacksmith and a sawyer. She wrote of Mr Pearce 'wheelwright and builder, living at Corsley Heath' who employed over twenty inhabitants besides another twenty workers not resident in the parish. 'The work carried out by Mr Pearce at his Corsley workshop is mainly that of cartbuilding; he also undertakes house carpentering, painting etc.'[2] A splendid photograph of the workforce was also included (p.157 above). She omitted to say that Mr Pearce had also tenanted a limekiln and quarry at Cley Hill, belonging to Lord Bath, since Michaelmas 1904. Unfortunately women's work is invisible in the Valuation survey, and whilst Davies also writes of the laundry-work, charring, gloving, nursing and midwifery as well as domestic activities, there is nothing to enhance her descriptions.

Other properties can certainly be identified in this way, but other chapters in Davies' account can also be amplified. Thus, Chapter XVI, 'Social life in Corsley', could be supplemented by descriptions of the pubs or of the Reading Room, which was let on a ninety-nine-year lease at 1s per annum from Lord Bath from Michaelmas 1891. It had been built in 1892, but was 'not much frequented' according to

1   PRO IR 58/73333, Hereditament nos. 190-4.

2   PRO IR 58/73334, Hereditament no. 238. The quarry is Hereditament no. 235; Davies, *Life in an English Village*, 122-4.

Davies.[1] The church and chapels were described in the Valuation Field Books also. The Baptist and Wesleyan chapels were fully described. The Wesleyan chapel at Lane End was a stone, brick and slate building in fair repair by 1914. It had a rectangular chapel room with pitch pine furniture and a small raised dais and preaching desk. There was also a small gallery, and a schoolroom at the rear. Davies described the chapel as having services normally taken by lay preachers from the neighbourhood, and occasionally attended by a travelling preacher. The Baptist chapel at Whitbourne, 'brick, tile and part stucco', had a small organ and an adjoining room for Sunday school and prayer-meetings. It was surrounded by a burial-ground and beyond that was a 'deep tank for use in the rite of baptism'. The Field Book referred to it as a 'circular baptistry in [the] graveyard'.[2]

At this remove in time, one could also now add many names to the anonymous individuals cited. The data obtained from the Field Books therefore allow some comparable examination of a near-contemporary secondary source, and in this case largely confirms that many of Davies' statements held good some five or six years later. Nearly all aspects of her enquiries as published in 1909 can be added to in some way by using the Valuation Field Books.

[Reprinted with the author's permission from his *Land and Society in Edwardian Britain* (Cambridge Studies in Historical Geography 25), Cambridge Univ. Press, 2005, pp.273-82. Brian Short is Emeritus Professor of Historical Geography at the University of Sussex.]

1   PRO IR 58/73335, Hereditament no. 346.

2   PRO IR 58/73333, Hereditament nos. 137 and 138

Bibliography

Primary Sources

The National Archives (TNA)
MH32/111 correspondence between Byam Davies and Local
    Government Board

British Library Newspaper Library
Daily Express

Kensington Archives
Kensington News & West London Times
West London Press
Royal Borough of Kensington register of electors

London Metropolitan Archives
LCC/Min/4359 Sub Committee on underfed children
LCC/Min/3170 Sub Committee on children's care
LCC Education Committee Minutes

London School of Economics
Fabian Society Archive Coll Misc 0862
Fabian News
Fabian Women's Group H25 meetings, H27 attendance lists and H 28
    annual reports
Fabian Summer School Visitors Book G9

Fabian lecturers C62/1
Davies M F, *School Care Committees: a guide to their work* 1909
Frere, M, *Children's Care Committees* 1909

University of London, Senate House
VCH archives. A19, 1506, Wiltshire early correspondence

At Wiltshire & Swindon History Centre, Chippenham
Wiltshire VCH collection WSA 1946A/1/1
Salisbury & Winchester Journal
Warminster & Westbury Journal
Corsley school log books WSA F8/500/84/1/1
Corsley parish council minute book WSA 1097/20
Electoral register Westbury division WSA A1/355/152
Diary of Rev Attwood WSA 1229/1
Parish of Corsley poor rate book WSA G12/510/21
Kelly's Directory Wiltshire 1903, 1907, 1911

At Wiltshire Heritage Museum Library, Devizes
Cuttings Book volume 13
Scrope, George Poulett, 'Extracts of letters from Poor Persons who
    emigrated last year to Canada and the United States' 1832 in
    Pamphlets on the Poor Law etc

Secondary Sources

Black, C (ed) *Married Women's Work* originally published 1915,
    Virago reprint 1993
Critall (ed), *Victoria County History of Wiltshire* Vol 8, 1965
Davies M F, *Life in an English Village*, Unwin, 1909
Davies M F, *School Care Committees, a guide to their work*, Burleigh,
    1909a

Freeman M, *Social Investigation and Rural England 1879-1914*, Boydell for the Royal Historical Society, 2003

Grice H, *Corsley House: a history*, 1999

Hutchings V, *Crocodiles and Chicken Chasers*, Corsley & Chapmanslade Millennium Book Committee, 2000

Page and Ditchfield, eds, *Victoria County History of Berkshire* Vol 3, 1923

Pease E, *History of the Fabian Society*, Fabian Society and George Allen & Unwin, 2nd ed 1925

Short B, *Land and Society in Edwardian Britain*, Cambridge Univ Press, 1997

Some Publications Quoting or Using Maud Davies's Work

Beckett, J 'Rethinking the English village' *The Local Historian* Vol 42 No 4 2012

Britain 2000, The Office Yearbook of the United Kingdom

Broadberry S and Burhop C, 'Real wages and labour productivity in Britain and Germany 1871-1938: a unified approach to the international comparison of living standards' *Journal of Economic History* Vol 17 No 2 2010

Burnett, John, *Plenty and Want*, Penguin 1968

Burnett, John, *Idle Hands. The experience of unemployment 1790-1990*, Psychology Press 1994

Cohen, S and Fleay, C, 'Fighters for the poor' *History Today* January 2000 p 36

Collis, Robert, *Identity of England*, Oxford Univ Press 2002, p 305

Freeman, Mark, *Social Investigation and Rural England 1870-1914*, Boydell for the Royal Historical Society, 2003 ch 4

Freeman, Mark (ed) *The English Rural Poor 1850-1914*, 5 vols, Pickering and Chatto, 2005, Vol 5

Hendrick, Harry, *Images of Youth: age class and the male youth problem 1880-1920*, Oxford Univ Press, 1990

Mannell, Stephen, *All Manners of Food: Eating and Taste in England and France from the Middle Ages to to Present.* University of Illinois Press, 1996

Mills, Dennis, *Lord and Peasant in Nineteenth Century Britain*, Croom Helm, London 1980

Oddy D J, *From plain fare to fusion food: British diet from the 1890s to the 1990s.* Boydell 2003

Oren, Laura, 'The welfare of women in laboring families: England 1860-1950' *Feminist Studies*, Vol 1 1973, p 107

Perkin, Joan, *Women and Marriage in Nineteenth century England*, Black, 1983, p 192

Perkin, Joan, 'Sewing machines: liberation or drudgery for women?' *History Today* December 2002, p 41

Powell, W R, 'Local History in Theory and Practice' *Historical Research* Vol 31, May 1958, p 41

Short, Brian, *Land and Society in Edwardian Britain*, CUP 1997

Strange, Julie-Ann, *Death, Grief and Poverty in Britain 1870 - 1914*, CUP, 2005, 36, 254

Thompson, F M L, *Cambridge Social History of Britain 1750-1950*, CUP 1993, p 214, 216

Twells, Alison, *British Women's History 1780-1914: a documentary history*, I B Taurus, 2007

Underdown, David, *Revolution, Riot and Rebellion: popular politics and culture in England 1603-1660*, 1987, p 7 n

Winstanley, Michael, *The Shopkeeper's World 1830-1914*, Manchester Univ Press, 1983, p 199, 202

Index

This is based on the index to the 1909 edition, with the original pages renumbered and index entries to the additional material incorporated into it.

Accounts, overseers 287-9
Adults, numbers of, in poverty 174, 175, 176, 177, 179-81
Aged, in receipt of outdoor relief 205
provision for 205, 206, 207, 208
Agricultural and industrial population 75, 89, 90
Agricultural labourers, wages and earnings of, 152, 153, 154
Agricultural produce, destination of 145, 146
Agricultural riots in Wilts 116
Agricultural wages 86, 94, 152, 153, 154
Agriculture 89, 123, 142, 143, 144, 145, 146, 147, 148, 149
after enclosure 91, 92, 93
employment of boys in 116
employment of women in 116, 124
medieval 57
Allotment, under enclosure award 91-2
Allotments 169, 170
Amusements, obsolete 131
Ancestors of Corsley men, occupations 253-259
Ancestry of Corsley householders 246- 259
Apprenticeship 79, 80
of pauper children 78-9, 113
Arable, conversion of, to pasture 123, 124
distribution of 51
Arable and pasture, distribution of 92
Area of parish 49, 296-7
Artisans 156
earnings of 157-9
proportion of, in poverty 181
peports on characters of 201, 202, 203
reports on children of 203
Atwood, Rev G 45

Bailey, Farmer 129
Bakers, women 163
Baking 76

Ball, Farmer 129
Bank, school savings 244
Baptist chapel, 305
bequest to 129
Baptists 96, 97, 269
'Barley' times 115
Barton, family of 76, 128
farming accounts 93-4, 291
farming by Mr 123
John 92
Mr 104
Mrs, endowment of new church by 126
Bath, Marquis of ix, 100, 297, 300, 303, 304
Beacon on Cley Hill 61
Beadle, appointment of 100
Beer, consumption of 264-5
Bell, casting of 100
Bellringers 98
Benefice, list of presentations to 283-5
Benefit societies, see Clubs
Bickenham Field 57, 91
Birthplace of Corsley people 250-2
Blacksmith, savings of 130
Blacksmiths 159
Boat train 39-40, 41
Boer War 2
Booth, Charles 2
Bounds, beating of the 112
Bowley 2
Boys, agricultural wages of 154
employment of, in agriculture 116-7
Brickmakers, earnings of 159
Budgets, family see Family Budgets
Bugley, manor of 59
Building trades 156

Calthrop, Miss M C C ix, 14, 22
Canada, emigrations to 117-8

Carey, George, clothier 68, 77
Carey, George, maltster 69, 77
    family 69, 76
Carpenter, John, dyer 83
    William, apprenticeship of 80
Carpenters' earnings 158
Carr, family of 63-4
    Mr 61
Carters' earnings 150-1
Carts and horses 130-1, 148-9
Catering, local 209-210
Celtic villages 53
Census reports 290
Chapel, Kingston Court 60
    Services 264
Chapels, loation of 52-3
    Nonconformist 125-6, 264
Chapman, William, apprenticeship of 80
Chapmanslade 52, 296
    episcopal church built at 126
    manor of 59
Character and its relation to poverty 182-208
    tables of reports on 187-201
    of artisans, reports on 201
Charwomen, wages of 160
Chedlinhanger field 57, 91
Children, earnings of 117
    number of, in poverty 175, 176, 177, 178,
    179, 180, 181
    of Corsley people, migrations of 261-2
    of Corsley people, occupations of 253-60
    pauper, put to service 113
    proportion of, in poverty 271-2
    small proportion of, in Corsley 271
Chipps, hamlet of 123, 303 see also Landhayes
Church, account of 279
    old parish 99
    rebuilding of 99
    seating order 280-3
Church of England 96, 97, 268-9
    Services 96, 97
Churches, Episcopal, building of new 186
    location of 52
Churchwardens accounts 95
Clark, William 42
Clements, Mr 304
Cley Hill 49, 50, 51, 60-1, 304
    barrows on 54
    beacon on 61
    Celtic settlement on 54
    game played on 131
    limekiln on 88
    name of 49

Cley Hill Farm 52, 56, 92, 123, 165, 295, 303
    eviction at 63
Cley Hill Field 57, 91
Cloth factory, closing of 121, 290
Cloth-making and agriculture 84
Cloth trade 55, 76-72, 82-85, 116, 120, 122-3
    decline of 116, 120, 122-3
    description of 82-3
    wages in 85
    Wiltshire 62
    Wiltshire, disorganisation of 67-8
Clothiers, immigration of 69
Club, Corsley Walking 119
Clubs 119, 241-4
Coal and timber trade 51
Coal hauliers 144
Coal-mines, Radstock 51
Commonfield agriculture 60-1
Common fields, ancient 53, 57, 60-1
    enclosure of 56, 82, 91-2
Commons, see waste lands
Conclusion 271-5
Coney Warren 61
Configuration 50, 51, 52
Congregational Church 96
Congregationalists 269
Coombs, owner of silk factory 123
    Mr 129
Coope, John 92
Corn production 91, 123
Corsley Heath 53, 55, 74, 304
    enclosure of 55, 72
Corsley House 1, 6-7, 24, 52, 115, 297
    building of 104
Corsley, manor of 59
    monuments 66
    park 60
    stock 65-6
    Walking Club 119
Corsley parish council 23, 27
Cottage gardens 168-170, 300
    rents 168
Cottage property, owners of 166
Cottages 165-168, 299, 301-2
    size of 166, 299, 300-1
Court Leet 88-9
Cow keeping in Corsley 123
Cowley, Mr 304
Cracumbe, Godfrey 277
Cricket 281
Cunningham, W 17

Dairies Factory, United, in Frome 143

Dairy farming 123, 124
Dairy produce, destination of 143, 145, 146
Dairying 143-6
Dairymen, earnings of 151
Dartford 52
Davies, Byam (father) 1, 6, 9, 24, 25, 45-6, 297
Davies, Cecil (sister) 7
Davies, Frances (mother) 6, 7, 10, 25, 45
Davies, Mrs Margaret 40, 41
Davies family 7, 8, 10, 33-4, 44
Day labourers, wages and earnings of 154-5
Dearle, N B 22
Deer, wild, in Corsley 60
Deerlip, origin of name of 60
Deficiency of school-children, definition of 183
Destitution not condition for granting relief 113
Diet, cottagers 210-240
    inquiry as to 138
    of labouring families 117
Doctors 244-5
Dodeman, Henry 277
Dogs, relief and charity refused to persons keeping 114
Domesday survey 56-7
Donkeys, old men provided with 88
Dredge, Mr 129
Dressmakers, earnings of 162-3
Dressmakers' apprentices, earnings of 163
Drink, reports on 184-5
Dyeworks 83-4

Earnings, inquiry as to 136-8
Earnings of agricultural labourers 152-4
    artisans 56-9
    brickmakers 158-9
    carters 150-1
    children 117
    cowmen 151
    diarymen 151
    day-labourers 154-5
    dressmakers 162-3
    glovemakers 161
    labourers 149-155
    laundresses 159-60
    under-gardeners 154
    women 117
    women at nursing 162
    women at sewing 161
    women in Corsley 164
    woodmen 154-5
Ecclesiastical unification 60
Education, state of 203-4

statistics of 127
Elliott, William clothier 70
Emigration 290
    at parish expense 117-8
Emigrations to Canada 117
Employment of women in agriculture 94, 124-5
    See also Labourers, Artisans, Women etc
Enclosure, expense of 92
    of commonfields 56
    of Corsley Heath 55, 74-5
    of parish 82, 91-2
Enclosure award, allotment under 92
Entertainment, provided at public houses 265-6
Entertainments 264
Eviction at Cley Hill Farm 63-4
Expenditure of family incomes 213-240
Eyres, Mrs 129

Fabian Society 1, 2, 6, 25-29
Fabian summer school 26
Fabian Women's Group 25,26
Factories in Corsley 122-3
Fairs, Corsley 131
Families, history of 246-262
    incomes of 172
    size of 248-50
    vitality of 273-5
Family budgets 209-245
    mode of collection 138
Family life 263-4
Famine of 1801 115
Farmers 142-4
    mode of living 129-30
Farming accounts 93-4, 291
Farms, breaking up of 124
    consolidation of 56, 91
    particulars of 145-6
    size of 144
Food, menus of 212-240
    minimum cost of 173
    preparation of 210-1
Food supply, local 209-210
Football 267
Forest, see Selwood Forest
Forest land, hamlets in 53
Forester, extortions of 55
Friendly societies 119, 241-4
Frome 50, 303
Fussell, a dyer 122
    H A Fussell, dye-works of 83
    family 128-9

Games, obsolete 131

Garden, account of profits of 169-170
Gardeners 155, see also Under-gardeners
Gardens 167-170, 300
    proportion of food furnished by 210
Garrett, Albert 302
Geographical position of Corsley 49, 57
Germanic villages 53
Gipsies 131
Gipsy fights 131
Girls, employment of, in industry 117
Glove-making, earnings of women at 161
    rates of payment for 161
Goddard, Canon E H 21
Godwell, manor of 59
Great Western Railway 50, 58, 128
    effect on rural population of 128
GWR shares 5 fn 14
Greatwood, James, will of 84
Grice, Hugh 24, 40
Groom-gardeners 155
Guardians, Warminster Board of 122

Hall, Hubert ix, 12, 14, 15
Hamlets, distribution of 52
Harris, Mr 304
Hiring of labourers, annual 102-3
Holdings, small see Small holdings
Honesty, reports on 185-6
Hopkins, John, clothier 70
Horses and carts, number of 130-1, 148-9
House property of paupers 113
Households, identification of 138-9
    incomes of 172
Houses, distribution of 51-2
Housing 74, 101-104, 165-8
Howes W T, District Valuer 296
Hundred Oke 57 fn
Huntenhull manor 59, 302 see also Huntley
Huntley 53 *see also* Huntenhull
    workhouse at 104

Illiteracy 203-4
Immigration 69-70
Incomes, family 171-2
Incumbents, list of 283-5
Industrial and agricultural population 75, 89-90
Industries 125
Industry, employment of girls in 117
    employment of women in 117
Inefficiency, see Deficiency
Inhabitants, classification of 139
Inn, establishment of 76
Inoculation 111-2

Inquiry, method of 135-9
Inquiry form 135-6
Inquisition in 1337, 277
Insurance 244
Ironworks, Westbury 50

Jamaica 39, 40
James, A E 303
Journeymen, living in of 103
Judicial situation in Corsley 57

Kebbel, T E 21
Kershaw, Rev ix, 19, 23
Kington, family of 56
Kington, Sir Reginald de, bailiff of forest 54
Kington Court chapel 60
Knowles, Lilian ix, 12

Labourer, presence of, in eighteenth century 70
Labourers 149-155
    annual hiring 102
    earnings of 149-155
    proportion of, in poverty 179-180
    proposed allotment of, among ratepayers 121
    wages of 149-155
Labourers, wages in kind, estimation of 150
Landhayes 56
Landownership 297
Lane End 53, 302
Laundry-work 159-160
Lease of lives, cottages let on 166
Leases, in survey book 70-2, 75
Leatham Mr 19
Leighs Green 52, 53, 55, 300, 302
Limekiln 88
Littleton, William de 277
Living, how got by inhabitants of Corsley 140-164
    minimum cost of 172-4
    standard of 130
    table of minimum cost of 174
Lodgers 168, 267
London County Council 30, 33
London School of Economics ix, 1, 6, 10 – 13, 295
Longbridge Deverel [Deverill], inquisition at 55
Longhedge 53, 55
Longleat ix, 50, 165, 297
Longleat estate, timber-hauling from 144
Lye, family of 62

McKillop, John ix, 13
MacTaggart, Miss C S 44
Magistrates, relief ordered by 114

Maiden Bradley, convent of 277
    Prior of 57
Mann, H 2, 29
Manor, grant of, 276
    Farm 60, 165, 303
    Farm as an inn 77
    House 60
Manorial rents and fees 65
Manors, purchases of, by Sir John Thynne 285-6
    of Corsley 55, 57, 59
Market gardeners 147-9
    vitality of children 273
Market gardens, formation of 123
Marketers, women 163
Marketing 147-9
Married Women's Work 6, 27-8
Masons, earnings of 158
Meares, Robert 76, 92
Medical attendance 244 - 245
Medical Clubs 244
Medieval agriculture 57
    records 276-8
Men, unmarried 264-5
Menus, of cottagers' meals 212-240
Methodists 95
Metropolitan Railway 42
Midwifery, women's earnings at 162
Midwives 245
Migration of children of Corsley people 261-2
    of families 250-2
    in parish 168
Militiamen 113
Milk, facilities for obtaining 209-210
Mill, Corsley 57
Mitchell, Miss Winifred ix
Monuments, Corsley 65-6
Moody family 130
Mothers' meeting 267
Music, church 98

National School, establishment of 126
Newcomers in parish 268
New York 39, 40
Nonconformist chapels 125-6
Norridge, manor of 59
Nursing Association, Cley Hill Benefit 245
Nursing, earnings of women at 162

Occupations of ancestors of Corsley men 253-8
    of children of Corsley people 253-60
    of inhabitants 62, 70, 75, 140-2
Overcrowding 101, 167-8
Overseer, paid assistant, appointed 115, 121

Overseers' accounts 287-9
Oxford, Richard 295, 303

Page, William 14 – 18, 24
Painters, earnings of 158
Parish, A W 297
Parish Council 269-70
Parish Registers 72-4
Park, Corsley 60
Park Barn, origin of name of 60
Pasture, conversion of arable to 123-4
    distribution of 51, 303
Pasture and arable, distribution of 92
Patrons of Church, list of 283-5
Pauperism 121, 204-6
Paupers, proposed allotment of, among ratepayers
    121
Pearce, wagon works 304
Philipps (Dimsdale), Elsbeth 14-15
Phipps, C N ix
Pigs 302
Plumbers, earnings of 158
Political situation of Corsley 57
Pony traps, number of 147-9
Poor Relief, see Overseers' Accounts
    during famine years 115
    history of 111-5
    ordered by magistrates 114
Poor House 79
    Workhouse becomes 109
Poor Law, administration of, in eighteenth
    century 77-9, 81-2
    New 120-1
Population 140, 166, 290
    changes in 72-3
    consequences of growth of 101
    decline of 120, 124
    distribution 51-4
    ebb of 56
    growth of 71-2
    number of 81
Potato-ground 94, 123
Poverty, causes of 274
    definition of 172-7
    number of families in primary 174-6
    number of families in secondary 177-8
    prevention of 274-5
Poverty and prosperity in Corsley 271
Prevention of Destitution 32, 34
Primary poverty 172-7
Prosperity, causes of 272
Provision dealer, account-book of 86-7
Provision dealers, local 76, 87

Public houses 52, 263-7

Quarter Sessions 50

Rabbitt warren 61
Radstock, coal hauled from 144
Radstock coal-mines 51
Railway *see* Great Western Railway
Rates in aid of wages 115
Rates, to be paid by tenants 121
Reading-room 263, 304
Records, medieval 276-9
Recruits, militia 113
Rectory 104
Reformation, consequences of 59
Registers, parish 72-4
Religion 268-9
Religious revival 81, 95 - 100
Religious services 268-9
Rents, allotments 199
    Cottage 168
    Manorial 65
Rents in kind 65, 71
Reports on character, tables of 187 -201
    of artisans 201
Reports on households 182 - 208
Riots, agricultural in Wilts 116
Roads 58, 88-9, 121
    employment of paupers on 121
Rowntree, Seebohm 2
Royal visit 100
Rural problems enquiry 29

Sainsbury, James 129
Sandhayes 52
Sandpits in roads 89
Savings Bank, school 244
Sawyer 159
School, location of 52
    National, establishment of 126-7
    savings bank 244
    Sunday, establishment of 97
School care committees 30-34
Schools, private 127-8
Seating order for Corsley church 280-3
Secondary poverty 177
Seignorial unification 59 et seq
Selwood Forest 50, 54, 60
    disafforestation of 65
    Sir Reginald de Kingston, bailiff of, 54
Sewing, earnings of women at 161
Sexton, appointment of 100
Ships   *Arcadia* 39

     Prinz August Wilhelm 39
     Majestic 39
     Baltic 39,40
Shopkeepers, women 163
Shopping of cottagers 86-7, 209
Sick benefit societies, see Clubs
Silk factory 85, 116
Sims, James 302
Singer, Thomas, dye-houses of 83
Small holdings, beneficial effects of 272
    formation of 124
    number of 124
    suitability of soil for 124
    work of women on 124
Smallpox 111-2
Snelgrove, Mr 304
Sobriety, reports on 185
Social life 263-70
Societies, friendly 119, see also Clubs
Spanish invasion 61
Sparey, account-book of 86-7
Stock, Corsley 65-6
Stones, quarrying of 89, 112
Studley, grant of manor to prioress of 276
    prioress of 277
Sturford Mead 52, 165
Sunday customs 269
Sunday School, establishment of 97
Survey Book, leases in 70-2

Table of pauperism 205
Tables of reports of character 187-201
Taunton, clothier and miller 122
    factory of, Mr 82
    family 129
Temple 53
    Episcopal church built at 126
Tenancy, systems of 166, 297, 298
Tenants, occupations of 70, 75
Terrier of 1828 92
Thanksgiving, day of general 100
Thatcher 156
Thrift, reports on 185-6
Thynne, Sir John, purchases of land 59-60, 285-
    6, 303
Timber merchants 144
Timber trade 51
Townsend Dr, police surgeon 41
Townshend, Caroline 43
Townsmen, immigration of 70, 76
Trades and crafts 76-7
Tradesmen's token 68
Turnpike Act 88

Under-gardeners, earnings of 154
Unification, ecclesiastical
    Seignorial 59 et seq
Upton, manor of 59
Urban influence in country districts 128

Valuation Office survey 4-5, 295
    timing of survey 296
    hereditaments surveyed 296, 299
    area surveyed 296-7
Vestry, distribution of votes at 99-100
Victoria County History 1, 5, 6, 13-18
Vill of Corsley 55
Village types 53
Visitors 168

Wages 85-6, 121
    agricultural 94, 117, 149-55
    artisans 156-9
    brickmakers 158-9
    carters' 150-1
    charwomen's 160
    cowmen's 151
    dressmakers' 162-3
    inquiry as to
    labourers' 149-155
    laundresses' 159-160
    under-gardeners' 154
    women's, see Earnings of women
Warminster 50, 303
    a corn market 50
    Board of Guardians 122
    Market, dress of frequenters of 130
    Quarter sessions at 50
    Union 120
    Union Workhouse, establishment of 110
Waste lands 61
Wastes, enclosure of 72
    squatting on 55
Water meadows 51
Water supply 302
Waterloo, Battle of commemorated 100
Weavers, earnings of 85
    immigration of 69
Webb, Sidney and Beatrice ix, 1, 11, 13, 19, 25, 295
Wellesley Buildings 37-8, 40
Wesleyans 95-7, 125, 269, 305
Westbury 50
    ironworks 50
Weymouth, Viscount 100

allotments under enclosure 92
Wheelwrights, earnings of 158
Whitaker, Thomas 76
Whitbourne 53, 305
    extent of AD 1364 278
    manor of 57, 59
Whitbourne Baptist Chapel, bequest to 129
Whitbourne Hill 302
Whitbourne Moor 52,53,55
    silk factory at 116
Whitbourne Springs 52, 129
    workhouse at 105
Whitbourne Temple Farm, breaking up of 124
White, Mr A B 23
White, Ellen 300
White slave trade 6, 34 – 36
Whitehall Residential Hotel 37-8
Widows in receipt of outdoor relief 204-6
Wiltshire, agricultural riots 116
    workhouses in 104
Wiltshire cloth trade 62
    disorganisation of 67-8
Wise woman 131
Women, earnings of 117
    Employed in agriculture 94, 124
    Employment of, in agriculture and industry 116-7
    Employment of, in agriculture discontinued 124
    Failure of work for 125
    Migration from Corsley of 125
Women's work 159-164
    Remuneration of 164
Wood, Corsley 56
Woodmen, earnings of 154-5
Wordsworth, Canon Christopher ix
Work, parochial provision of 78, 88, 112, 121-2
Workhouse, committee to regulate 109
    disuse of, as place of employment 109
    establishment of 104
    expenses per head at 109
    food supplied at 108
    history of 105-110
    inmates of 105-110
    local, disuse of 110
    Warminster 110
    work done at 107
Workhouses in Wiltshire 104
Writers' Club 36-7

Youdall, Jack 131
Young, William, innkeeper 76

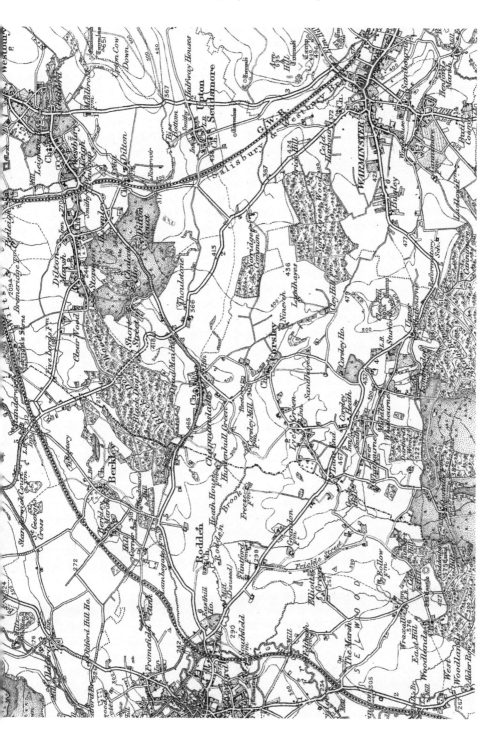

Ingram Content Group UK Ltd.
Milton Keynes UK
UKHW040226060523
421276UK00002B/26